So...You Are Tired of Being a Lame Duck

The Disaster Manual for Attention Deficit Disorder and Attention Deficit Disorder with Hyperactivity

Mary Jane Grange, R.N.

About the Cover

Authors usually try to represent their entire book by the picture which they have
chosen for their book cover. A picture is worth a thousand words. My picture on my book
cover follows this tradition. Parents and step parents are dealing with multiple children
and/or spouses with attention deficit disorders. Parents and step parents are losing their
confidence in their ability to parent. Step parents and biological parents have become like
driftwood—neither root nor branch. Step parents are expected to accent their homes while
confined to a corner of their property and then walled-off with stone walls. Step parents are
expected to watch others bloom, but not bloom themselves. The Lord expects fruit on these
branches. (John 15:5; Malachi 4:1-6; Doctrine and Covenants 2:1-3) Like Ephraim and
Manasseh, parents and step parents must become branches that grow over the many walls that
children and step children have built between parents, step parents and children and step
children. (Genesis 49: 22-26)

Order this book online at www.trafford.com
or email orders@trafford.com

Most Trafford titles are also available at major online book retailers.

Printed in the United States of America.

ISBN: 978-1-4269-3625-8 (SC)

ISBN: 978-1-4269-3626-5 (E-BOOK)

*Our mission is to efficiently provide the world's finest, most comprehensive book publishing
service, enabling every author to experience success. To find out how to publish your book,
your way, and have it available worldwide, visit us online at www.trafford.com*

Trafford rev. 7/6/2010

 www.trafford.com

North America & international
toll-free: 1 888 232 4444 (USA & Canada)
phone: 250 383 6864 ♦ fax: 812 355 4082

To My Family

Acknowledgments

I am indebted to many for their assistance in my second manuscript. I am very grateful for the assistance of Brother Morris Kjar. He has answered many questions with the patience of a dove.

I would like to thank Owen and Colleen Asplund and their family for not being afraid to give a home to a lame duck–somebody about to be tried and tested. Your preparation for life was most helpful and also your examples. My husband and I will love you forever.

I would like to thank my daughter and her husband for the many meals they prepared for us or shared with us so I could spend a full day writing or researching. I would like to thank my grandchildren for helping us with yard work, too. I helped them with their homework. They helped us with our homework.

Lastly, I would like to thank my dear husband, Joseph. He is an inspiration and has the patience of Job with me most of the time. Thank you for letting me stay home and be a wife, mother, and grandmother instead of accumulating campers, vacations, and a lot of adult toys. Thank you for letting me have the time and money, which you worked hard for in the cold and the heat of the day, so we could be active in the Lord's Kingdom. My extended family and I thank you for the time and money to do our genealogy. Thank you for listening many, many times to versions of my manuscripts. Your insights and love have always been helpful.

All quotes and footnotes from individuals or companies have been used with permission. The text of the four scriptures, The Holy Bible, The Book of Mormon, The Doctrine and Covenants, and The Pearl of Great Price are in public domain. I do not translate doctrine for The Church of Jesus Christ of Latter-day Saints. I understand this. I do try to apply its teachings to my life. To apply them, I must understand them.

Mary Jane Grange, R.N.

Our Greatest Glory Comes
Not in Never Falling,
But in Rising
Every Time We Fall.

–Author Unknown

Table of Contents

Prologue

Each of us receives a wake-up call in our lives. Some receive many wake-up calls before they decide to heed them. One of my many wake-up calls occurred when I was called a lame duck. Naturally, this comment came from someone that I loved very much, and I wanted them to like and love me, too.

Years later, I met this person again. They were married now. I was still a lame duck to them. Their feelings had not changed, even though I had changed. I had joined The Church of Jesus Christ of Latter-day Saints, and I had received a college degree. In spite of the years and these accomplishments, their feelings about me had not changed. Their feelings and behavior toward me when I was young were justified by telling me I had an attention deficit disorder. I was too difficult to get along with now and as a young child. Naturally, I was very hurt.

I began wondering if this is how everyone felt about me. When I was young, I could not walk right, dress right, run right, sleep right, read right, and eat right. Yes, I quit trying to do anything around these people to avoid painful criticisms. The sad thing is, I had prayed for help, and I was clearly impressed to do things a certain way.

Essentially, I was given a "coat of many colors," just like our great-great grandfather of many generations ago, Joseph of Egypt. However, I was not allowed to experience the mantle of that coat. When I tried to experience the mantle of being a daughter, sister, student, mother, step mother, and friend, I was treated as an outsider. This was done by people who were supposed to be family, friends, teachers, and neighbors. Yes, I lost my temper. Anyone would. It took me years to realize that this is a natural cycle which occurs when everyone goes their own way.[1]

Naturally, everyone's behavior was justified because I had an attention deficit disorder. Kicking my butt literally and figuratively was going to cure this. At that time, I realized that I may be a lame duck, but I was trying. Unfortunately, I also realized that no matter what I did or said: I would always be a lame duck to this person and many others. As a result, I lost a lot of confidence in myself and in others.

I did not want to be a lame duck anymore. It was not profitable to be a lame duck. I decided that I needed to learn how not to be a lame duck. I must admit that I tried reinventing the wheel several times. I also tried putting a few round pegs in square knotholes and a few square pegs in round knotholes. I even tried learning how not to be a lame duck without my parents and family. This continued until one day. I read the following scripture.

> *But behold, if ye will awake and arouse your faculties, even to an experiment*
> *upon my words, and exercise a particle of faith, yea, even if ye can no more than*
> *desire to believe, let this desire work in you, even until ye believe in a manner*
> *that ye can give place for a portion of my words.*

Alma 32:27, The Book of Mormon

---

[1] Isaiah 53:6, The Holy Bible, p. 926.

This scripture touched my heart. I sensed this was the key to changing my life. I had to experiment on the Savior's words. I had been experimenting on the words of man and had many failed experiments. The Savior taught me to experiment with the words of my parents and step parent. I suspect this is what the Savior meant by honoring your parents.

My experiments on the Savior's words has taught me a lot. I have had some very interesting experiences because I made a place for the Savior in my world. I discovered that I did not have to live life with the emotions of a junior high school or high school student. I also discovered that not being a lame duck or being a little more graceful is a process. It comes step by step and degree by degree until we have accomplished what we want to do with our lives. Hopefully, we have done some things that our Heavenly Father would like us to accomplish, too.

High Schools and Universities call the awkward period of time in our lives freshman. Lame ducks or freshmen are not what you think they are. Freshmen are inexperienced, untried, and about to be tested. No matter what age and in spite of the best intentions, we are all lame ducks or freshmen. Why? We are all learning something new. Awkwardness always comes when learning something new.

Just because others call you a lame duck, that does not mean that you are a lame duck. Maybe you are a lame duck. Maybe they are a lame duck. This can be changed. Just remember. Others are feeling the same way that you are. They are inexperienced, untried, and are about to be tested, too.

As a student nurse, I wondered if our lame duck behavior and even some psychiatric disorders were a result of attention deficit disorder. I began a study of attention deficit disorder. Since I am not a general with advanced degrees, I again used the greatest medical textbooks of all time which I can depend on. Ancient prophets saw our day, especially Isaiah. Prophets saw our difficulties. They saw our difficulties in learning. How would prophets teach us to learn with an attention deficit disorder? Could those ways be applied to secular learning as well as spiritual learning in our day?

As a young member of The Church of Jesus Christ, Floyd Earl Young, Jr. taught my seminary class in Laramie, Wyoming. He taught us that if we want to learn more about The Book of Mormon, we should write a paper using The Book of Mormon. To learn more about attention deficit disorders, I decided to use all four standard works of the Savior as text: The Holy Bible, The Book of Mormon, Doctrine and Covenants, and The Pearl of Great Price.

Most people read these works to prove The Book of Mormon is true or not true. Many have already proved The Book of Mormon is true. It is now time to move on and learn more about ourselves, our problems, and their solutions with The Book of Mormon and other standard works. The Book of Mormon is not a testament to replace The Holy Bible. The Book of Mormon is another testament of Jesus Christ. I do not want to live without The Holy Bible anymore than you do. These books are meant to be read side by side.[2]

I have watched nations change and individuals depart from the teachings of the Savior and the original Twelve Apostles. Yet, we are still squabbling over the truth of The Book of Mormon. While we are arguing over The Book of Mormon, the Ten Commandments given to Moses has been attacked. Many people want us to declare the Ten Commandments has no

---

[2]Ezekiel 37:16-17, The Holy Bible, p. 1080.

significance in our lives. I have wondered if it is <u>The Holy Bible</u> that is the true target to be destroyed, not <u>The Book of Mormon</u>. If we loose confidence in <u>The Holy Bible</u>, we really will go astray with attention deficit disorders. We also can be victimized needlessly. If <u>The Book of Mormon</u> is false then anything claiming there is a Savior will be attacked. Be glad there are two witnesses of Christ's Sacrifice for us and a record of the writings of the original Twelve Apostles.

Every book has a goal. Our goal is to discover what attention deficit disorder is and what attention deficit disorder is not. Years later, when we are old and reflecting on our lives, we will discover what attention deficit disorder and attention deficit disorder with hyperactivity really are. Once defined, we can find solutions to our attention deficit disorders.

So what really is attention deficit disorder? How soon does attention deficit disorders begin in our lives? If I had to describe attention deficit disorders it would be this definition: Attention deficit disorders are our reactions to our environment, specifically, our first reactions to our first exposures to stress and opposition. If we get our way and stress and opposition continue, we continue with the same reaction. An attention deficit disorder affects everything in our life. It determines the choices we make and the kind of initiative that we have.

Attention deficit disorder is most usually defined as the inability to stay on task. However, I have seen healthy children who have not been given any tasks to perform. There are also healthy children who refuse to perform tasks. Is this really attention deficit disorder or a matter of choice?

Step families have many troubles with attention deficit disorders. At the end of my first book, <u>The Medicine Wheel for Step Parents</u>, I mentioned that I have more help for step parents in my second and third books. In my first book, I pointed out that there are double the "dictators and imitators" in a step family. In a step family, there are double and triple the children with attention deficit disorder and attention deficit disorder with hyperactivity. The children in step families refuse to follow tasks. To keep peace in the family, children are not given any tasks to perform. As a result, they are learning to run away instead of learning to perform and endure.

Considering how step children treat step parents and vice versa, all of your children and step children may have an attention deficit disorder. A step parent may have a spouse and an ex-spouse with this disorder. As expected, an ex-spouse will always have many excuses to justify that his wants and needs are more important than his children's needs. An ex-spouse may also be dealing with multiple individuals with attention deficit disorder in his or her new family.

Responding to all of the individuals with attention deficit disorder in your family can be a nightmare for any mother or step mother. Treating these individuals by psychiatry, counseling, and medication will cost a fortune. The children manipulate their counselors as well as their parents and step parents anyway. Parents and step parents are forced to let their children roam the many stages of attention deficit disorder.

We all have a great-great grandfather in common who had to endure the hardships of eleven brothers and some sisters with attention deficit disorders. Their attention deficit disorders were caused by age and very hard hearts. Let us explore his story and see if we can benefit from his experience. We will learn some new ways to act, not react, to the attention deficit disorders in ourselves and our children. We will discover the layers of attention deficit disorders which accumulate until we say enough!

Chapter One

"Your Coat of Many Colors"

One of the first "Bible stories" that I learned and can remember from my childhood is the story of Joseph of Egypt. At that time, I just loved the story about his "coat of many colors." I was not aware that he, Joseph of Egypt, is our great-great grandfather many times removed, either by birth or by adoption.[3]

Naturally, Joseph of Egypt has a natural lineage by birth, as we all do. Jacob is his father. Isaac is his grandfather, and Abraham of old is Joseph's great-grandfather. Abraham was told by the Lord that all families of all nations would be blessed through Abraham. This blessing was given to Isaac. Isaac gave this blessing to Jacob.

Jacob was a dreamer. Jacob's blessing that all families would be blessed through his seed was a dream and is known as "Jacob's ladder." This blessing, known as "Jacob's ladder," was given to Joseph and his descendants. Joseph's descendants begin with his sons, Manasseh and Ephraim.

However, let's continue with the story of Joseph and his "coat of many colors." Joseph had a gift. He was visionary and could interpret dreams. He also told on his half brothers and their evil ways. He did not do this maliciously, or the dreams would have stopped. He would not be able to interpret other dreams. He read and tried to understand the scriptures he had then.

His brothers hated him and felt sorely vexed by his presence. They did not want to be judged by Joseph's standards. They had a different pace in mind for their lives. Joseph's brothers had guilty consciences and behavior to hide from their father. I imagine that it was a game to see who could get Joseph to break a commandment. They could tell on him then.

Jacob is accused of loving his son, Joseph, more than the eleven other boys and other daughters. I do not believe this is true because Jacob would not be a worthy, effective high priest or father. I do believe that Jacob remembered his dream that is known as "Jacob's ladder." It is very difficult to get excited about children who have given up their birthright because of adultery, fornication, and murder.

However, Jacob had one son who would do as he asked, and Joseph wanted to learn. Naturally, if the child is going to do the work, a parent spends more time teaching him. A child also progresses more if he listens to his parents and has compassion for his parents. Every parent has a dream of teaching all of their children this way.

In today's language, Joseph would be known as a teacher's pet. The teacher, his father, Jacob, would always be viewed as showing favoritism to Joseph. This is how the other sons justified their jealousy and behavior.

Joseph's brothers were very envious of a many-colored coat given to Joseph by his father. His "coat of many colors" probably represented the work Joseph had done with Jacob, his father.

---

[3]Romans 8:15-17, The Holy Bible, p. 1426; Ephesians 1:5, The Holy Bible, p. 1481.

It also represented every day who the next presiding high priest would be. Executors of an estate can understand this. Joseph would be the executor of his father's estate, spiritually and worldly.

Jacob probably wondered considerably how his dream of blessing all families would be accomplished since only one of his children seemed to be faithful in keeping the commandments of God. One does not have to be in rocket science to figure this out. It is going to be Joseph, the faithful one. However, the story of Joseph begins before his "coat of many colors." It begins with Joseph's family history.

Jacob, Joseph's father, was the younger of twins. Jacob's twin brother was Esau. Esau sold his birthright for a mess of pottage. Jacob had to flee because Esau was so angry when he realized what Jacob had done. Jacob went to his mother's brother's house. Laban had a very attractive daughter, and Jacob fell instantly in love with her. He agreed to work seven years to marry her. On the day of his marriage, Jacob was given Leah to wife. He had to work another seven years for Rachel, the one he loved. Leah and Rachel are sisters, probably twins.

While working for Laban, his father-in-law, Jacob's wages were changed ten times. His wages were decreased because Jacob would not have complained if they were increased. His cousins, the sons of Laban, grew jealous. They were afraid that Jacob, a worker, was going to take their glory. Laban probably changed Jacob's wages so many times to ease his sons' anxiety. Jacob noticed that their countenance was changing toward him, and he grew concerned. Jacob finally was told to leave by God.

There was just a couple of things Jacob had to clear up. One of those things was his wages. Laban and Jacob agreed that Jacob could have certain colors of sheep or cattle. Jacob did the work. Jacob let the color of cows in to breed the cows which he was allowed to take. Through trickery of his own, he got his wages back. However, he had to flee Laban and his sons.

Another thing that Jacob had to clear up was the feelings between he and Esau, his twin brother. Fortunately, Esau was forgiving and welcomed Jacob and his family back.

Jacob had two wives and two concubines. These four women produced twelve sons and some daughters. Reuben lost the birthright because of adultery with one of the concubines. One of his daughters had sex with someone that was considered beneath the "chosen people." If the sex had been with someone of the chosen people that would have been all right. Though the man wanted to marry her, two of Jacob's sons killed all the men in the city in which the father of the guilty man lived. They also killed the guilty man and his father.

One of his sons by Rachel, the favored wife, was Joseph. Joseph was a dreamer like his father. Joseph is known for two dreams. Joseph dreamed they were in the field tying sheaves. Eleven sheaves bowed to him. Most people discuss their weird dreams with others. Joseph did the same. His brothers immediately took offense.

Joseph dreamed a second dream. This dream was probably to comfort him after many derogatory remarks were made to him. He was only seventeen. Joseph dreamed that the sun, moon, and eleven stars bowed to him. This time, Jacob took offense and sent him to his brothers who were tending sheep.

The brothers saw Joseph coming. They probably were talking about him and were already inflamed. Seeing Joseph coming in his many-colored coat, they became more enraged and decided to kill him. Reuben, the oldest, wanted to put him in a pit and get him later when everyone had cooled down. Reuben left, possibly to check on some sheep that were straying. He left Joseph in a pit with the angry crowd of brothers. He may have been afraid of his brothers.

The angry brothers sat and ate by the pit that Joseph was in. Food usually has a sedating effect, especially in the heat of the day. Judah decided to sell his brother to Ishmaelites on their way to Egypt. Joseph was sold for twenty pieces of silver, the going price of a slave in that day. Joseph's brothers told Jacob that they had found a piece of his torn "coat of many colors," and they gave it to Jacob. Joseph must have been killed by a wild animal. They assumed Joseph would be dead because they knew he would be mistreated in Egypt.

There are some things that we need to keep in mind to appreciate this story. First, Jacob's favored wife, the one he wanted, died in childbirth with Benjamin. This is always in the back of your mind, no matter how long ago it occurred. Second, parents have a sense that gives them the ability to feel when their children are lying or have passed away. Third, Benjamin did not tell what really happened to Joseph for fear of his half brothers. Fourth, Jacob, a prophet and a seer, would immediately consult with the Lord about Joseph. He probably knew where Joseph was. He could not bring him home because Joseph's brothers would do something worse to Joseph.

Three wives had to deal with a husband who was already grieving over a dead wife. Jacob was already grieving over his children's behavior. Joseph, the one in whom Jacob figured his own dream would be fulfilled, was now dead or missing. Three wives got to deal with the countenances of guilty children, the behavior that goes with a darkened countenance, and a grieving husband who was suspicious of his sons and could no longer trust them with Benjamin.

These wives were considered as not knowing anything. They were the ones who did all the work such as tending and chasing sheep, the gardening, bearing children, housework, moving or cleaning the tents, and cooking. After all this work, they certainly were not capable of handling any decision-making about the family. My question is: With all this negative behavior, sin, unfairness, and complete fabrications, how did Jacob and Joseph and their mothers become the bad ones for centuries? The dreamers and the workers became the bad guys and the bad gals. The sinners became the good guys. Joseph's family resembles society today.

For most people of the world, Jacob of Israel is one of their great-great grandfathers, many generations ago. He had twelve sons who are referred to as the tribes of Israel. The twelve tribes have intermarried and are related so much that even the twelve sons of Esau are now related, and Jacob is one of their grandfathers, too. The tribes of Ephraim and Manasseh have intermarried with people of the Orient. Jacob is now one of their great-great grandfathers. How extensive, I do not know.

Jacob received the birthright from Esau through trickery. He experienced trickery when he had to marry two wives to get the one he wanted. Step families can appreciate the pain this caused Jacob. We do not need to keep this battle going. The Lord and Esau ended it long ago.

The younger received the birthright again. When Joseph of Egypt was reunited with his father, Jacob of Israel, Joseph had two sons, Manasseh and Ephraim. Just before Jacob died, he blessed Joseph's two sons. Ephraim received the birthright, but was the younger. Joseph reminded Jacob that Manasseh was the older. Jacob said, "This was the right way."

Though a prophet was expressing the will of God, this has started many generations of hatred and jealousy in many countries. Countries of Manasseh's descendants are offended and are tired of this. I can understand the descendants of Manasseh's feelings. I know I am tired of the eldest or the youngest receiving everything. I am tired of the same small groups of people receiving everything and telling me it is God's will. Those in these small groups wonder why the rest of us are not progressing. Course, I am a middle child. However, let's go on with the story.

We do not know why Jacob pronounced the blessing this way. We must take it on faith that Jacob knew what he was doing because he was a prophet. Ephraim's blessing on Manasseh's head would not help the lands that the tribe of Manasseh would eventually populate. Manasseh's blessing on Ephraim's head would be of no worth for the lands that Ephraim would populate. Each had a role to fulfill in Jacob's blessing. Both received a blessing

One reason that this blessing was pronounced this way is because Joshua who traveled forty years with Moses was of the tribe of Ephraim.[4] Ephraim and his descendants were blessed because Joshua was faithful. Joshua was sent by Moses with eleven spies to check over the Land of Israel. Joshua was the only one who came back with a report of how wonderful the land was. He brought fruit back to prove it. Ten others came back to Moses and said the land was terrible because the inhabitants were stronger than they were. The Isrealites wanted to go back to Egypt. Bondage was better than starving to death.[5]

The Lord blessed Joshua and his lineage for showing up for work, being obedient, and optimistic. The tribe of Ephraim is blessed abundantly because of Joshua's efforts. This tribe is predominantly in North America, another land of abundance. It takes an abundance of many things to bless the people of the world. Jacob probably saw these events in the future. As a prophet, he was a seer.

Ephraim was not the only tribe to be blessed with doing something for the Lord. The Israelites carried the ark of the covenant, their tabernacle, with them. The ark of the covenant was called the tabernacle of testimony. It was made of gold, and the mercy seat was its covering. The tribe of Levi was given authority to attend to the care of the tabernacle, its vessels, and anything pertaining to it.[6] They even camped around it. The Book of Numbers records instructions given for the care of the Tabernacle.

Ephraim has been given the blessing of carrying the gospel to everyone on the Earth. They, too, have been given instructions in their duty. The tribe of Levi was in charge of the tabernacle. I wonder what the other tribes will be in charge of after the gospel has been carried to all parts of the earth. There have been many inventions to assist the tribe of Ephraim. I wonder what inventions will come to assist the other tribes in their work for the world. Naturally, where much is given, much is expected.

Why am I writing about Joseph of Egypt in a book about attention deficit disorder and attention deficit disorder with hyperactivity? We are related to Joseph of Egypt through the tribe of Manasseh and the tribe of Ephraim. For many generations, Joseph's descendants, have been diagnosed with attention deficit disorder and attention deficit disorder with hyperactivity. Remember. We are also the descendants of Abraham, Isaac, and Jacob.

By today's standards, Joseph of Egypt would have attention deficit disorder. He was a dreamer and impulsive, as youth can be. Joseph also had "steel trap memories for complex issues." Joseph could understand things at seventeen that his adult brothers could not. This is why his brothers hated him. Yet, his attackers and critics of his family were the ones accepted as

---

[4]Numbers 13:8, The Holy Bible, p. 213.

[5]Numbers Chapters 13 and 14, The Holy Bible, pp. 213-216.

[6]Numbers 1:50, The Holy Bible, pp. 192-193.

normal. Isaiah specifically instructed us not to call evil good, good evil, put darkness for light, light for darkness, and put bitter for sweet, and sweet for bitter.[7] What is this keeping us from?

Everyone has been given a "coat of many colors." In our day, our "coat of many colors" is called "a man of many hats." Like Joseph of Egypt, children in The Church of Jesus Christ of Latter-day Saints are given their "coat of many colors" when they are blessed at six weeks of age by their father who holds the Melchizedek Priesthood.

We are given additional colors in our "coat of many colors" when we are baptized and when worthy male members are ordained to the priesthood at age twelve and at age nineteen. Members over age sixteen who are worthy, mature, and make a request to their bishop are given more information about their "coat of many colors" in a patriarchal blessing by a stake patriarch. You receive colors in your "coat of many colors" with every ordinance and covenant you keep with your Heavenly Father. Your "coat of many colors" will be a source of comfort and honor. You do not have to resort to trickery and oppression to meet your needs.

"We are climbing Jacob's ladder." I know there is a beautiful song about climbing Jacob's ladder. This is a misnomer. We are not climbing Jacob's ladder. Jacob's ladder is a twelve or thirteen rung ladder. We only know of three rungs, Ephraim, Manasseh, and Judah. Ephraim and Manasseh were adopted by Jacob as his own.

Jacob's ladder has angels descending and ascending. This describes our births and our deaths. We are born into one of the twelve tribes of Israel. When we are born, we come to this earth in an orderly process. When we die or leave this earth, we leave in an orderly way, too. When angels come to this earth as ministering angels, they come in an orderly process also.

We are not like the angels of the adversary ascending and descending in a disorderly way to create havoc upon the Earth. We did not descend Jacob's Ladder to take peace from the Earth and our homes. Angels of the adversary climb over or step on the very people we are supposed to help and bless with our "coat of many colors." These people are included in Jacob's ladder. Jacob's ladder is not power or status. Jacob's ladder is a blessing, not a curse.

We are blending Jacob's ladder. When the ten tribes are returned to us, and they will be, we will be one large blended family under the direction of our Heavenly Father, His Son, Jesus Christ, the Holy Ghost, and the First Presidency on the Earth at the time–just like we are now. The ten other sons are known as the ten lost tribes of Israel. They are not lost except through their behavior. When they receive their contrite heart and spirit, they are found again. They also receive their "coat of many colors" in a patriarchal blessing–just like you and me.

All will be a part in the blessings for the families of the Earth. Since we are all descendants of Abraham, Isaac, Jacob, and Joseph, let's find out what attention deficit disorder is and what attention deficit disorder is not. This will reveal your "coat of many colors."

Since, most of the world belongs to the tribe of Ephraim and Manasseh, I suspect that we will resemble Joseph of Egypt when we find our "coat of many colors?" Joseph of Egypt found and harnessed his coat of many colors. Can we harness our "coat of many colors" like our forefather, Joseph of Egypt, harnessed his "coat of many colors?" Will a "coat of many colors" help the attention deficit disorders we experience?

---

[7]Isaiah 5:20, <u>The Holy Bible</u>, p. 868.

Chapter Two

Your Alpha and Omega

There are many modern day definitions of attention deficit behavior and attention deficit behavior with hyperactivity. There are definitions of attention deficit disorder on the Internet. Your doctor or child's school teacher has good information, too. Attention deficit disorder is abbreviated with the letters ADD. This description was prepared by Rebecca Chapman Boothe. I obtained it from our family doctor. I added the italics.

WHAT DOES ADD LOOK LIKE?

"People with ADD are often noted for their *inconsistencies.* One day they can "do it" and the next day they can't. They can have *difficulty remembering simple things, yet have "steel trap" memories for complex issues.* To avoid disappointment, frustration, and discouragement, don't expect their highest level of competence to be the standard. It's an unrealistic expectation of a person with ADD. What's normal is that they will be inconsistent."

Typically, they have problems with *following through on instructions, paying attention appropriately* to what they need to attend to, *seem not to listen,* be *disorganized, have poor handwriting, miss details, have trouble starting tasks* or with tasks that require planning or long term effort, appear to be *easily distracted* and *forgetful.* In addition, some people with ADD can be *fidgety, verbally impulsive, unable to wait their turn,* and *act on impulse* regardless of consequences. But, remember–not all people with ADD have all of these difficulties, nor all of the time."

Because society has traditionally thought of a person with ADD as being hyper, many children without hyperactivity are sometimes thought of as *day dreamers* and *absent-minded professors.* Non-hyperactive children with ADD most often seem to be girls (though girls can have ADD with hyperactivity and boys can have ADD without hyperactivity.)"[8]

Additionally, because of the ability of an individual with ADD to "*over focus,*" or "*hyper focus on something that is of great interest* or highly stimulating," many untrained observers assume that this ability to concentrate negates the possibility of ADD being a concern, especially when they see children *able to pay attention while working one-on-one* with someone, doing something they enjoy, or who can sit and play an electronic game or watch TV for hours on end."

ADD is not a learning disability. Although ADD obviously effects the performance of a person in a school setting, it will also *effect* other domains of life,

---

[8]Prepared by Rebecca Chapman Booth, http://www.add.org/content/abc/basic.htm, 1998.

which can include *relationships* with others, running a home, *keeping track of finances* and *organizing, planning, and managing* most areas of one's life.

WHAT CAUSES ADD?

ADD is a neurobiological disorder. The most recent research shows that the symptoms of ADD are caused by a chemical imbalance in the brain. To understand how this disorder interferes with one's ability to focus, sustain attention, and with memory formation and retrieval, it is important to understand how the brain communicates information. Each brain cell has one axon, the part of the cell that sends messages to other cells; and many dendrites, the part that receives messages from other cells. There is a space between the axon and the next brain cell (they do not connect or touch). This space is called a neural gap.

Since these nerve endings don't actually touch, special chemicals, called neurotransmitters, carry or transmit the message from the end of the axon to the dendrites who will receive it. With ADD there is a flaw in the way the brain manages the neurotransmitter production, storage or flow, causing imbalances. There is either not enough of them, or the levels are not regulated, swinging wildly from high to low.

HOW IMPORTANT IS A THOROUGH EVALUATION?

Very...it is also extremely important that it is individualized and designed to uncover co-existing conditions, such as learning disabilities and behavior, mood or anxiety disorders (depression, generalized anxiety, obsessive-compulsive disorder, oppositional defiant disorder, etc.), or any other problems that could be causing symptoms that look similar to the symptoms of ADD.[9]

Nurses and doctors have a briefer description of attention deficit disorder and attention deficit disorder with hyperactivity. We use these terms to describe the heartbeat of a patient. An irregular heartbeat can be regularly irregular. In other words, the irregularities follow a pattern. People with attention deficit disorders are regularly irregular, too. Their irregular behavior follows a pattern.

List the concerns you have for your child and step child's behavior at home and at school. Notice if these behaviors follow a pattern. List what behavior you would like to change in yourself. Does parents' and step parents' behavior follow a pattern? Are children and step children copying what patterns they see in your home or on television and movies? For example, parents complain of children and step children spending too much time with friends. Do parents and step parents spend more time and speak more kindly to their friends than family and step family? As you study the topics and answer the questions in each chapter, you will begin to harness your coat of many colors instead of an attention deficit disorder harnessing you.

---

[9]Prepared by Rebecca Chapman Booth, http://www.add.org/content/abc/basic.htm, 1998. Her quotes are used with her permission.

Chapter Three

Physical Causes

There may be a physical cause for your child's lack of attention and your child's difficulty to concentrate. A difficulty with attention or in concentration is known as the inability to stay on task. The inability to stay on task is also called attention deficit disorder and attention deficit disorder with hyperactivity. Some of these possible causes of attention deficit disorders will need to be evaluated by physicians. I am aware this is expensive.

Your child was premature. Mothers often attribute their child's learning problems to prematurity. An estimated date of confinement or delivery is plus or minus two weeks. A mother delivering more than two weeks before her delivery date will have a premature child. Infants delivering sometime after thirty-six weeks usually do fine.

Prematurity can be defined by an infant's body weight. An infant weighing under five pounds with very little muscle and fat pads is always considered premature though the mother sometimes carried the infant full-term. The difficulty arises in determining when the egg was released and fertilized. Women do not keep track of their menstrual periods. Memories become shortened in the shock of finding out that one is pregnant. Thus, physicians rely on ultrasounds.

A premature infant is usually the result of a problem pregnancy. The mother has taken medications to prolong the pregnancy, to prevent high blood pressure and seizures in the mother, and to develop the infant's lungs quickly. The infant will be given medications to preserve its life after it is born. We are talking about very delicate tissue. A lack of oxygen and medications affects your child's brain development. It takes a few minutes to put an infant on a respirator.

Even the smallest premature infants are surviving. Visual problems occur when an infant receives one-hundred percent oxygen to survive. Others may have a form of cerebral palsy. Parents usually are told their premature infant will catch-up by age five if they are walking by eighteen months. There are more things than motor skills for premature infants to catch-up on.

All organ systems are premature if your child is premature. Developmental lags are not noticeable when children are playing, and things are running smoothly. It is when children are under stress that problems are noticeable. School is supposed to be that first stress. This is not true in this day. Stress brings out the recessive genes that may be dormant.

However, if your premature child can learn how to be an expert on Nintendo or in sports, his learning problems are probably not due to prematurity. Even premature infants must learn how to make proper choices in their lifetime. Full term infants cannot exist indefinitely on reflex or hand and eye coordination. They must coordinate their hands, eyes, brains, and feelings with their environment and with other individuals trying to coordinate the same things.

Is your child's attention span a matter of development? As a nurse, I cared for mothers who claimed their infants were toilet-trained at three and six months. We live in a fast-paced world. We do not need to make our child's world any more fast-paced than it already is.

Parents are working two or more jobs. This fast-paced world often does not wait for normal growth and development. Your child's development will follow some guidelines, but each child is different, and each child will learn at a different pace. There are a lot of changes going on in your child's body that you can and cannot see. These changes must come before cells become an embryo, an embryo becomes a fetus, and a fetus becomes a newborn, a newborn becomes a toddler, and a toddler becomes preschooler, etc. This continues until your child dies.

Your child's development is like learning how to play a musical instrument. Your child requires a certain amount of one-to-one assistance until the material clicks with his coordination and confidence. With practice, effort, and sacrifice from both parent and child, the child is able to begin work alone. Since each instrument is different, this will vary. Human beings will always need some morale boosters along the way, too.

Power struggles with parents accompany different age levels. Does your child have to stay off task for your attention? Mothers who are hurried, frustrated, and are working do not have the time to spend with their children. Is there an over-achiever in your home? One is not an under-achiever if they do not perform like an over-achiever. In your desire for quality time with your children, remember that a child has to be more than just physically fit to be successful in this world. Parents need to be more than just physically fit to keep up with children.

One of the physical causes of lack of concentration and not performing tasks at age level is an excessive intake of sugar. There is much debate as to whether sugar affects children's behavior. As a mother, grandmother, and dental patient, I know that sugar affects children's behavior. When my child and grandchildren eat sugared cereal or candy, they become hyperactive. When all three meals and their snacks have been sugared cereal, pop, and candy, their hyperactivity worsens. They have ingested large amounts of sugar and carbohydrates that are energy boosters which have no substance.

Children usually consume caffeine with their sugared drinks along with what they have eaten. For their body weight, they have just received an overdose of sugar and caffeine, similar to an overdose of medication. All overdoses have side effects. Caffeine is a medication. It is often given to individuals with migraine headaches. Caffeine also affects cardiac output.

In addition, children have not learned self-control or social control. This type of energy overdose without any controls is not your imagination. It most always happens when parents are too tired to cook a nourishing meal, are not home, or parents do not feel like dealing with children who have the energy to bounce off the entire wall of China. Naturally, children become argumentative with you when you are argumentative with them about their behavior. This can be called attention deficit disorder with hyperactivity.

Adults, eating the same amount of sugar and caffeine, do not receive this much energy benefit. They are tired, and their body does not respond as quick. Without caffeine, they become sleepy because they have only received an overdose of sugar for their body weight. Elevated blood sugar makes one sleepy. Diabetics are familiar with this symptom.

Now, if you recall, I stated I believed sugar affects children's behavior because I was a dental patient. I have had to have dental crowns because of tooth sensitivity, ranging from moderate to severe tooth pain. What is the first question your dentist or dental hygienist asks you? That question is: "Have you had or do you have any tooth sensitivity to sweet?" Now, if sugar is irritating to a nerve in a tooth to the point of severe pain, sugar affects other nerves in the body when there is an elevated blood sugar. If sugar causes teeth to decay and ache, sugar causes other things in the body to deteriorate. Your aching joints are an example. Now, if sugar causes teeth and joints to ache and deteriorate, sugar can and does affect children's behavior. Sugar causes children's behavior to deteriorate, too. A diet low in water-soluble vitamins, fat-soluble vitamins, and the vitamins given to us by sunlight will potentiate high-sugar intakes.

Try some honey. My grandchildren are not as hyperactive on pure honey. They are more satisfied. They do not receive a sweet overdose for their body weight, and the sugar is in a form which their body can use. Their energy has more stable plateaus rather than peaks and valleys. The honey has to be pure honey. Processed honey has been pasteurized, destroying most of the good nutrition. Other good cereal substitutes are bagels and cheese or homemade bread and peanut butter. Learn how to make homemade bread again. This does wonders for your family. It takes some extra planning. If the pioneers in wagon trains could do it, we can, too.

If the Lord did not want us to have sugar, He would have told us about this in scriptures. He did. It is found in the Doctrine and Covenants Section 89, the Word of Wisdom section.

And again, hot drinks are not for the body or belly.
Doctrine and Covenants 89: 9

This does not specifically say sugar. It does not specifically say caffeine, either. Everyone has assumed that it is the caffeine or the temperature that is harmful in hot drinks. Caffeine is harmful. However, it is the sugar in those hot drinks that is harmful, too. In fact, sugar, caffeine, and carbonation potentiate each other. This means the effects of a drug or any chemicals are multiplied by administering the drugs at the same time.

Patients having surgery receive a pre-operative medication using the same principle. Potentiation is why after one can of caffeinated drink, one is rummaging through every cupboard looking for something sweet. The craving for something sweet is not as bad, but is still present after one sugared drink. Children's behavior is noticeably different between a sugared drink, diet drinks with caffeine, and drinks with caffeine and sugar. We can see from the increase in diabetes that sugar is a serious problem. In fact, the pioneers of 1833 were doing the same things we do now. Let's look back in history.

The pioneers did not have running tap water. Their pumps pumped water from wells or creeks. This water was contaminated or muddy. The taste was not so good, and they would become sick if they drank water straight from the creek. Pioneers learned that if they boiled their water, they did not become sick with dysentery or cholera. They added sugar to cover the taste.

Pioneers always heated their homes with fireplaces. Their homes would have several fireplaces to heat and cook with. This kind of heat is very drying to the throat, especially to the ones who worked by the fire all day and then slept near the fire at night. Mothers learned to keep a cast iron teakettle brewing all the time near their fireplace and on the old cook stoves. This teakettle added moisture in the air. Otherwise, pioneers and their children would wake up sputtering and choking in the middle of the night because their throat was severely dry. A baby with a cold could die from a plugged airway with dried nasal and throat secretions.

Mother would make drinks from various plants to cover the taste of creek water. Teas from plants are bitter. She added sugar to the various hot drinks which the family was consuming daily by their fireplaces. Mother began buying green tea which was imported from the Orient. The flavor was better, but these teas still required sugar. This tea contained a large amount of caffeine. This drink was an energy booster for farmers who worked sun-up till past sundown in their fields.

My grandmother would only allow her grandchildren a few sips of green or orange tea. From experiences like I mentioned above, she knew children were inattentive and unmanageable with this kind of drink. However, this was all her family had to quench their thirst. My father would give this tea to us. He was always working two jobs and was never home with his unmanageable children. Sadly, he deliberately gave this tea to us to spite my mother and grandmother. No one was going to tell him how to raise his children.

Does this sound like society today? Though we are working sun-up till past sundown, the same ingredients cold are still not for the body or belly. The ingredients are harmful to our health physically. These energy boosters which have no substance are expensive. They do not give anyone the fuel to pay attention, to concentrate, and to retain, but they do give someone the fuel to run faster than they can walk. These energy boosters give children fuel which makes everyone who comes in contact with your child run faster than they can walk, too.

Is your child getting adequate sleep? Some children need more sleep than other children. Make sure they get at least eight hours of sleep. If your child has a television or phone in their room, they may be spending hours on the phone or watching television when you think they are asleep. Teachers can tell the difference when your child gets a good breakfast and adequate sleep. As a Sunday School teacher, I could tell which twelve year old child was up late and who had a quick bowl of sugared-cereal before they came to church.

Your child may be sick. There can be many reasons for children to be inattentive and unable to stay on task. Pollution, allergies, lead paint, or any kind of chronic disease that has not been identified can be the culprit. Have a good physical exam and blood chemistry to check for health problems. Parents working two jobs cannot stay home with sick children. They would lose their job or be unable to make their large house payments, car payments, trip payments, or buy season sports tickets, etc.

Your child may have an allergy. Children are allergic to more than just medications. They are allergic to anything that exists. With pollution and flu season, your child can have a sinus infection from November to April. Children with allergies usually are given a decongestant so everyone can sleep. This is a long time to be on a decongestant every year. This eventually will affect the kidneys. Children with stuffy noses and headaches and those who are taking decongestants will not perform at their best.

More and more children are diagnosed with thyroid disease. Here is a list of symptoms of a hyperactive thyroid. Children can become excitable, aggressive, and impulsive. Adults become nervous and jittery. Symptoms of hypoactive thyroid are: Children are overweight, tired, have an extreme cold insensitivity, and become fatigued easily. This can be seen as lazy and out of shape. The increase in thyroid disease may be a left-over from underground and above-ground nuclear testing. However, thyroids deal with heat and basal metabolism. Thyroids do not have to work efficiently because of quick home heating and the use of quick energy boosters.

Your child may have a hearing loss. This may not be noticeable until the child is in school. He cannot hear well from the back row. Your child cannot hear well when the teacher turns and faces the blackboard. Parents may feel their child has selective hearing. A child may hear better when their parent yells. This does not mean he will listen even if he hears his parents. Children do not acknowledge their parents and step parents know more because of experience.

If anyone in the home plays loud music consistently, the three inner ear bones become loose. When there is a lot of noise or chatter, these bones wiggle. The child can hear, but he cannot distinguish words. Naturally, if he makes mistakes, has difficulty learning, and becomes behind in school, he or she will be laughed at and ridiculed by children and adults.

Your child may have a problem with his or her vision. The degenerative eye diseases do not come on suddenly. This happens over time. It can be a result of eye infections, especially when a child has frequent ear and upper respiratory infections. Pollution will irritate the eyes as well as the lungs. All the medications that children and adults are on affects the eye and optic nerve. Children may have a lazy eye. The most common visual problems are plain old near-sightedness, far-sightedness, and astigmatism. The most common way to tell if your child needs glasses is to read with them. They cannot differentiate between an Ii and the l, n and h, r and a, b and d, g and p. Children will also strain and position their head to the side.

Visual exams and glasses are expensive. Parents do not like to buy glasses every year. Children break or lose their glasses frequently. It is hard enough to buy school clothes and shoes. Everything is expensive. Some parents prefer to pay for recreation or adult toys.

Does your child have dyslexia? Dyslexia is the inability to recognize letters and words on a written page. This results in your child reading below level. Common examples are the switching of the b and d letters. Naturally, when your child mispronounces a simple word, he is laughed at and teased, often unmercifully. Their behavior, impulsive or withdrawn, can be a cover for this handicap and treatment. The problem occurs when this inability persists.

Adult form of Dyslexia. There are many adults who have hidden the fact they cannot read well because of dyslexia. I suspect that there is also an adult type of dyslexia. This includes shapes, not just letters–especially the shapes of cars and trucks. There have been many accidents where adult and teen drivers claim they did not see an oncoming car. In reality, the adult or teenage driver was in too much of a hurry at an intersection. They stopped less than a "California stop" at the stop sign or stop light. Like a computer, the brain could not process go, stop, and go that quickly. The oncoming car appeared to be in the other lane. The brain switched the shape into the opposite directions–just like it does with letters. An oncoming car now appears to be going in the opposite direction. The hurried or fatigued driver quickly proceeds–to a crash. For this reason alone, it is imperative that you and your children take the time to learn how to read to train your brain. There are too many cars with the same shape, but different names. Blink and think to give your brain time to process reality. Your life and the lives of your children and others depend on your ability to read and recognize shapes correctly.

In defense of your child, children learn at different speeds. There is no five second rule in reading, just as there was no five-second-rule for your child when he learned to turnover, sit, crawl, and walk. Children have to spend a certain amount of time with someone on a one-on-one basis to accomplish the task of reading–just as he did the other tasks in his life.

Attention deficit disorder is confused with a learning disability. Children with learning disabilities have problems speaking rationally and appropriately, not with forming words. They usually swear all the time, especially at inappropriate times. They have problems with writing, spelling, and arithmetic as well as inattentive, impulsive behavior. A lack of oxygen at birth or stress in the home may cause brain damage. This could be failure-to-thrive syndrome which is seen in babies not being loved, touched, or stimulated. They usually will not work at learning.

Children with learning disabilities cannot or will not listen to their parents and teachers. Adults will not listen to employers or their spouse. They are poor readers and cannot organize thoughts even in a one-on-one relationship. Children with learning disabilities have poor memories and are never satisfied. They do not have a disorder in seeing or hearing. They have problems in acquiring or expressing knowledge. They may have no desire to acquire knowledge. Thus, they may refuse to go to school. These children are unable to grasp patterns in learning. They cannot relate printed text to spoken words and cannot interpret written words. These individuals will not do the repetitions of learning which installs the same things in the brain, but in different formats. They cannot see the hurt they have repeatedly caused in others.

There are individuals who can memorize long lists of movies and television programs which they have seen, including the cast of characters, what other movies these characters are in, the scripts, and the songs. Yet, they claim they have a learning disability and cannot learn or work. This is not a learning disability. They do not have a desire to learn or work. The easiness of the way has overtaken them, and they have fallen into the pits of laziness and idleness.

Autism. Many children are diagnosed with autism. They have no speech, do not respond to affection, and do not like to be touched without advanced warning. They may not make eye contact with you. Autistic children stop developing mentally, but they continue to develop physically. Since they have no speech, autistic children express emotions with crying and hitting. They are unaware that their behavior can hurt others. The cause may be a genetic disorder, birth trauma, or environmental causes. Milder forms of autism can be diagnosed as attention deficit disorders or Asbergers Syndrome. Doctors may help you with these symptoms. I seriously doubt immunizations cause autism. I feel that pesticides in GMO seeds, the hybrid seed, has an affect on our children. Children are diagnosed after eating the fruit/vegetables of the hybrid seeds..

Pesticide Sprays. Home owners are using too much pesticide sprays in their homes and on their lawns. Not only are these sprays killing our natural pollinators such as the honey bees, but humans are experiencing some of the same symptoms that bugs do after being sprayed with pesticide. Bugs become disoriented, have twitching legs, and respiratory problems. I have watched home owners spray yards in the middle of the day. Women are spraying too close to the plant. The chest area is full of blood vessels. Sprays volatilize into a gas at certain temperatures. Home owners cannot control where these gases travel. We could be giving our children a chemical from of autism. This could also cause breast cancer in both men and women. Our state will always have programs to control disease, mosquitoes, crickets, and grasshoppers. We must decrease our use of pesticide sprays.

Lead Paint. At this time, we are concerned with lead paint and other things in our children's toys, clothing, and bedding. Lead paint has always been a concern because young children suck on and eat anything. Lead use to contaminate our soils and waters from leaded gas and industrial waste. Lead paint and solder in our food cans give children high lead in their systems which affects every organ. Families also stretched their flour during World War II with lead paint shavings. Children who have suffered from lead poisoning are sluggish, listless, anemic, and have learning disabilities. Adults have mood disorders and neuropathy in their extremities. The treatment is to remove the source of contamination.

Does skull structure make a difference in the capacity that our children can learn? I have read some articles with individuals dealing with children with dyslexia. Their children have had brain scans, and they have some difference in structure of the skull. I am not qualified to judge or state an opinion in this matter. Talk with a neurologist. Retardation usually accompanies serious problems with skull structure. Do not leave your infant in his car seat for extensive periods of time. This flattens the skull.

I would like to remind everyone that minor differences in skull structure can be a matter of our ancestors and their ancestors. We are descended from the twelve tribes of Israel. There were four different mothers from these twelve tribes plus many grandparents. There was and is a lot of intermarriage occurring. I have ancestors from Germany, England, Norway, Holland, and the United States. Skull structure could be the differences in our heritage. A rule of thumb that I was taught in nursing school of course is head measurement. If you have a seven foot father even this may not be accurate. So doctors measure the distance between the eyes. This distance is usually the same size as one of your eyes.

Attention deficit disorder is a problem of self-control. Self-control of emotions does not happen as quickly as potty-training. Self-control is a life-long process. Parents and step parents may not be allowing time for self-control to develop. Parents have not learned self-control. Parents may be encouraging a lack of self-control by rewarding this behavior. If parents do not control their emotions and habits, children feel they do not need to control their emotions.

Your child may be in emotional shock. Children have many fears without being ridiculed and tormented for not wearing the most expensive clothing and having the perfect figure. Many of these fears are caused by that natural state of progression called awkwardness.

Unfortunately, children do not tell parents what is going on with them at school until things become big problems, or the teacher calls home. Children may seem alright when they come home, but they may be experiencing too much opposition causing emotional and social shock. It is hard to accept that your peers do not like or accept you. It is difficult to be a scapegoat for everything wrong in the classroom. Even young children know when this is happening. This will be covered more extensively in a chapter titled, "Social Shock."

Many parents have their children on medication for attention deficit disorder. Families do need stability in their home. An extremely hyperactive child wears the patience of everyone. Medications are sometimes an accepted method of treatment. I have wondered if the rates of random sexual activity, teenage pregnancy, and teenage suicide could be decreased by putting children and teenagers on a medication for an attention deficit disorder instead of birth control. Birth control may even counter the effects of these medications. This is something parents and step parents need to discuss with their physician. Research the internet for information.

Your child will learn faster and retain more if he is manageable. Parents can provide a more stable environment for everyone if the child is manageable. Other recommendations for treatment are counseling. The family is taught behavior modification. *Most doctors recommend avoiding over stimulation of your child and providing consistency and order in the home.* Strive for moderation in all things in your home. This is something that can be learned.

Parents, do you know how your child learns? Mother can tell anyone who listens about every sweet thing her child has done from birth to walking. She can tell anyone how her child learned to walk and talk. There were patterns to this. These patterns more than likely will show up when a child is learning concepts which will stimulate his brain.

Dr. Michael Ballam, a musical professor at Utah State University, teaches in his lectures and audiotapes that there are nine basic ways that individuals learn. Those ways are audio, visual, mathematics, tactile, interpersonal, intra personal, spacial, linguistic, and music.[10] Audio learning is by hearing, visual learning is by seeing, and mathematical learning is by numerical order. Mathematics is the process by which we learn how to add to in order instead of divide up in order or in chaos. Intra personal learning is learning by knowing our self, our assets, and our limitations. Interpersonal is learning by dealing with each other in various capacities such as school, work, family, and marriage. Spacial learning is the ability to learn about the relationships of different spaces in our environment. A child can learn more through spacial learning if the emphasis is not on how things are divided in his life, but how things are similar and are added to. We learn by adding precepts, not dividing, isolating, and discarding precepts.

Linguistics is the ability to communicate with others and to even teach them. Individuals also learn by music—not just by listening, but by singing, humming, and performing. Learning to play a musical instrument forces a child to use all areas of the brain, both hemispheres of the brain, and to coordinate them in concert together. However, some people learn more visually or by audio methods. Usually, learning is a combination of audio, visual, and something else. That something is parents and their example of learning. This is where our talents come from. Some are artists, writers, architects, doctors, lawyers, musicians, singers, and scholars—like parents.

There are many things that come from the way we learn and when we refuse to learn. Do you spend enough time with your child that you know how he or she learns? It is just as important for parents to know this about their children, as well as teachers. If a child learns by audio, and you are teaching by video, there will be problems with learning. When there are problems with learning, there are always problems with behavior. The child has to cover his weaknesses in some way. This increases his anxiety and your frustration with him.

Concentrate on learning how your child learns. Create an atmosphere for learning. Work on the other chapters in this book. Raising children has never been easy, except on television or in the movies. This is in thirty minute segments with a very nice house payed for, job security, utility bills paid, and children who are popular, who are A-students, cooperative, and who are on several sports teams. This is not reality.

Parents have heard of the following principle: "If you want your child to change, parents have to change." Could this principle apply to learning, too? If you want your child to learn, parents must learn, too. If parents cannot learn in the world in which they have taken their children, do not expect your child to learn in that world. Parents may have to change what they are learning. This is accomplished by the tenth method of learning. We will discuss this in another chapter. Naturally, it includes all of the nine areas that we discussed in this section.

List any physical causes that you suspect affects your child or step child's behavior. What are you potentiating in your environment? This includes medications for the heart, blood pressure, asthma, diabetes, cancer, arthritis, depression, boredom, pain, street drugs, food preservatives, and pesticide sprays. How much sugar and caffeine are you and your children consuming? Is your child or step child smoking and using illegal drugs? Does your child or step child have a desire to acquire knowledge? Does your child or step child work only at things that interest him? Who is encouraging or rewarding your child's lack of self-control? Are you willing to give yourself chemical autism and risk others' health for a chemical high?

---

[10]Dr. Michael Ballam, <u>More Music and the Mind</u>, Cassette Two, Side A, Phoenix Productions, Logan, Utah, 1999.

Chapter Four

The Big, Bright, Beautiful World

In all the smog, there is a big, bright, beautiful world out there that the Lord has given us to use as shelter, food, and enjoyment while we attend this mortal school on Earth.[11] Each country, each landscape has its problems, its challenges, and its assets–its people.

Children are curious about everything. They have many questions about their world. Children also like to take things apart to see how they work. Children and step children also like to take parents and step parents apart to see how they work and to stop them from working.

Everyone becomes trapped in curiosity. There is so much to choose from in this world. Parents forget how much time is involved in paying for these things. They forget how much time is involved in participating in and traveling to these things. School work becomes an after thought. They will make it up afterwards. As a result, children learn a little about a lot briefly, but there is no time to study and ponder. Families feel sports is where learning takes place.

There are so many things that distract children and even adults. If a parent is distracted, too, a family can be controlled by excessive curiosity with things that really are just novelties, passing fancies, or fantasies in their lives. Our forefathers always said: "Curiosity killed the cat." Perhaps this is one of the reasons that the Savior has cautioned us to stay away from being caught up in the mysteries of the world.[12]

It is interesting to note that the opposite of curiosity is apathy. When someone is apathetic, they do not have normal emotions, concerns, or interest in others. They are indifferent or unmoved for someone who is pathetic or for whom they should have pity. These things are all symptoms listed in the attention deficit disorders. Could our indulgence in excessive curiosity in things and substances actually cause the opposite of what we want to accomplish in our children?

Children cannot learn leadership skills in hobbies, novelties, and passing fantasies. Skills of competition are not the same as leadership skills. Though hobbies can be very interesting and entertaining, children learn leadership qualities from their spiritual, emotional, and social experiences. Leadership comes from work, service, sacrifice, and persistence.

In these experiences, a child has had to work for what he received. He has had to work with others, too. It is easy to work on fun things. Children have to learn how to work, obey, and persist when it is not so fun. This is what will get children through the misfortunes in their lives, especially when parents are no longer with their children. Children will not have to turn to various addictions, depression, and thoughts of suicide.

Some children receive opportunities to learn leadership skills in school. Because of time, competition, money, and popularity, only a few get the opportunity to learn how to be a leader. Children know when they are being left out, or there is no hope for them in the classroom.

---

[11]Doctrine and Covenants 59:18-20, p. 109.

[12]1 Corinthians 13:1-2, The Holy Bible, p. 1454.

There are fewer opportunities for children to learn leadership skills because spiritual matters are heavily regulated by current laws. This clashes with the brotherly kindness aspect of our lives. This conflict causes a distorted vision that everyone is an impediment to our progress because they have some impediment. They are not worthy of any consideration, kindness, and do not deserve a turn to learn leadership skills. No wonder, children cannot wait their turn.

Spiritual leadership skills are important because this is where a child learns how to be a good follower. One has to be a good follower, a good listener, and allow others the space to learn before they can be a good leader who can direct and instruct others. Remember. Leaders must inspire confidence in others at a time when their followers are struggling and not so cooperative. If children cannot do this when they are not struggling, children certainly will not be able to do things that help themselves and others when they are struggling.

It is in the spiritual aspects of our personality, that all will have opportunities to learn and become leaders. This learning comes from contrite spirits, not egos. There will be opposition as we learn spiritual skills, but opposition is the process by which *all of us* learn all things.

Besides consuming large amounts of children's time, hobbies and passing fantasies conflict with the most important spiritual learning process in our lives, the Sabbath Day. Hobbies and recreation have replaced observance of the Sabbath Day. If hobbies and sports are not played on Sunday, Sunday has become their day of travel. There are blessings associated with keeping the Sabbath Day holy.[13] These blessings we do not fully comprehend, but they are attached to this important day in every week of our lives. If we do not observe the Sabbath Day, these blessings are lost to us.

These blessings are very important patterns which children of all ages need to recognize other patterns in their life. Remember. Children with learning disabilities and attention deficit disorders have difficulty recognizing patterns. Do their families keep the Sabbath Day holy?

First, the Lord set the pattern for His children. The Lord labored six days and rested the seventh day. Even God, Himself, kept the Sabbath Day holy when the World was created. He could have justified breaking the Sabbath that one time. There was a War going on in Heaven. The world was being prepared for us. I am sure that He had some loose ends He could have worked on. He didn't. He rested to show those who would have their spiritual matters regulated heavily in their lifetimes the correct pattern to follow. By resting, the Savior was prepared for the World on each and every one of His Mondays.

After the Lord set the pattern, keeping the Sabbath Day holy became a commandment.[14] Keeping the Sabbath Day holy is one of the Ten Commandments. The Sabbath Day became a holy day for ourselves and for others, too. All, including families, those who work for us, our animals, and the stranger within our gates are not to work.[15] We are to assemble and be instructed or reasoned with in our churches.[16] This has to be done at a meeting place where we

---

[13]Doctrine and Covenants 59:9-20, pp. 108-109.

[14]Exodus 20:8-11, The Holy Bible, pp. 109-110.

[15]Exodus 20:10-11, The Holy Bible, pp. 109-110.

[16]Deuteronomy 16:8, The Holy Bible, p. 279.

can hear spiritual messages. It is a special way to train ourselves to plan ahead and choose priorities. We are in control of our spirits. Our wants, needs, and desires do not control our spirits. However, instead of getting better, the Sabbath became heavily regulated.

Second, the Sabbath Day is a reminder of the redemption of the Jews from bondage with the Egyptians.[17] We have been in bondage to many things and many people, too. It is well that we remember what the Lord has brought us and our ancestors and our descendants through. We need to thank God for freeing all of us from the many things which people have held us in bondage. This is an excellent pattern to teach children bondage versus gratitude.

Third, the Sabbath Day is observed on the first day of the week in memory of the Resurrection and Ascension of the Savior. He arose from His tomb on the Sabbath. Those in authority of His church changed the Sabbath Day observance from the seventh day of the week to the first day of the week. However, if the Savior had arose on any other day of the week, we still would have been asked to observe the Sabbath Day. We still would be asked to remember and renew the covenants that we made in our spiritual progression. We do this by actual worship and partaking of the sacrament. This helps us remember that the Sabbath was made for man–not man for the Sabbath. (Mark 2:27)

Fourth, we are to rest from our temporal labors.[18] The Sabbath is a constant reminder of the need for spiritual sustenance. It is a duty before God to rest from our labors. The Lord has always instructed us to not run faster than we have strength.[19] He ought to know. He created our bodies. He knows how the body functions, and He knows the body and mind has limits. Those bodily functions are improved with rest. Our Savior wants us to rely on Him for rest and salvation, not a smorgasbord of hobbies and recreation.

It is extremely unfair to others when individuals do not rest in body and mind from their labors. All have worked with co-workers who show up five minutes before they are to start work. They are sunburned, exhausted, and haven't slept because they have been driving all day Sunday and early Monday morning to get to work on time. While at work, they cannot carry their load. These individuals are burning the candle at both ends. They expect others to do the same to help them out. In other words, you do most of their work for the shift. They get the paycheck which will help pay for their next vacation in two or three weeks. Naturally, you get the privilege of helping them out again or carrying their load. If you complain, you are the trouble-maker. If you do not do their work, the oncoming shift is overburdened. Good service is compromised. Some of these services can mean the difference between life and death.

By now, I am sure you are wondering what does keeping the Sabbath Day holy have to do with attention deficit disorder in children and adults. Remember those sunburned, exhausted, coworkers who have not slept or ate in over twenty-four hours. Their children were with them. Their children, too, are sunburned, exhausted, and impatient. They are not prepared for school and cannot carry their load. If children were not with their parents, they were most likely with individuals who did not keep the Sabbath Day holy to entertain many children. The children

---

[17]Deuteronomy 5:15, The Holy Bible, p. 262.

[18]Doctrine and Covenants 59:10, p. 109.

[19]Doctrine and Covenants 10:4, p. 17; Isaiah 40:31, The Holy Bible, p. 909.

stayed up late and ate junk food, too. In any case, children do not rest while parents were away. Homework was skipped also.

Parents have the idea that they can make up this lost work in their children. Being together for frequent hobbies and vacations makes up for an education. Elementary education is not that important anyway. It does not matter if their children cannot focus or pay attention in school. Parents will make up this work in their children when it is convenient for them. This is where children learn that education is not fun, and they learn study skills which are some very bad study habits.

We need to realize that keeping the Sabbath Day holy is a sign that we know there are others following behind us in this life. If we do not observe the Sabbath, rest from our temporal labors, and learn spiritual matters, we will not be able to carry our load. We leave our work for others to complete, as well as their own work. We will not be able to teach our children how to carry their burdens. We will be too tired and too angry with them because they are not able to carry their load.

Others, who follow us, will have a heavier load to carry, especially our children and grandchildren. They have their own salvation to work out. Our children have their set of problems to solve. They have their own families to raise and support. Their covenants are as important as our covenants. Observance of the Sabbath Day is a way that we are honest with our fellow men. Better health and more opportunities to learn, grow, and serve with clear minds will result.[20] If we delight in the Sabbath, we will find our sacred honor.[21]

Our Sabbath is not so delightful. Parents feel like they are fighting with children all day long and accomplishing nothing on their Sabbath. Parents, the Sabbath begins at midnight. If you and your children are up late into the Sabbath partying, and then arise with only enough time to eat a bowl of sugared cereal, your Sabbath will not be a delight.

Teachers have been telling parents for years they cannot teach your children on an empty stomach or sugar-high foods. Children are not manageable, and they do not pay attention. It is that way with the Sabbath School, too. Parents might as well face the fact that the things they and their children learn at their Sabbath School are going to save their lives spiritually. Their presence in church and home will even save their lives physically and their lives financially, etc.

After your child has eaten a bowl of sugared cereal, his healthy, but empty digestive system quickly absorbs sugar. It is a quick energy booster, but your child has just received an overdose of carbohydrates for his body weight, and your child is still fatigued from the weekend.

By the time your child dresses after breakfast and arrives at church, any food value for learning and retaining is gone. The only thing that remains is the high blood sugar. With a healthy body which produces insulin, a high blood sugar will soon decrease, too. It will be replaced by a low-blood sugar level. Your child has no fuel to learn by, and his only thought is to get out of this meeting, get home, and get some more food quickly while Mom fixes dinner. What does your child eat–more sugared-cereal or sugared toaster items?

Your Sabbath has become encumbered. Mother feels she is stuck in a rut because she will not be keeping the Sabbath Day holy by fixing a large meal for breakfast and dinner. Mother

---

[20]Doctrine and Covenants 89:18-21, p. 176.

[21]Isaiah 58:13-14, The Holy Bible, p. 931.

is tired, too, and in a hurry herself. She would like to relax on the weekend. The <u>Doctrine and Covenants</u> again has the answer for us.

> *13 And on this day thou shalt do none other thing, only let thy food*
> *be prepared with singleness of heart that thy fasting may be perfect,*
> *or, in other words, that thy joy may be full.*

<u>*Doctrine and Covenants*</u> *59:13*

The term, singleness of heart, does not mean that mothers cannot fix meals for their families. It means focusing your thoughts and spirits on the Sabbath. Thinking and pondering require fuel. The family can help. This can be a time of great closeness. Cooking *with* someone is a pleasure. Many discussions can take place. Children can learn how to cook instead of taking a nap or playing video games. They can experience some one-on-one time with parents. Your food does not have to be elaborate, but needs to be nourishing and something of substance. Your children can also learn how to clean up after cooking and eating.

We learn many time-lines in our life time. I have had to learn time-lines in history for different centuries and learn religious time lines for classes. Here is an important time-line that we need to learn about ourselves. It will bring us better health, and may save our life some day.

OUR LIFE-LINE

Birth	Accountability	Priesthood	Mission		Marriage	
b	8	12	19	21		Death

Boys Temple Endowment at mission (19y)–Wear protective garment
Girls Temple Endowment mission (21y or older) or marriage–Wear protective garment

WHAT PROTECTS US IN OUR LIFE-LINE

<u>Keeping the Sabbath Day Holy</u>
<u>Word of Wisdom</u>
      <u>Endowment</u>
     <u>Scriptures</u>

"Throw out the life-line." These are beautiful words in a Protestant hymn by Edward S. Ufford by the same title. The chorus in this hymn describes someone who is drifting away. They plead for someone to throw out the life-line because someone is sinking. This song does not mean throw the life-line away. Keeping the Sabbath Day holy and keeping the Word of Wisdom in our lives are our life-lines which will prevent us from sinking or drifting away from truth and reality. These life-lines will also keep us from drifting away from learning and from our families and step families. Our health will be preserved by these two lifelines.

Word of Wisdom. In February 1833, Joseph Smith was meeting with a group of men who would later become prophets. This group was known as the School of the Prophets. They used tobacco. His wife Emma did not like the smoke and cleaning up after them. She complained to

Joseph. *Joseph also noticed they were not performing up to level, and the spirit of the Lord was not there.* He inquired of the Lord. He was given the 89th section of the <u>Doctrine and Covenants</u> as direction. Following this section was optional at first. It became a commandment when Heber J. Grant was president. This section is known as the Word of Wisdom. This Word of Wisdom has given health to many members of The Church of Jesus Christ of Latter-day Saints..

The Lord's Word of Wisdom was given to us as a warning for there would be evil-designs that exist in the hearts of men and women in the latter-days. The Word of Wisdom is for the weakest of saints, a baby or the sick. Simply put, alcohol, tobacco, coffee, tea, and strong drinks are not for the body. Drugs are not either. Though they may partake of what is not good for them, everyone seems to agree on most of this.

We have been disputing about strong drinks since this Word of Wisdom was given. The seasons are changing. Partaking of the same ingredients in a cold drink is still breaking the Word of Wisdom. We have replaced our faith, our hope, our charity, our patriarchal blessing, our prayers, and our temple endowment for a forty-four ounce or two-liter size caffeinated drink. We do this several times a day. Faith, hope, charity, prayer, patriarchal blessings, and our endowment are supposed to strengthen and stimulate us when we are tired–even when our fatigue comes from working two or more jobs or staying up all night with a sick baby.

If we persist, we will never advance. There are hidden treasures of knowledge and wisdom that we will never obtain. There are doctors who are trying to find cures for our health problems. They will never find them because their research is affected by the things that we insist on taking for energy when we are running faster than we can walk.

When we fast or anoint the sick, we pray for help. When our loved ones improve or we stop fasting, the first drink we seek is a caffeinated drink. Babies are given flat caffeinated drinks for upset stomachs and diarrhea. It is no wonder that our prayers are not answered, and we have the health that we do. It is no wonder, we cannot stay on task and control our thoughts.

When we are sick, the first drink that we should obtain is water–water that has minerals still in it. Clear liquids such as apple juice and grape juice should follow. Full liquids such as soups and juices which have pulp in them come next. A soft diet and a regular diet with meat in normal proportions follow. The Word of Wisdom says to eat meat sparingly. Our bodies require amino acids which are found in protein so this wisdom probably means proportion size. We have an increase in Type II Diabetes which is caused by improper portion size and stress. Even Benjamin Franklin has said that we should not eat or drink to the point of dullness.

Has your Sabbath Day become encumbered? Do parents and children have spiritual dyslexia? Spiritual dyslexia is exchanging sweet for bitter, darkness for light, and good for evil. Keeping the Sabbath Day holy and eating according to the Word of Wisdom keep us from spiritual dyslexia. Are your meals and snacks encumbering your progress and your health? Are you eating comfort foods or foods that cause dullness?

Are you and your children's hearts failing because you are running faster than you can walk? Are your hearts waxing cold with family members and their many crisis'? Are you moved by your family members' pain and suffering? Can family members stay on task with a cold, failing heart? Can you teach and comfort your family in the trials of social shock with a cold, failing heart? Is your cold, failing heart a result of the things you digest?

Chapter Five

Social Shock

As a registered nurse, I have taken care of many patients in shock. The most common forms of shock are hemorrhagic shock, caused by blood loss; dehydration, caused by fluid loss; and anaphylactic shock, caused by an allergic reaction. In addition, there is also septic shock, which is caused by an infection. Any kind of drug or chemical that we ingest which effects the heart's ability to pump will in some way lower or raise the blood pressure drastically. This is called chemical shock. Cardiogenic shock results when the normal rhythm or pathways of the heart are interrupted. Respiratory failure and cardiac failure causes severe shock. Even fainting is a form of shock. I suspect there is also a carcinogenic shock, too. (Cancer related)

Each type of shock has some basic rules to follow and some special instructions of care to follow. It is easy to take care of a patient who is in shock and does not communicate with you. With oxygen, intravenous fluids, blood transfusions, and keeping an eye on the patient's intake and output, the patient usually recovers. Eventually, the patient wakes up and is in shock that he was in shock. He wonders what happened. We have to reassure him that he is going to be all right several times.

A patient in shock becomes fearful when he is in situations that he or she has no control over. These situations will affect him or her the rest of his life. If his employer suspects that his health will affect his job in any way, he will be terminated. His livelihood will be gone. His retirement will be gone. He is worried his friends and family (in that order) will not like him anymore. In most cases, he has some terrific fears for a condition that will be gone six weeks after surgery. As soon as he is back at work, and everything seems back to normal, his "emotional shock" subsides, until he get the "financial shock" of his bill.

Patients in shock can become angry and will not let anyone help them. They also cannot follow simple instructions. This can be frustrating. It is difficult to reason with these patients. Nurses have had to think of some pretty elaborate stories to talk a patient into letting them help them. Some patients in shock realize the nurse is giving them the old razzle-dazzle. Finally, the patient has to be restrained to the bed and sedating medication given.

Shock in our neighborhoods and communities happens the same way as in a patient. No matter what people do and no matter what age group, nothing seems to follow the expected path. These people have a dehydration of spirit. Ezekiel called this condition dry bones.[22] For most people, spiritual dehydration is caused by not ingesting daily things that will restore their spirit.

For many people, it is a massive hemorrhage of spirit. It is frustrating to do good and receive criticism. It is maddening, even for children, to always be told they could do better and more by others who are doing even less. It is heart-rendering to have one's performance judged by the money your parents make which affects the clothes you wear, the friends you have, the cars you drive, the toys you have, and even the hair-do you have. It is frightening and deflating

---

[22]Ezekiel 37:11, The Holy Bible, p. 1080.

to the spirit to be judged by the color of your skin, how thin you are, or how well you can score on a sports team. Even children know that only a few are allowed to excel under these circumstances. There are only so many players allowed on a team.

With all of the criticisms that children receive, children wonder what chance do I have when I get bigger. The world is growing larger. That world has already told me that I have no place for various reasons. Children feel like a pebble in the sand which is tossed to and fro by the waves of the Atlantic Ocean. Adults would withdraw into their own protective shell if the same things were happening to them which our children are asked to endure. They are asked to endure this without any spiritual training.

Even parents feel like a piece of dust in the Earth. Your family's problems feel like gigantic boulders or even mountains.[23] Let me ease your mind a little. If you are feeling like one of the sands of the sea or of the dust of the Earth, your family is right on target. We are all like sands of the Earth.[24] According to Abraham's blessing, Abraham's descendants would be as numerous as the dust of the Earth and would people one great nation. In Abraham, all families of the Earth will be blessed.[25]

I find it very interesting. No matter what color of our skin, God has always provided for each generation of the many sands of the sea. He wants all of His children back. One generation effects another. He does not provide more for any one generation. We are all equal in His sight. He blesses our efforts. Those blessings are not equal because our efforts are not equal. We have been given our free agency. Free agency will be discussed in another chapter.

Families will be tested in all things. Our free agency is being tested. Jesus had His trials. His free agency was tested. We are going to have our trials, too. One person may have shed His blood for all of Heavenly Father's children. However, this one person, as great as He is, is not tested for all of Heavenly Father's children.

Families may not feel so blessed in their trials while being tested. Their trial may seem like a kangaroo court. They feel like their hands are tied like Isaac, and the verdict is in the pouch. We do not know how to remove the boulders and mountains impeding our progress in our testing. These boulders and mountains can cause an emotional shock.

I call this emotional shock in our neighborhoods and communities, social shock. I have often wondered if attention deficit disorder is social shock with fear. Attention deficit disorder with hyperactivity is social shock with fear and anger. One is the victim. One is the victimizer. Sometimes, it is convenient to be the victim. Sometimes, one has no choice, but to be a victim. Sometimes, it is convenient to be the victimizer. Sometimes, one has no choice, but to be a victimizer.

As expected, it is difficult to learn when one is a victim or a victimizer. Because of the fear of man, children withdraw into a world that is safe and accepting. Anyone who is a victimizer also has difficulty learning. Their hyperactivity comes from the feeling that they have to cover their tracks or behavior because of guilt. They cannot look others in the eye. They

---

[23]Matthew 17:20, The Holy Bible, p. 1217.

[24]Genesis 13:16, The Holy Bible, p. 19.

[25]Genesis 12:3, The Holy Bible, p. 17.

become very nervous and fidgety. Something has replaced the learning process in both victim and victimizer which effects their entire life.

It's the "fight or flight mechanism" within us. It is the adrenal gland's reflexive response for danger. The Lord did not give this protective mechanism to fight or flight over the minor things in our lives. The Savior gave us this response to prevent injury when we get burnt, or we are in danger. The danger or injury comes from not recognizing good and evil.[26] He did not want us to be standing around thinking: "Now, should I exit quickly when my house is burning down?" Should I criticize my family instead of helping to put out the fire in our home?"

Everyone has been burnt so many times by everyone else at places of learning, we have now turned something good, such as learning, into something bitter. Our hearts are waxing cold toward one another because of this.[27] In other words, attention deficit disorder and attention deficit disorder with hyperactivity comes without, not within a child. It is learned. It is taught. It is forced upon everyone, not just a child.

Children have not had enough positive attention and time to develop social skills on their own to discard attention deficit behaviors. As a result, without quality attention from parent, teacher, and neighborhood, a child will become a teenager and an adult with an attention deficit disorder. Everyone wants to treat the child. No one wants to treat the society he came from. This would step on too many toes and affect too many pockets.

The child is expected to develop without opportunities to develop. No one plays with a child with attention deficit disorder or attention deficit disorder with hyperactivity. No one talks to them, sits by them, eats with them at lunch, or includes them in any way, unless they have to. The isolation is very painful. This limits their exposure to learning experiences. The child is graded on the same scale as children who have a multitude of opportunities to develop and an emotionally safe environment to live in. This is extremely unfair.

To add insult to injury, the parents are working several jobs to pay for their own life styles and hobbies. They are away from their children for long periods of time. They assume a child wants their parents' lifestyle and hobby. To compensate, they put a child in sports where he can learn leadership skills and some hobbies, too.

While in sports, the child is not played with or is belittled, teased, and taunted in front of his parents and peers. Parents can't hear from the bleachers what is being said to their child. They would not understand the slang that children have deliberately created to hide this teasing in front of adults anyway. When the game is over, feelings of anger, resentment, and inadequacy are supposed to leave. This is what being part of a team means. The "ten second rule" does not apply to this kind of hurt. It will be years for the child to heal from the insults they received at school and at home.

When children do complain to their parent or teachers, he is told to toughen up or "cowboy up" and take it. In reality, any cowboy would have decked the child or adult who had called their child or themselves such demeaning remarks. It is not how the Savior handled mocking, but these individuals would have deserved it. However, hitting others does not make us feel better, and we get in more trouble.

---

[26]Isaiah 5:20-21, The Holy Bible, p. 868.

[27]Matthew 24:12, The Holy Bible, p. 1230.

Children do not have any respect for teachers. There are some reasons for that. It is not attention deficit disorder. We all have had incidents with school teachers that both parents and children could not understand. Parents and students forget that teachers are people with families who have problems and money worries. Teachers are tired when they must work two jobs, too.

When parents and students become angry with their teachers, they wonder if teachers are competent to be teaching their children something important like mathematics, science, or English. Many students feel that mathematics, science, English, history, etc. are not that important, or this teacher would not be teaching it.

Children do not realize that teachers do not know the whole story. They are trying to manage, as well as teach, hundreds of children, not just your child. Children and parents do know when the teacher does not want to know the whole story. It was easier to teach and to believe somebody in designer clothes and who is making straight A's.

No one knows when families are going through personal trials and enduring much emotional shock. No one cares. They have their own problems and their own agendas. If children report offending children, they are labeled a "snitch" and are isolated anyway. Parents do not believe their children could tease and taunt other children anyway. Timid children who once were helpful and good natured quit doing things around others and for others. The school teacher becomes more angry with them than the offending children.

Teachers are not in as much control of their class as they think they are. Teachers have to set limits with all of the children in his or her class. They know who is the class manipulator and class bully, as well as the class clown.

Our children's peers like to play the "bait and switch game" with each other. "The bait and switch game" is the battle for friends, popularity, and control of the teacher and her classroom. Children do not have to be in a gang to be extremely jealous and territorial. This "bait and switch game" causes a lot of distress in our children.

In the "bait and switch game," children tell other students, particularly timid ones, how terrible their teachers are to them or were to a sibling. They also tell how terrible other children are to them. When a particular child agrees how terrible others are and adds their own comments, the classmate runs, not walks, to teachers and classmates and states, "Bill or Suzie said: 'This, and this, and this about you.' He or she thinks you are terrible." Naturally, the classmates and the teacher do not have good feelings about Bill and Suzie. They are on the look-out for problems. These children are avoided and shunned. Everything they do is condemned.

This behavior continues and happens in the work place, our neighborhoods, our churches, and our families. I am sure it has happened to everyone at some time in their life. This is a hard environment for your child to learn under. It is a hard environment to live in. This is a hard environment to work in.

This is not attention deficit disorder and attention deficit disorder with hyperactivity. This is managing territory with the "fight or flight mechanism." Individuals are fighting with lies and gossip. If we are busy running from things or fighting with people physically and psychologically, there is not much room in our minds to learn or time to do the things we need to be doing. Usually, territory is controlled by evil-speaking against many of the Lord's anointed. The Lord will not bless us if we control others this way.

Children are dealing with crime, death, and divorce in their homes. These are very hard situations for adults to endure. Though children are taught right and wrong actions, children are forced to live with more wrong than right actions. Our children are becoming immune to right and wrong because they have to ignore crimes of siblings, parents, step parents, community leaders, and other infamous people in the news. If children do not let people hurt them by various behaviors, they do not see others being hurt by their behavior and attitudes.

It is a common practice to give high energy, caffeinated drinks and candy to children just before a scheduled visitation. Step parents give decongestants and/or alcohol to settle down a child who is bouncing off the wall. At the end of the visit and as a return gesture, the step parent or biological parent gives the child high energy drinks and candy to give the custodial parent a dose of their own medicine. Of course, the child also receives the third degree at each location. This is a hard environment to live in. It is a hard environment to learn in, especially when the child goes to school the next day after this treatment every weekend.

We have read of accounts from the news media about step mothers abusing and even killing young step children. I admit I do not know their full stories. Let's look at this further. Step mothers ultimately receive the responsibility to care for young children at night since fathers work. No matter how much a step mother loves her husband and his children, it is not the responsibility of a step mother to care for a step child who is an infant or toddler. Infants and toddlers are acutely aware of strangers. Screaming infants and toddlers on caffeinated drinks and candy are not fun when the child is familiar with you. The child cannot tell you what is wrong. Step mothers are tired, too. They usually have to work because of child support. Do not pass an infant or toddler back and forth like livestock. Fathers should wait for overnight visits when the child is older. This is a consequence of divorce.

If I as a nurse expected my patients to function, while they were in shock, as they normally do, I would be fired. We are expecting our children to function while they are in physical, emotional, social, intellectual, financial, moral, and spiritual shock. The child in social shock is not suppose to notice that he is in shock or complain. Some children can recover from this shock with some support systems. Some children cannot recover. There are more and more children all the time who are not recovering. They seek addictions for their pain. The glimmer of the world will not compensate, all though many children and adults try.

It is sad to note, the things that would restore and heal the spirits in our children are to be avoided. Spiritual things are even regulated by law. In countries where children are excelling intellectually, worship of their form of deity is not prohibited by law. Only in the United States of America are spiritual things considered offensive. In fact, it is not cool to believe in God. We must believe the things that Hollywood wants us to believe in.

We are raising little spirits to become dynamic, productive spirits, but we feel their attention deficit disorders have no spiritual connections. The only things left for our children to defend themselves or have any acceptance and attention are: to continue with the childish things in their lives, exist on pride, or pick up various weapons of rebellion. Children do not understand that there are better ways to control or alleviate the emotional shocks in their lives.

Keep track of the physical, spiritual, intellectual, and emotional intake and output of parent and child. Are you and your child trying to develop personalities with entertainment and by only being a spectator? Does everyone have opportunities to develop without competition?

Who is trying to control everyone by either being a victim or victimizer? Is your step family learning how to deal with opposition? Is your family immune to right and wrong? Do family members have to develop a hard heart to ignore the crimes in families and community?

Chapter Six

"Those Childish Things"

Attention deficit disorder and attention deficit disorder with hyperactivity are often a result of not putting away childish things.[28] We can only serve one master, either the adult within us or the child within us.[29] Adults always have some "kid" left in them. This makes life interesting and gives adults a little sense of humor. However, we are always growing up. For the most part, adults put away childish things.

Even young children put away childish things. This is the pattern of normal growth and development which leads to maturity. Young children stop sucking on a bottle. It is easier and quicker to chew food. Children find out they can eat on the run if they eat table food. Table food tastes better. Children also have better nutrition and more energy with food they chew. Mothers know that it is easier to toilet-train a child who is eating table food. Children have put away some childish things already, and they are only one or two years old. No matter what age, crisis' will come and crisis' will go. Some will even stay around as we raise and provide for our families. There are some childish things that we must give up in order to raise ourselves and our families. This is where your acceptance and satisfaction with yourself lies.

First, it is easier to put away childish things if we have learned how to read, write, do arithmetic, articulate in a language, and are familiar with geographic areas of the world. This develops our brain and gives us something of substance to rely on in times of stress. With reading, writing, arithmetic, history, and the ability to communicate in a language, children become aware that there are others on this planet besides them.

If we have done this in proper order through our various school years, we will be preparing for our future, our spouse's future, and our children's future. Our parents' future will be more pleasant, too. If we cannot provide for ourselves and rely on ourselves, we will not be able to provide for a spouse's future, our children's future, and an aged parent.

Second, one has to accept himself, his limitations, and develop his assets. Everyone has been given at least one gift within themselves. We all have something to offer each other. All have opposition to overcome. The Apostle Paul taught us in Galatians 6:3-5 to accept ourselves. We do not have to inflate ourselves. We bear our own burdens.

Third, a belief that one can always catch-up their homework and chores when it is convenient for them is childish. Any sports fan knows how hard it is to catch-up in a game when the score is twenty-one to eight with three minutes left to play. Likewise, it is difficult to play catch-up as an adult all the time when the scores of life are in that same range. It is more difficult for children to play catch-up all the time. They become frustrated, lose interest, and become distracted. *Their fans leave. Sports teaches a child to play catch-up, not leadership skills.*

---

[28]1 Corinthians 13:11, The Holy Bible, p. 1454.

[29]Matthew 6:24, The Holy Bible, p. 1196.

Fourth, hitting is a childish thing. Hitting indicates anger. Hitting indicates jealousy. If you are playfully hitting someone, it means you are angry with someone for some reason. The problem may have happened long ago. It is time to forgive and forget. Let others experience the mantle of their calling in their family and neighborhood with peace in their home and their community. This is maturity.

Hitting when we are adults is extremely childish behavior. It is also unlawful. We have brains, speech, and emotions to develop other means of expressing our feelings of displeasure. An appropriate tender touch and soft answers will take this anger from you. These methods will have better results.

Fifth, we have to learn how to stop on the green light.[30] When we were young, our parents and grandparents would not allow us to play across the street until we had learned to cross the street. We had to remember to look both ways. Because of the speed of cars, children are now taught to look left, then right, and left again, depending on which side of the street they are crossing from.

If there are lights at the intersection which we want to go through, we had to learn that red means stop, yellow means caution, not speed up, and green means go. There are times that we must stop on the green light. We will not know when this will happen until seconds before a decision must be made. Cars and pedestrians are in such a hurry. They do not acknowledge that the light has changed, and it is now someone else's turn to go. This is called defensive driving.

If we do not do any defensive driving, we will hit a pedestrian or another car. We could kill someone else or ourselves. We get the "joyful experience" of dealing with a car mechanic or a car salesman. A car payment will be for five or six years. The entire family is inconvenienced while waiting for the car to be repaired. In addition, we have to come up with our part of the insurance money. All of these situations occurred because we did not do defensive driving.

Likewise, we have to learn how to do some spiritual defensive driving. We have to learn how to look both ways on our spiritual journeys. We may have the green light. We may have the right to choose to go ahead. Our parents may have the money for emotional repairs. If we insist on going in the direction we are heading, we will collide with others in the intersection of their life. It may be our turn to use the intersection correctly, but we will still be hurt.

The Holy Ghost will be there to guide us and tell us when to stop quickly or go quickly. Nothing can compensate for this guide at an intersection of one's life. This education is an education in its self. It can be applied to our emotional, financial, moral, and spiritual safety, as well as our physical safety. There will always be an emotional payment due when unnecessary risks are taken. You may be diagnosed with an attention deficit disorder if you have not learned there are times when you will have to stop on the green light.

Sixth, excessive competition is a childish thing. This indicates that we have to be better than anyone else at everything to be accepted or noticed. Excessive competition is a sign of stress in yourself or your family. Individuals have not been born to win a blue ribbon at everything they do. Life is a test, not a contest. We will not win at every thing. We will work more than we play. We are to work out our salvation and decide which kind of vessel or person we want to be. There are many things in this plan of salvation for us to work out. We will learn more from our mistakes than we will learn from winning at every thing we try.

---

[30]Leif Nelson, Kearns, Utah Stake Mission Leader, May 2001.

Seventh, climbing and running away are childish things. Children usually climb to obtain what they cannot have. They run away when they cannot obtain what they wanted. Children also like to explore the unknown. They are very familiar with what is on the ground within their reach. They want what is out of reach.

Climbing and avoiding responsibility with extreme sports are so prevalent that search and rescue teams are now billing for their services. The areas in which the rescuers perform their services have put rescuers in great danger. Adults and teenagers still persist in climbing. They are the center of attention. Their view is spectacular. It does not matter how many broken bones they endure or that they have burdened their family with a traumatic death or long-term injuries.

Families are asked to wait alone while one finds themselves on their climbing adventures. Many climbers have forsaken families and left them to fend for themselves while they were climbing something just because it was there. Many of these climbers have been killed. They lost their focus while seeking fleeting fame and pleasure. Their focus should have been on their families. They have to be there to focus on their families and love them. They would have been much more famous had they stayed with their families.

Climbers and runners have not been able to lay aside those childish things of restlessness, fidgety behavior, climbing, and fame. It takes a strong person to lay down those high school dreams of fame to raise a family. It takes an ever stronger person to show their family how to lay down their high school dreams and weapons of rebellion. There is a higher unknown within us that is higher than any mountain including Mount Everest. This is why the Lord told us to avoid the mysteries of the world. The Savior did not cast himself off the temple, the mountain of the Lord, when tempted by Satan. Risky behavior is not part of His pattern for us.

Children will climb up, over, under, and on top of anything. Adults climb over people. They do this by many methods. The most common methods are having no regard for man and evil-speaking of the Lord's anointed.

Eighth, children have no fear or regard for man.[31] Parents often laugh about how their child is not afraid of anyone or anything. Children are not brave, but are experiencing bravado. Outbursts, yelling, and screaming are parts of having no fear or regard for man. Any broken commandment results from having no regard for man. Children develop no regard for man because they have been burned spiritually and emotionally. They are burned spiritually and emotionally by their consequences and again by gossip about their consequences.

Gossip occurs within families, friends, neighborhoods, newspapers, and every media that children use. There is so much gossip that children do not know who to believe or trust anymore. Gossip tells a child that a particular person is not worthy of respect. Children do not stop and count how many people around them are not worthy of respect in their life. If children would stop and count, they would become very suspicious.

Gossip has become such a way of life. Children or adults could not count on one hand anybody, including himself, that is not picked apart, considered failures, and not worthy of kind treatment in their families and neighborhoods. This is confusing to anyone, especially children.

It is no wonder that it is so difficult for youth to trust anyone, especially their own family. Children hear gossip about their own parents and grandparents from their parents and brothers and sisters, grandparents, and the neighborhood. Children must develop an insensitivity and a

---

[31]Luke 18:4, <u>The Holy Bible</u>, p. 1309; <u>Doctrine and Covenants</u> 101:84, p. 200.

lack of respect for their own parents to protect their feelings. Since children have no fear of their parents nor regard for them, this affects how parents can discipline their children. Parents who want to discipline without spanking and hitting have to have respect from children. Otherwise, the stern looks of their parents do not mean a thing to the child when he is misbehaving.

The child will have to give up childish behavior, impulsiveness, restlessness, etc., when someone he or she loves gives them a stern look. A child may not have any regard for man until a boyfriend or girlfriend gives him or her a stern look. The child will do anything for acceptance with someone he or she regards. This may lead to some broken commandments. However, your child has no regard for man or woman. This habit will continue with their spouse and children.

Many people feel that children who have no regard for others and break commandments and laws, particular the moral ones, have an attention deficit disorder. I find it very interesting. There are people who will not acknowledge the Ten Commandments and who seek to have ever reference to the Ten Commandments outlawed in public gatherings. These individuals, the ones who have no regard for the Ten Commandments, have no regard for the ones breaking these commandments are the quickest to point out that someone has broken a commandment. They must. They have an attention deficit disorder and do not deserve kind treatment. They holler this from the rooftops through our various media over and over. More than presidents have been impeached or thrown out of their calling this way. Many parents and spouses are impeached, too.

Ninth, evil-speaking against the Lord's anointed is one of the most harmful, childish things in our lives. Speaking evil against any of the Lord's anointed is unproductive and lingers into adulthood. With the help of scriptures, let's define what an anointing is. I will next define who the Lord's anointed is. We will also define what is not evil speaking of the Lord's anointed.

Anointing is the application of oil to the head of a person. It is a sacred experience. Kings were anointed to their callings by prophets. Men were anointed to be prophets. This is done by one having the authority to perform these anointings. Someone could not just anoint someone to become a king every time they were displeased with the present king or prophet.

The sick are anointed and blessed by two elders or high priests who have the proper authority to do this ordinance.[32] Anointing is a way to consecrate, ordain, hallow, and sanctify leaders and the sick among us. This anointing sets individuals apart and recognizes someone as one who has special needs and requires special blessings. Anointing is also a secular ritual. Travel was difficult in ancient times. There were many weary, dusty travelers. Anointing was a sign of hospitality. Anointing was also part of daily personal grooming.[33]

We sustain leaders by not speaking evil against them. Naturally, there is a Supreme category in leadership. Jesus Christ, the Savior and Creator of this World, is our Heavenly Father's Anointed One. He is our Leader and Great Shepherd. Jesus Christ volunteered to sacrifice His life for His Heavenly Father's children. Jesus Christ was picked to represent our Heavenly Father on the Earth.[34] In the tribe of Judah, their promised deliverer of the Jews is known as the Messiah. Since we all belong to a tribe within the House of Israel, Christ is the

---

[32]James 5:14-15, The Holy Bible, p. 1543; Mark 6:13, The Holy Bible, p. 1250.

[33]Luke 7:46, The Holy Bible, p. 1288; Ruth 3:3, The Holy Bible, p. 379.

[34]Revelation 12:7-10, The Holy Bible, p. 1577.

promised Savior or deliverer of us all. Christ comes from the Greek word, "Christus" which means to spread over" and refers to Jesus The Christ Jesus The Christ is the Anointed One by which we gather under his wing. In remembrance of His Sacrifice, we do not speak the Lord's name in vain.[35] Swearing is speaking evil against God's anointed, the supreme authority of this world. Unkind thoughts about the Savior and Creator of this World are extremely idle anyway.

There are other leaders that we must sustain. They are our prophet and his counselors, the twelve apostles, the seventies, the presiding authorities, our stake president, and his counselors, our bishop, and his counselors, and those in ward and stake positions.

However, this is not all. Every member of The Church of Jesus Christ of Latter-day Saints, who has been to the temple and endowed, has also been anointed. Our patriarchal blessings tell us what we have been anointed to. Anyone who has been blessed by elders of The Church of Jesus Christ of Latter-day Saints has been anointed. This includes many parents.

Parenthood is such a sacred position. It was included in the law of Moses which is also known as The Ten Commandments. Every parent is one of the Lord's anointed. The powers of procreation that are shared and instilled within parents did not come in a light moment or a "by the way process." These powers are not a biological clock that is ticking within us. These powers were given to us in a very hallowed moment.

Non members have not been endowed, anointed, or had their patriarchal blessing. Patriarchal blessings reveal what they would be anointed to. We do not know what or if we were anointed in some way to those things before we came to this Earth. So, we are not to speak evil of anyone. The Lord's anointed refers to all of us.

What is evil speaking of the Lord's anointed? Most people think this refers to lack of support and back-biting of leaders of their church. They are right. We are to support our leaders preceding us as well as current leaders. If we stay away from church meetings, we are speaking evil against the Lord's anointed. In order to stay away from our meetings, we had to speak that thought and those excuses to our mind for not attending meetings and supporting leaders.

Loud laughter against someone is evil speaking of the Lord's anointed. Isolating, bullying, and stonewalling others with their confidences and your half-truths and lies are all ways of evil speaking of the Lord's anointed.

The Lord's servants are set apart and are entitled to revelation, but they also have to learn step by step, and degree by degree, just like we all do. This takes time. As they are learning, they are dealing with crisis' for many people while working and raising a family. Is our backbiting depleting their energy, as well as our own? Are our expressions of feelings causing confrontations? Are we trying to stir up or anger individuals against their leaders? Other individuals may be clinging to them for emotional stability. When we disagree with leaders, we are assuming that we know more than the Lord's servants. We may not know the full story. We are not allowing this servant of the Lord time and a pleasant atmosphere to learn his commission or duties? We are not allowing them to experience the mantle of his or her calling in peace?

Gossip is speaking evil against the Lord's anointed. We are not going to be blessed with a clear-thinking mind to use for: smart mouths, malicious teasing, passing on half-truths or personal information, isolation, or for swearing. We do not like to listen to gossip about our loved ones. The Savior does not want to listen to gossip and swearing about one of His children.

---

[35]Matthew 5:34-37, The Holy Bible, p. 1194.

42

Members of The Church of Jesus Christ of Latter-day Saints believe in ministering angels.[36] If a member of your family has died, such as a parent, grandparent, sibling, child, or grandchild, they will most likely be the ministering angels that will be assigned to you and other members of your family. There are not too many family members who like hearing others swearing against their loved ones in their presence. These ministering angels leave, as anyone would, if they overheard someone speaking against their family in mortality.

We have free agency. Are we not entitled to express our opinions? Yes. However, it is through evil speaking of the Lord's anointed that our initiative or the ability to stay on task becomes negatively oriented. It is then easier to tempt our free agency with other things.

We have rights. If we have learned how to stop on some green lights, we can do what we have been instructed. We are instructed in the scriptures to love all men, not just those we love. We were told not to judge anyone also. All are to speak peace to one another, become unified, bear one other's burdens, and to let virtue affect our thoughts as well as our actions. We cannot do this with an authority complex which causes us to speak evil against the Lord's anointed.

It has become a national pastime to speak evil against our national leaders. It is interesting to note, there are scriptures telling us not to speak evil against dignitaries.[37] It takes a strong person to break this habit in their lives when they are exposed to it everyday on the television, in the newspaper, movies, and in idle chit-chat. Once formed, this habit will not remain with just dignitaries. Speaking evil against the dignitaries of our lives invades all parts of our lives, such as family, friends, neighborhoods, and churches. If we do not want to be taught to speak evil against the Lord's anointed, we are going to have to turn off the television.

Families wonder why some families succeed and some families fail. Yet, parents seem to be trying to do the same things for their families. The amount of evil speaking against the Lord's anointed in the home will gauge the amount of success for a family. Speaking evil against parents destroys a family. Children do not know who to believe. They fall for anything. Parents become angry. They speak evil against the Lord's anointed. Parents may have done the anointing on their own children.

There are consequences that come with backbiting, gossiping, and not supporting our leaders in our families, churches, communities and country. Families and leaders are destroyed by gossip and evil-speaking of the Lord's anointed. No one knows who to believe. I do not know what the going price of a family or a good leader is in the Lord's Kingdom. I am not a seer. I do know that one of the consequences of evil speaking against the Lord's anointed is that no one supports you when it is your turn to lead. (Matthew 7:1)

What is not speaking evil against the Lord's anointed? If someone chooses not to remain silent when something is wrong, and a leader needs help, it is not speaking evil against the Lord's anointed. The accusation that you are speaking against the Lord's anointed is not a command for you to look the other way when others are breaking rules or committing secret combinations.[38] It is not being lukewarm about the principles of the gospel. At times, we will have to stick up for

---

[36]Moroni 7:25. p. 523; Moroni 10:14, The Book of Mormon, p. 530.

[37]James 4:11, The Holy Bible, p. 1542; 2 Peter 2:10, The Holy Bible, p. 1553.

[38]Doctrine and Covenants 101:97, p. 200.

the Savior and His gospel. It is one of those tests. By our silence, we are speaking against God's Anointed, Jesus Christ. We can disagree and still be respectful for the burdens a leader bears.

Speaking evil against the Lord's anointed is a test to see how well we follow the commandments of men. It is an excellent measurement to see how many are on your side in an argument. If speaking evil against the Lord's anointed is so detrimental, peeking against the Lord's anointed or pornography is even more harmful. A lack of virtue with or against the Lord's anointed is an even larger entrapment for the body and spirit.

Tenth, sexual promiscuity is common to children. There is a natural curiosity about sexual matters and how the private body parts function. There is an unnatural curiosity about sex common to children. Random sexual partners begin at the junior high level. This sexual activity is given as much thought as a new toy. Abusive behavior between boy and girl friend occurs at the high school level. This keeps on going into adulthood. Until one is ready to give up this kind of conduct in his life and the many other childish things in his life, he or she will never be blessed with the maturity and thinking of an adult. He or she will be functioning at a teenage level in a world of adults. Childish things cause us to function with pride.

I wonder if this is how the elect are deceived. The elect are deceived by gossip and by evil speaking of the Lord's anointed. Individuals are deceived by thinking they cannot do well in school. They are deceived when they have no regard for man. They are deceived by excessive play, hitting, climbing, risky behavior, cramming, and unauthorized sexual activity.

If we want to think and speak as a man and not be deceived, we have to give up those things that are common to children. Don't let the childish things in your life replace faith, hope, and charity.[39] People will think you have attention deficit disorder. There is a world of knowledge and experience in faith, hope, and charity that is very exciting and rewarding. We do not have to function with childish pride in our adult years.

> *When I was a child, I spake as a child, I understood as a child,*
> *I thought as a child: but when I became a man, I put away childish things.*

1 Corinthians 13:11, The Holy Bible

List what childish things that you need to put away to help your children and step children mature and put away childish things. How much gossip or speaking against the Lord's anointed occurs in your step family? Are any of your elect (chosen ones) in your family deceived by untrue gossip and the various medias? How are you handling their behavior?

---

[39] 1 Corinthians 13:13, The Holy Bible, p. 1454.

44

Chapter Seven

A Matter of Pride

We constantly struggle between pride and honor. Many times, honor seems to be losing to pride. Individuals fighting the battle of pride versus the battle for honor will be viewed as one with an attention deficit disorder when they choose pride over honor. Though children cannot be tempted by Satan before the age of eight, pride begins young. Parents are teaching pride when they least expect it. Children copy their parents' example and the example of all individuals who parents have exposed their children to in their short life.

Our children may be only four or five years of age, but they are exposed to siblings, grandparents, aunts, uncles, teachers, neighbors, friends, doctors, dentists, and Hollywood. Our children are exposed to many people before the age of eight years, the age of accountability. From these people, their opinions are formed.

There are many others to whom our children are exposed. Parents purchase pride for their children. Our children soak up television programs, movies, videos, and sports like a sponge. What are individuals in these media working under? The principle of pride. They claim they are exposing to us what happens when we are prideful. In reality, they are driving us to provide to try and provide ourselves with some dignity and make sense of things.

Each character has their own way of achieving dignity, self-respect, and the attention they deserve. They feed their pride with arrogance, conceit, egotism, immodest, immoral, and even criminal behavior. They boast or glory in their mistakes or their own strengths to the point of snobbery. These characters are condescending of others. With a cute, catchy phrase, some music, and designer clothes, these characters become the cream of the crop and very attractive to children.

Children do not realize this story is written from a script. The story will only be popular for a moment in time. This fleeting script can and will be changed to suit a producers' needs now and in the future. It does not matter what the ones who purchased this entertainment need.

Children are in for a rude awakening when people do not respond to them the same way the people in movies or cartoons respond to their favorite, cute, insubordinate character. This causes a lot of conflict. Naturally, children resort to what they have been taught, seen, or experienced. Pride. It becomes a vicious cycle. The Savior describes this pride cycle in the scriptures.

> *37 That they may be conferred upon us, it is true; but when we undertake to cover our sins, or to gratify our pride, our vain ambition, or to exercise control or dominion or compulsion upon the souls of the children of men, in any degree of unrighteousness, behold, the heavens withdraw themselves; the Spirit of the Lord is grieved; and when it is withdrawn, Amen to the priesthood or the authority of that man.*

Doctrine and Covenants 121:37

THE PRIDE CYCLE

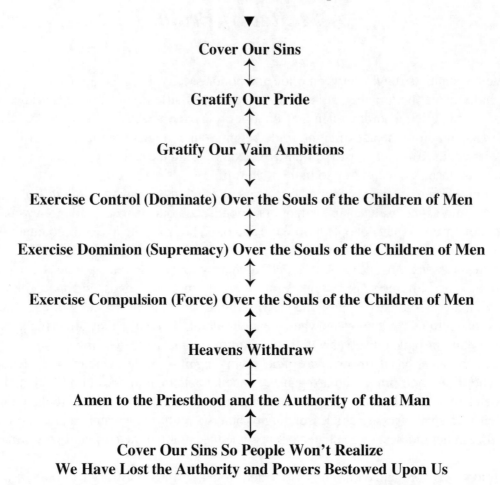

Powers of Heaven Bestowed Upon Us

▼

Cover Our Sins

↕

Gratify Our Pride

↕

Gratify Our Vain Ambitions

↕

Exercise Control (Dominate) Over the Souls of the Children of Men

↕

Exercise Dominion (Supremacy) Over the Souls of the Children of Men

↕

Exercise Compulsion (Force) Over the Souls of the Children of Men

↕

Heavens Withdraw

↕

Amen to the Priesthood and the Authority of that Man

↕

**Cover Our Sins So People Won't Realize
We Have Lost the Authority and Powers Bestowed Upon Us**

The arrows are going both ways. The arrows should be going in many different directions. We do not jump from one step to the next step cleanly, leaving us only one step in the pride cycle to struggle with. When we choose to cover our sins with pride, we pick up the entire muddy cycle. The mud we track all over becomes a pit of spiritual quicksand and an attention deficit disorder. As we try to cover our mud, our sins, and get out of the spiritual quicksand we are in, we feel we must gratify our hurt pride and our vain ambitions at the same time. Anxiety, fear, doubt, and frustration occur. We now exercise control, dominion, and compulsion over others to relieve the tension that is building. This has to be covered, too. Our behavior is justified to make up for the loss of the blessings of our Savior and the authority and power within us. Individuals in the pride cycle cling to whatever they have placed their hopes in while dashing the hopes of others.

This is a painful process to be in. There is not much room for learning in individuals who are caught in the pride cycle. It takes a lot of energy to deal with the emotional stress, conflicts, and mocking within the pride cycle. One may not know they are in the pride cycle, they just hurt. One looks for many ways to try to ease this hurt.

In the study of psychology, we learned about famous psychologists and psychiatrists and the behaviors they observed in patients. These doctors suspected their patients adapted to stress with these behaviors. We call these behaviors defense mechanisms. Defense mechanisms help us adapt to the discomfort in our pride cycle, not just painful memories. Defense mechanisms began as a way to escape chores at home and control our parents, siblings, friends, and teachers.

Repression. I remember learning that Dr. Sigmund Freud considered sex as the problem in every situation, and repression was the basic defense mechanism. In repression, we force thoughts and impulses into what we call the back of our mind, the subconscious area. They often do not stay there. This is because there is a conscious and an unconscious part to repression. No one likes to be put down or controlled so strictly that their natural development is curtailed. We may try very hard to keep painful memories in the conscious mind from going back and forth between the conscious and the unconscious parts of our mind. Anger, jealousy, fears, gossip covetousness, and lack of mercy brings repressed memories to the surface in various ways.

We are thinking that an individual using repression as a defense mechanism is unable to remember painful experiences. Remember. There is a conscious part to repression. Repression is the conscious stonewalling behavior and put downs we see in feuding families, step families, spouses, friends, employment situations, governments, etc. Consciously, individuals restrained and oppressed others to impede their progress. Naturally, those who are stonewalled, isolated, and manipulated, become angry when their progress and development are impeded, and they resist. More controls are added which creates the need for secret combinations in the relationship. These controls also need to be justified. Hence, the secrets that accompany stonewalling, manipulation, and isolation. These secrets involve many defense mechanisms.

Through the secrets of repression, an individual justifies and redirects the hostility to others and away from himself. He escapes the guilt and the fear he feels when he fails to act kindly or in socially approved ways with family and friends. We all have had ideas forced on us, and we were told these ideas were for our own good. Many of these ideas were to repress or control us. When one represses others, he discovers how painful the pits are which he dug for others. I suspect that individuals refuse to acknowledge the pain which they are experiencing and have caused others. If they acknowledge, they must admit guilt and make restitution.

Many parents and step parents and teachers have been so severely restricted in their homes and classrooms by immature children that even the natural development of parents, step parents, teachers, and friends has become impeded. It is no wonder that the natural development of children and step children is impeded by repression.

Aggression. When negative feelings surface or circulate, the individual becomes an aggressor and copes by aggression, ranging from accusations, physical attacks, verbal abuse, rage, and homicide. These conscious actions of attack and control are for the benefit of the aggressor. *In projection.* Individuals justify repressive acts by projecting their feelings on others. Children may talk about their sibling hating them. In reality, it is they who hate their sibling.

Reaction formation involves doing or feeling the opposite of what someone has asked them to do. This ties families and step families in knots. Compulsiveness and extreme behavior are characteristic of reaction formation. This also sounds like the behaviors in attention deficit disorder. Pornography and homosexuality are examples of reaction formation. Individuals react to the side effects of the many cardiac drugs, anti-depressants, blood pressures medications, steroids, and illegal street drugs which they or their family members are taking. Others have offered a service to replace the lost function of individuals, specifically energy and impotence.

47

Both men and women are afraid in heterosexual relationships. Both become tired of never being asked for a date or having a date accepted. If men are using street drugs or prescription medications, they are afraid of being impotent with a female. Though men are impotent and women are single, they still have a desire to form their own family.

Rationalization finds a reasonable reason for behavior that is not the real reason or for behavior which is illegal. In other words, in other defense mechanisms we have been trying to convince others of the validity of our actions. We now must convince ourselves that we are helping others after we forced them to believe we were helping them.

Children may be only three years old, but they are expected to give us a reason when they misbehave. If children have a good excuse for their irrational behavior, they get out of doing things, and they avoid trouble. Excuses worked for them. Excuses will work for them always.

Fantasy. When people react to our poor excuses with anger and isolation, they occupy their time with the defense mechanism of fantasy. They daydream of physical exploits, toys, attractiveness, amusements, ways to make money with little effort, etc. Much time and money is wasted on unfulfilled desires. If they achieve these dreams, they force their dreams on others. Instead of fantasizing, they could have checked their patriarchal blessing.

Compensation. Many individuals compensate for their deficiencies by overcoming insurmountable obstacles. Individuals may not be a sports hero or a Hollywood beauty queen, but people like to excel at something even if they are handicapped. *Intellectualization* is a form of compensation and is a way to make up for physical deficiencies. Usually, we overcompensate and decide that we must excel where we are weakest or are deprived. We also *sublimate or redirect* our behavior in socially accepted activities. Two examples of sublimation are: war into sports and desire to learn into teaching.

Regression. However, for some reason regression occurs, no matter how hard we try. Since we are older, our behavior is bigger, bolder, and worse. Regression is the reappearance of a previously abandoned habit. Examples of regression are: bed wetting when a new baby is born, trying to quit smoking over and over; a thief begins to steal again, adults returning to juvenile and infantile behavior. All seem *fixated (fixation).* When confronted with the same frustrating situations, their responses are always the same–instead of looking for new solutions,

There are other steps in the defensive process of self. These, too, are called defense mechanisms. Those mechanisms are *denial, depression, justification, compartmentalization,* and *procrastination.* When the human mind has decided that its pride needs defending, it will invent or redefine anything to avoid unpleasant circumstances, even work, and make it look good.

Impotence is becoming a defense mechanism. Impotent individuals are helpless and have an absence of function–not just sexually. Individuals are impotent: physically, morally, socially, intellectually, financially, emotionally, and spiritually. If they do not know how to work or will not learn how to work then someone has to do things for them. They can play while others work. We all have been bullied into doing homework for other children. We have done others' work on the job, but they collected the paycheck. Some of these paychecks are very large. This is beyond laziness and impudence, it is impotence. It is profitable for them to be helpless. The impotence and impudence of others are severe burdens for parents and step parents and spouses.

The sad thing is, these fifteen to twenty steps have been replaced by five steps that will help the situation forever. These five steps will improve our health, too. In fact, the prophet, Isaiah, warned us about exchanging good for evil, light for darkness, and bitter for sweet in the latter days. Specifically, his warning reads as follows.

20 ¶ Woe unto them that call evil good, and good evil; that put darkness for light, and light for darkness; that put bitter for sweet, and sweet for bitter!

Isaiah 5:20, The Holy Bible

What are the five steps of good that have been exchanged for fifteen or twenty steps of evil, bitterness, and darkness which psychologists and psychiatrists admit only denies, distorts, or falsifies reality for us? These five good, sweet steps are the five steps of repentance.

It is difficult for patients to walk around or function with many, bulky, unnecessary bandages. If we do not cleanse our wounds first, no amount of bandaging will keep the infection process away. It is that way with spiritual wounds, too. If you recall, repentance is known as the cleansing process for the soul. Let's look at this more closely and compare our bandages with the Savior's bandages. Our mind is telling us to heal our wounds by protecting our wounded selves. Our Savior tells us there is another, better way.

REPRESSION OF SINS	*REMISSION OF SINS*

1. Refuse to admit there is a problem
    denial
    apathy
    fantasy
	1. Recognize–acknowledge your problem,
	              identify your problem

2. Rationalization
    justification–excuses
    procrastination–postpone
	2. Remorse–feel guilty, but contrite

3. Reaction formation–hopelessness, anger
       helplessness
    depression
	3. Regret–sorrow,

4. Regression–habit returns
    repression–have positive and negative
          feelings about subject
    fixation–same anxiety, same response,
          different day
    projection–others' feelings, others' fault
    aggression–physical and verbal attacks
	4. Refrain–avoid, resist, abstain

5. Redirection–Redefining
    compensation–weak areas
    sublimation–socially accepted ways
    intellectualization
	5. Restitution–restore, amends,
	       forgiveness
	       mercy
	          for self
	          for others

Recognize is the basic step for repentance. Denial is the opposite of recognize. Could it be that denial is the most basic of all the defense mechanisms, not repression? Even a very scared patient who is suffering a heart attack retreats to denial.

When we should be remorseful about our mistakes and excuses, we rationalize and look for other excuses. Depression is the result. Depression is not the same as regret. Regret is a godly sorrow while depression is a despair over fear and anger with man.

At a time when we should be practicing self-control and restraint, old habits return. No matter how hard we try, we cannot handle the anxiety for all our old predicaments, our new predicaments, what others are thinking about us, that we are imperfect, and our children are imperfect. We will not be able to restore ourselves by redefining socially and spiritually accepted behaviors and concepts. It does not work. We still must make restitution. Restitution comes from repentance.

Now what does repentance and repression have to do with attention deficit disorder, especially in young children? Young children, as young as four years old, have to have designer clothes, designer shoes, designer toys, and have popular friends to be popular. Children are very anxious when they do not have those things. They will steal for them in spite of what their parents and step parents have provided for them. They are using defense mechanisms that they should not even be exposed to at their young ages.

Children know or fear they will suffer much grief and embarrassment for their lack of designer things and designer friends. They will fight over friends and things to achieve their goals. It does not matter how many other children they hurt or leave out in this process of achieving their designer environment.

Moreover, children like designer things. They are in the pride cycle. They become angry with parents who do not provide these things for them. The spirit of the Lord withdraws because children are exercising control, dominion, and compulsion over the souls of the children of men, specifically their parents, siblings, teachers, and potential friends. Children cover their misbehavior very young.

Children have not had the time, the experience, or the opposition to learn to stay out of this pride cycle. Parents may be working several jobs to pay for these defense mechanisms. If parents become too tired, they do not have the time to teach their children about repentance.

Parents try to exercise control, dominion, and compulsion over their children when they are not home or do not have the patience to deal with them. Parents do this by giving them an endless list of rules. Then, parents purchase more defense mechanisms (pride) or stories about pride (movies) to occupy their children. Children have decided these defense mechanisms work better than repentance. Parents feel they work better than repentance, too.

Children can sense when a parent or a sibling has lost their authority or their power in their own home. Parents, children, or spouses exercise control, dominion, and compulsion over their families and friends with such habits as drug addiction, alcoholism, smoking, gambling, verbal abuse, physical abuse, immorality, excessive recreation, and excessive shopping. *This controls families, step families, communities, and nations as well as the ones participating in these addictions. This is not free agency or the spirit of the Lord would not withdraw when we do these things.*[40]

---

[40]2 Nephi 2:27, The Book of Mormon, p. 59.

Isaiah can help us with attention deficit disorder. Isaiah saw the things the psychiatrists are seeing. Isaiah saw that there were more children of the desolate. He wrote for the parents, step parents, and children of the desolate in this day. We do not have to pick up defense mechanisms which leads to weapons of rebellion or exist on pride. We can pick up our scriptures and read Isaiah.

I am aware that Isaiah is difficult to read, especially when someone is reading at the third grade level. However, Isaiah left a key to understanding his book. Most books give the reader important information in the first chapter. This information in the first chapter defines the actions of the other chapters. Isaiah wrote this way, too. This key to finding comfort by the words of Isaiah is found in Isaiah 1:2. The Savior and possibly Isaiah nourished and brought up children. Their children rebelled against them. Isaiah saw our day and wrote for parents who had rebellious children. Other prophets, Lehi and Nephi, had rebellious sons and brothers. It made life difficult. They read Isaiah as a comfort and included parts of Isaiah in 1 Nephi and 2 Nephi. Isaiah's teachings were a great comfort to them.

Isaiah seems sad. He is sad. In his lamentations over his children and the Lord's children, Isaiah skips from his own day, the Savior's day, and our day. Parents would be diagnosed with an attention deficit disorder if we did this. Now, Isaiah seems to have more meaning, especially Isaiah 9:6. Now, the governments of homes and countries are upon our shoulders for our experience. Anyone with problems with their families and step families can relate to Isaiah and learn from Isaiah. Isaiah is warning us to not exchange mercy for pride.

Sadly, children are known to be cruel. Children with attention deficit disorder do not have that light, sweetness, and goodness which Isaiah told us to not trade for darkness, bitterness, and evil. There are trading dark for darker, bitter for more bitter, and evil for more evil. Yet, they control their parents' and their step parents' home. Children do not automatically acquire the light and sweet and good in their lives as they develop. They need to be taught or given this light by instruction and example. This light is called mercy.

Mercy is why remission of sins works in our lives, and repression of sins does not work. The remission of sins brings us mercy. The repression of sins brings us pride, depression, and man's idea of justice. Repentance brings mercy for ourselves and others. We were born on Earth to control our bodies and minds through mercy, not justice. It is okay to extend mercy to ourselves by being repentant to God and others. It is okay and wise to be merciful to family even if other family members are angry with their family.

At what stage of the pride cycle does each member of the family seem to reside? How do parent and child react when they are in the pride cycle of life? How does your child's pride affect your family? How does your pride affect your family?

What defense mechanisms do you and your children use to justify your behavior and your pride? What defense mechanisms do you and your children use to prevent others from controlling you? What defense mechanisms do you use to control others, especially parents and step parents Are you and your children and step children trading dark for darker, bitter for more bitter, and evil for more evil as you age?

How much mercy does your child or step child have for himself, others, his parents, step parents, siblings, and step siblings? Do you and your child have more mercy for idols than for your family and step family members and God? Do you and your child have enough mercy in your life to not be diagnosed with an attention deficit disorder?

Chapter Eight

Weapons of Rebellion

Individuals often use weapons of rebellion as a way to deal with emotional pain, conflicts, or boredom. They feel opposition to the authority figures in their lives is going to ease their discomfort. Weapons of rebellion have become a life style and a source of entertainment. Unfortunately, their pain and conflicts do not go away. They are quickly bored and go from one weapon or method of rebellion to another. In the process, individuals relying on weapons of rebellion are often diagnosed with an attention deficit disorder. They forgot that it was an important step in their life to learn to work together as a team. Every team has an authority and policies to obey.

Our weapons of rebellion determine our level of obedience. Individuals who are not obedient are viewed as rebellious and wayward, as well as having an attention deficit disorder. Obedience means a willingness to carry out the wishes or orders of those who are in authority over us, beginning with parents. Humility (meekness) comes from obedience. The opposite of obedience is not just disobedience. It is headstrong, insolent, and disrespectful.

One of the most painful of labels is the tag of being wayward and ungovernable. A wayward child insists upon having his own way in spite of parent's instructions, explanations, or family needs. A wayward child is stubborn, argumentative, resistant, disobedient, truant, and usually delinquent. The wayward child is smarter than his parents, teachers, and bosses, and his friends are, too. Wayward children cannot be relied on for simple tasks or in a crisis. Wayward children chase all hours of the night instead of conforming to the family rules or patterns. When confronted, they are unpredictable and blame their parent and step parent. Wayward children will most likely become wayward adults. They will have many problems in their life, and may marry a wayward spouse. Wayward children have many excuses for their wayward behavior.

Wayward children have had many afflictions because of their family.[41] We hear of many tragic stories in the newspaper or on the television of child abuse. For the most part, parents love their children. They want what is best for their children. They will work many jobs for their families. However, parents have their hands tied. Imperfect children feel they cannot reach perfection with imperfect parents. Imperfect siblings/friends who do not tattle are what matters..

Employers are not that kindly anymore to employees. They treat parents as a number. Governments do, too. If a parent has a second or third job, they are treated how a juvenile delinquent on a cleanup force is treated. Otherwise, a parent would not have second or third jobs. Climbing prices and whims of children have nothing to do with these second or third jobs.

In this day, employers feel the need to support owners of sports teams, public celebrities, and aging sports stars. Employers do not see the need to support their employees, especially as their employees age. It does not matter how long or how hard these employees have worked for them. When employers have to choose between health care, retirement plans, visual care, dental

---

[41]<u>Doctrine and Covenants</u> 31:2, p. 55.

plans, and tickets for private suites at the sports arenas, health care and retirement plans for employees are not considered critical. Health care can be deleted, or high deductibles can be given to their employees. Children do not understand the stress that work causes parents.

If the neighborhood treats a parent the same way governments and employers do, then children do, too. Children feel the neighborhood must know something that children don't. The rope really tightens around the parents wrists when their children do not listen to parents and go their own way. The financial chase over wants, needs, and desires can be an emotional nightmare. Naturally, children follow the sports celebrities instead of their parents.

Children have their free agency and their rights. One of the greatest gifts our Heavenly Father has given us is freedom of choice. Another term for freedom of choice is free agency. Our Heavenly Father and the Savior must have loved us very much. He also must have trusted us very much, too. Not only did our Heavenly Father give us free agency, he gave it to us without input. We have to ask if we want further information.[42] Many children do not ask.

We have resorted to weapons of rebellion. Unfortunately, many have confused free agency and rights with picking up weapons of rebellion. When we are exercising our freedoms, we do not have consequences. Freedoms bring more opportunities. These opportunities are that living water that the Savior talks about.[43] Martyrs have died while speaking boldly or gently for our many freedoms. They are free and will partake of "living water" on the other side of the veil.

Weapons of rebellion bring consequences in this life and in the life to come. Weapons of rebellion push us into a fiery furnace without any tools to fight fires. We are consumed. Our family or friends can be consumed by our weapons of rebellion, too. What are these weapons of rebellion that consume us? Those weapons are: lying, argumentative, controlling, and defiant behavior, cheating, stealing, vandalism, crime, adultery, fornication, drug addiction, homosexuality, and alcoholism. Even excessive shopping, excessive eating, excessive competition, and excessive recreation in one's life are weapons of rebellion.

Children feel that they can experiment in anything and everything they want. It is their right to sit in front of the television all day long, sleep late, experiment with drugs, alcohol, and sex when they want. Parents can bail children out. Isn't that what parents are for anyway? Individuals, their friends, their parents, or their children are not going to get hurt in any way by their behavior. Children will change when its really important. They have always had willpower when it was really important. Parents just did not see it. Parents need to change, not them.

Wayward behavior does not begin with pornography. It begins with lying, especially lying to yourself. Lying begets cheating. Cheating begets stealing. Lying also begets shame and confusion.[44] The very first thing that is stolen is your good name. Satan is now free to steal from you anything he wants. It will be like taking candy from a baby.

Unfortunately, lying begins in our "babies." Mothers and fathers know when their children are lying. Lying affects their countenance and their behavior. If the lying is frequent, this will be termed as a learning disorder as well as a psychological disorder. Your child may

---

[42]Matthew 7:7-8, The Holy Bible, p. 1197.

[43]John 4:10, The Holy Bible, p. 1330; Doctrine and Covenants 63:23, p. 116.

[44]Doctrine and Covenants 109:29-30, p. 224.

have a list of symptoms that will prove to a psychiatrist that your child has a disorder, but lying will be involved.

Parents know that if a child is lying, he is usually trying to hide something. When I was young, children tried to hide smoking and shoplifting. However, even the news admits the sexual atmosphere is different than ever before for our children. Sex, stealing expensive items, and drugs are what children are hiding in this day.

If children are smoking, they are smoking with friends who are also wayward. Wholesome friends will not come around because they do not want to lose their good name. Smoking and friends with no goals or self-control leads to fornication, or sex before marriage.

Wayward behavior does not just stop with fornication. Fornication leads to drug addiction. Sexual partners give each other drugs as a "favor." If children are drug addicts, children are most likely habitual sexual partners, as well as a habitual drug customer and distributor. This pays for their drugs and anything else they feel that is mandatory to have instantly in their life. It does not matter the cost to themselves or their families.

Teenage pregnancies and out-of-wedlock pregnancies are a result of using weapons of rebellion. Teenage pregnancies are not just a matter of poor planning, impulsive behavior, or loneliness. Couples who are having sex immaturely and prematurely become pregnant.

When children become pregnant out of wedlock, parents become very angry. Parents feel betrayed and embarrassed. This is not what they had in mind for their children, their grandchildren, or their own later years of marriage. Giving up one's own blood or encouraging a child to give up your own blood are very difficult experiences which no one ever gets over.

To add insult to injury, children blame parents for the very things that children decided they could experiment safely with. Nobody would notice, or they would not be caught. This blame only adds fuel to the fire. It causes a great distance between parent and child, both Earthly and Heavenly.

After five years experience on a maternity floor taking care of mothers and grandparents with out-of-wedlock babies, I feel that everyone should know what parents really are angry about. Parents with wayward children discover they do not have the children they thought they had. In addition, there are now so many demands by their children and fears for their children, parents cannot enjoy their own marriage. There does not seem to be any way or anytime for married couples to replenish themselves.

Parents cannot even have their own sexual experiences with their spouse, and they are the ones with the marriage license. It is very stressful for parents who are dealing with the financial and emotional nightmare of teenagers experimenting with anything they want to be accepted and popular. It is very difficult for parents to have sex while worrying about their children being exposed and eventually dying of AIDS. Their grandchildren could also be born with AIDS.

Sex is one way a married couple replenishes themselves. They are married and have been given the right to multiply and replenish the Earth. If they are no longer having children, parents still have sex. When parents are distraught over their children's behavior, they cannot function. Men become impotent. Women become frigid. Each blames the other. Both parents feel their spouse must not love them. Both go their own ways emotionally, when they should be united. Unity in marriage brings a special touch to a marriage and a family.

This special intimacy renews couples, their covenants, their commitment to each other, and their marriage. They can face another week with children and employers. This kind of intimacy can only happen in marriage. No matter how loving and committed a couple are, they will have some guilt attached to their sexual experience if they are not married. This is an involuntary response which one cannot control. Guilt and fear prevents renewal. There are always underlying fears that one's partner will leave the other for a better offer.

Women especially like to know that someone was not afraid to commit to them totally, though they may never express it. This is part of their self-esteem. Men feel the same. Renewal does not take place when there are no covenants, commitment, and marriage vows to renew. There is not a healthy substitute for renewing one's marriage.

My parents do not have the patience of Job. Your parents have a child or children who are headstrong and who feel they can experiment with anything they want. Their children are lying to get out of the home and cover their behavior. Parents have children as young as nine years of age smoking, having sexual activity, experimenting with drugs, alcohol, and any fad. Children will break any parental rule to accomplish these activities and show others that parents are not in control of them.

Parents are out or their minds with worry. They are sorry sometimes they even had children. Parents cannot have the experiences that renew them. While trying to keep out of bankruptcy with their children's behavior, provide a living with extra jobs, and a retirement for themselves, parents are blamed for children's behavior. Parents are told their children have attention deficit disorder and attention deficit disorder with hyperactivity. Parents are told that they probably have this disorder, too. Otherwise, their children would not be acting this way, and parents would not have to be working more than one job. The patience of Job does not come with this kind of behavior, anger, denial, grief, and limitations on healing.

Children do not have Attention Deficit Disorder and Attention Deficit Disorder with Hyperactivity because their parents do not have the patience of Job with them while children chose and experimented with various weapons of rebellion. Neither, do parents.

Children will not understand fully what parents are going through until they have a child or children lying, cheating, smoking, committing fornication or adultery, and stealing to purchase alcohol, drugs, and more cigarettes. Children may have their own new diseases and several jobs to learn the "patience of Job" with their children–in a world of very high prices.

While grieving over children and being angry with children, parents and children may be taking birth control pills or have birth control implants. As a student nurse and a registered nurse, I gave out instructions in the form of a pamphlet to many of my patients on various forms of birth control options. These instructions were designed for parents, particularly adult women, not children. This birth control was designed for their body weights and size. Women have to have a certain amount of body fat to store these hormones.

I have often wondered if birth control was a big pit for a marriage that was trying to start. If we could see the Lord's calculator and His statistics, how many marriages failed because of birth control? Birth control keeps one from having a baby by preventing the release of an egg or preventing implantation if conception has taken place.

Birth control pills and implants are convenient, but they have a price to pay emotionally. Many women have noticed that they are extremely moody, depressed, suicidal, and they have a decreased or absent sexual desire. Who wants to be intimate with someone who is irritable, depressed, and suicidal? Who wants to be intimate with someone who screams at you when you leave the cap off the toothpaste, or you leave your shoes in the middle of the living room floor?

Your first year of marriage is priceless. Your young husband does not understand the emotions that come with menstrual periods and birth control. Families become tired of walking on eggshells when around you. Husbands will here plenty of war stories at his employment. He will be given various methods on how to handle women. Most likely, it will not be the Lord's way. If husbands and fathers do not understand these emotions, children do not understand these emotions and these methods of treatment either.

My mother-in-law always taught us that each child brings his or her love with them. This is your accelerated learning class and dividend in one. It is soothing to learn new things and be proud of your accomplishments. Boats, campers, season sports tickets, and travel cannot replace this type of learning and this type of soothing. Remember. This is your boyfriend and children that we are talking about.

I know that you do not want to be abusive to your boyfriend, husband, friends, parents, or children. People can only take so much negative behavior in their lives. Counteracting normal hormones will always have an effect on your emotions. In the first days of birth control, there were complications and deaths due to birth control. I remember one patient in particular who died of so many blood clots, they could not count them on the x-ray. I saw the x-ray.

The dosages of the medications in birth control have been reduced. However, the patients are still having problems with moodiness, irritability, depression, and suicidal thoughts. Birth control in teenagers may be one of the causes of the increased suicides in teenagers. They do not have the body weights, fat storage, or size for this medication. They do not have the emotional skills or social skills developed to treat themselves when they are depressed. Even adult women get depressed on birth control. Smoking and birth control has serious side effects such as clots.

Boys do not like to be treated roughly by their girlfriends. They want a girlfriend, not a girl friend who is a nag. It causes serious doubt within boys to be treated so aggressively. Remember. At best, boys are two years behind girls emotionally and physically and all the other aspects of their personality.

It is hard to learn something new when someone is angry, guilty, moody, irritable, depressed, and suicidal. Retention is poor. Attention span is short. Under these circumstances, it is hard to be patient with a child who is moody and irritable. If both mother and daughter are on birth control, it is going to be very difficult in their home.

It is difficult to teach your children while feeling this way. One wants to just sit and vegetate in front of the television. Televisions do not talk back when you yell at them or make demands. Meanwhile, for every year your child does not receive help because of your emotional state, your child becomes behind in his school year. He withdraws or exhibits aggressive and impulsive behavior to fight those children who make fun of him or her or to cover his inadequacies. Your child views your behavior as normal and copies you. He is diagnosed with attention deficit disorder or attention deficit disorder with hyperactivity, and you are, too.

Always ask yourself: Do I really need this medication? What effect is it having on my body and emotions? What price will my family pay for me taking this medication? Do this for any medication. The love of a child in your home cannot be replaced by anything. It is something that you will be able to take with you to your Heavenly Home. There are not many things that we can take with us when we die.

Am I telling you to not plan for your children? No! As a nurse, I do not recommend having children every year. Having children and breast-feeding are lots of work and are hard on the emotions and physical body. This is between you, your spouse, and your Heavenly Father. If you do not plan with your Heavenly Father, you must rely on the visions of your future by yourself, your spouse, and others. At best, humans have twenty/twenty vision. This means you only see at twenty feet what you are able to see normally at twenty feet. I personally want to see beyond twenty feet for myself and family. I do not want hindsight to be my only vision.

Many have resorted to abortion. Women do not like the way they feel on birth control. Couples do not want to pay for birth control, or they are too impatient to use it. Couples do not want more children, but are unable to commit to having their tubes tied or a vasectomy. Women have felt compelled by their husbands and careers to have many abortions. This method of family planning has been justified because the spirit has not entered the body until the mother feels the baby move. This is known as quickening. Some feel the spirit enters the body when the baby is born.

Abortion is a most painful stone to carry around the rest of your life. I can remember elderly mothers still crying over the abortions they felt compelled to have or that husbands compelled them to have. Naturally, as a nurse and as a member of The Church of Jesus Christ of Latter-day Saints, I am against abortion. I worked hard on a degree that would help preserve life. I know the spirit enters the body at conception. I have felt the presence and absence of spirits in mothers about to miscarry or who have miscarried. Even their abdomen is not as firm anymore.

Pray about abortion to know for yourself when the spirit enters the body. Many will differ and argue. We are not arguing with society or Women's Rights. We are arguing with the Lord over the life of one of His children. No one will be happy and guilt-free with clear-thinking minds in this argument. Is there hope? Yes! There is repentance. Discuss this with a bishop.

There is scripture that tells us when the spirit enters the body. John the Baptist tells us. The Apostle Luke records it. After Mary, the mother of Jesus had conceived Jesus Christ, she visited her cousin Elizabeth. Elizabeth was six months pregnant with John the Baptist. When Mary greeted her cousin, Elizabeth's baby leaped in her womb.[45]

John the Baptist, as a fetus, recognized the spirit of Christ who was only now considered an embryo. Mary was just starting out her pregnancy. Therefore, Christ was certainly well within that first trimester. Some feel this was only the normal quickening of a pregnancy. Elizabeth was six months pregnant. However, the spirit of Christ had to be there for John to recognize it. In other words, Christ's spirit entered the embryonic cells at conception. His spirit did not appear at the time of quickening (about four months gestation) nor at birth.

With weapons of rebellion, you will always be in over your head. It will be easy to victimize you also. Individuals will be diagnosed with an attention deficit disorder because they cannot keep up the pace of things that are over their head. Individuals are carrying around the burdensome stones of lying, swearing, cheating, smoking, adultery, fornication, unwed pregnancy, abortion, homosexuality, alcoholism, and drug addiction while trying to swim in the oceans of life. Their swim will be unsuccessful, and they will sink without divine help. It will also be difficult to think clearly, pay attention, and retain.

Smoking, depression, alcoholism, and drugs will not cover up the stones of immorality and homosexuality which you have decided to always carry with you. Like tempers, weapons of rebellion accentuate or potentiate each other, and they grow bigger, bolder, and multiply. Our laws are multiplied to meet the demands of all the weapons of rebellions that we now have. Instead of changing and discarding weapons of rebellion, we want to discard the laws that seem to encumber us. It is not the laws that encumbers us, it is the weapons of rebellion.

---

[45]Luke 1:36-41, The Holy Bible, p. 1273.

With weapons of rebellion, individuals are in an environment that makes learning and retention very difficult. They have habits which make it difficult to concentrate and study. It is very difficult to learn when one is sad and tries to hide it. It is difficult to learn when one is carrying extremely heavy burdens physically and emotionally, socially, financially, etc. It is difficult to retain what you have while "robbing Peter to pay Paul." Individuals will also be diagnosed with an Attention Deficit Disorders when they are not able to forgive themselves, or they do not want to forgive others of their past mistakes.

We were not given bodies to carry the burdens of weapons of rebellion. We have been given a body to learn wisdom in all things. We do not need to learn how to be victims or victimizers in all things with all kinds of weapons of rebellion. If we persist with weapons of rebellion, we will lose precious gifts within ourselves. Weapons of rebellion are affecting how others view us, and we may not be that way at all. Weapons of rebellion are even affecting the way our country is viewed.

Individuals do not have to do or have everything they see in the smorgasbord of life to be a well-balanced individual with a great resume'. The Lord does not need a great resume'. He already knows your heart.[46] He needs you to have a humble and contrite spirit.

I know that you are growing up and want more experiences. Those experiences will come if you do not argue with the Lord or His servants, your parents, over using weapons of rebellion. This also includes church leaders and teachers. Be teachable and learn all you can.

Individuals of all ages want to be accepted while having their life's experiences. We are not living in a atmosphere of acceptance. This is why the Lord placed us in families. Having to pick up a weapon of rebellion before we can be accepted is not acceptance. It is victimization.

The consequences of many weapons of rebellion are painful. This is why the Lord told us not to covet.[47] Children and adults with goals do not need to covet another's knowledge, station, beauty, or various weapons of rebellion. Individuals just have to ask our Heavenly Father what you want to develop in yourself.[48] Acceptance will come. So will the blessings. You will find your place, your clear thinking mind, and the peace you desperately want if you will lay down your weapons of rebellion.

List the weapons of rebellion for everyone in your family. How are these weapons of rebellion affecting you, your family, and others? How much lying is going on in your home? How does your child react when he or she is lying? This behavior will occur when your child lies to you as an adult. How are parents reacting to children's and step children's weapons of rebellion and lies? Are your children controlling you, the family, and your finances with weapons of rebellion and lies? Is this why you really have to work two or more jobs to support your family? Are you teachable so you can learn the gifts of the spirit?

---

[46]Luke 16:15, The Holy Bible, p. 1307.

[47]Doctrine and Covenants 19:25-26, pp. 32-33.

[48]Matthew 7:7, The Holy Bible, p. 1197.

Chapter Nine

Gifts of the Spirit

Many adults and children have been told or will be told that they have an attention deficit disorder because they lack self-esteem. Many injustices have been justified with the "lack of self-esteem defense" by both victim and victimizer.

Self-esteem is the appreciation, regard, and respect that one gives to oneself and his or her personal accomplishments. It is your personal, but private "pat on the back" for a job well done under trying circumstances. It is by self-esteem that we love our neighbor as we do our self.

Self-esteem is reflected in how we take care of ourselves. Do we treasure some of our accomplishments? Is every task that we do greeted with contempt, scorn, ridicule, and self-loathing for ourselves. Naturally, others will treat us in the manner that we treat ourselves.[49]

Self-esteem cannot be bought.[50] Many mothers and fathers wish they could give self-esteem to their children. They would, of course, be willing to beg, borrow, or steal to do this. Parents would give their shirts off their own backs and work two or more jobs to accomplish this task. Building self-esteem this way results in self-esteem for parents, not children.

Parents can love their children and praise their efforts. Self-esteem still has to have a place to grow.[51] Your child's brain and personality has to be developed. Both parent and child must want a positive, gentle spirit to reside in their personality.

Self-esteem is very important. We know how painful it is to be unappreciated and unaccepted by others. It is terribly painful to not be able to appreciate one's efforts and accept ourselves with our limitations. Self-esteem gives us the confidence to try new things even in the face of obstacles. Self-esteem helps us decide what we want in life and can keep us from being deceived and confused. We must do positive things for a positive self-esteem.

I thought about self-esteem for many months. Since self-esteem is so important, I felt there had to be some scripture that would prepare the way for building a healthy self-esteem within ourselves. First, I thought of the Beatitudes. I soon realized if our life is totally based on just the Beatitudes, we would endure a lot of victimization. We would become victimizers.

I found a group of scriptures in 1 Corinthians 12 in The Holy Bible, Moroni Chapter 10 in The Book of Mormon, and Doctrine and Covenants Section 46. These scriptures are known as "The Gifts of the Spirit" chapters. They have a peace that seems so familiar. These scriptures seem to build on one another. They seem to connect to what we really want and need in life. The Savior has said: "The work I do, Ye shall do. Greater works than I do shall ye do."[52]

---

[49]Matthew 7:12, The Holy Bible, pp. 1197-1198.

[50]Moroni 10:8, The Book of Mormon, p. 530.

[51]Doctrine and Covenants 88:33, p. 167.

[52]John 14:12, The Holy Bible, p. 1353.

Teaching a child how to stay on task is that work. Parents must first learn how to stay on task themselves. Parents need to know how to get back on task when they are distracted. These works require experience in the gifts of the spirit.

Parents and children may not have an attention deficit disorder. They simply have not developed any "gifts of the spirit" yet. If they have, they may be afraid to use them. Someone laughing or ridiculing your child will undue your efforts with your child. This is why so much repetition is required with your children.

Can little children learn spiritual gifts? Yes. This is why adults are to be like children and be eager to learn. Gifts of the spirit take time, repetition, patience, love, and work to develop or perfect in adults. Remember this in your struggles. It takes time, patience, repetition, acceptance, love, and work just to get an infant to sleep through the night or a toddler toilet-trained. Their bodies and self-confidence have to mature. It is that way with the many other things that children learn over the years. The "ten second rule" or "three strikes and your out rule" does not apply to children.

Children may not appear to be listening or watching. Your infant, toddler, and young child will copy their parents' mannerisms. As they age, children are always surprised at how much they resemble their parents' attitudes as well as features. Children are copying their parents' examples. Children will learn the gifts of the spirit that parents are learning.

However, if parents try to mend themselves with things that are harmful to the body and spirit, their child will follow their footsteps. If parents want their children to learn how to mend themselves correctly, parents will have to turn off the television and movie theaters. Many children literally bounce off the walls like cartoon characters do and the current, favorite, but insubordinate character does. It is what they are most familiar with. It is a world that parents have taken children. This is not the world that the Savior told parents to train their children to.

I have free agency. Why do I need spiritual gifts? Spiritual gifts are given to all of us by our Heavenly Father and His Son, Jesus Christ, for our profit and learning.[53] We do not have to only use six percent of our brain power to provide for the needs of our selves and families. There are Heavenly gifts to help us meet these needs and develop our brains. All can partake. Rich or poor, bond or free, black, brown, or white, it does not matter. All will be given freedom with these spiritual gifts.[54] This is why the Gospel of Jesus Christ will be taken to every human being that came to this Earth before Christ comes again. Jesus died on a cruel cross so everyone had the chance to partake of these Heavenly gifts.

Heavenly Father and Jesus Christ did not want us to be ignorant. He also did not want us to be confounded or deceived while on this Earth by the commandments of men.[55] Some of these commandments are of the devil. The commandments of the devil always contain burdensome agendas instead of the welfare of people and families in mind. Dishonest people know their agendas are burdensome. Christ knew that we would become sick physically, morally, intellectually, emotionally, financially, spiritually, etc. with burdensome agendas. There are gifts

---

[53]Moroni 10:8, The Book of Mormon, p. 530; Doctrine and Covenants 46:1, p 85.

[54]4 Nephi 1:3, The Book of Mormon, p. 465.

[55]1 Corinthians 12:1, The Holy Bible, p. 1452: Doctrine and Covenants 46:7, p. 85.

for when we are burdened, sick, and to keep us from getting sick.[56] These gifts are given for the benefit of those who love the Lord and keep His commandments.[57]

Incidently, parents want the same things for their children. They do not want their children to be ignorant, confounded, deceived, or sick. They also want their children to benefit, profit, and learn from their experiences and relationships.

Why should I treat spiritual gifts in a sacred manner? Christ prepared the way so we could be partakers of these gifts.[58] Someone special died providing numerous gifts for us. His death is known as the Supreme Sacrifice. Parents know how hard it is to work and to provide for their children. Treat your spiritual gifts accordingly.

Patients who have received a transplant understand why these gifts are sacred. Someone died in order that they might live–not just exist. Someone special died so we could live abundantly. Besides, we do not want just one gift to cope with this world.

Self-esteem is a gift from our Heavenly Father. This gift comes from using spiritual gifts to build His Kingdom and to enrich our own lives. We can praise our children often. However, our children still have to build within themselves the kind of self-esteem which our children want–not what parents or anyone else wants for them. This requires work. Our children will have to work at things which result in positive accomplishments. They will have to work for themselves by themselves in the face of opposition. With spiritual gifts and self-esteem, sweet will be this work. However, self-esteem is not the greatest spiritual gift that we can receive.

Which spiritual gift is the greatest gift? To know that Jesus Christ is the Son of God, that He was crucified for the sins of the world, and that He has power over death is the greatest spiritual gift we could ever have. Some of His power is available to help us. Unfortunately, this gift is only given to some because they have not asked, and they do not believe on His words if they do ask.[59] Again, self-esteem is not the greatest spiritual gift to have.

According to the Savior, salvation in the Kingdom of God is the greatest gift.[60] After this, to become a seer is the greatest gift.[61] The fifteen apostles existing on the Earth at the time are known as prophets, seers, and revelators. They have developed the gifts of the spirit so they will not be overwhelmed with what they see in the future. They are able to teach and warn us.

Our memories are too short to be seers. We react with denial instead of acting with faith in Jesus Christ. Faith in Jesus Christ develops things in us that we are not aware that we had within us. The Savior volunteered to die for us to have the time to develop these unseen spiritual gifts within us. If He was willing to do that for us, these gifts must be important for us to learn.

---

[56]1 Corinthians 12:9, The Holy Bible, p. 1453; Moroni 10:11, The Book of Mormon, p. 530; Doctrine and Covenants 46:19-20, p. 86.

[57]Doctrine and Covenants 46:9, pp. 85-86.

[58]Ether 12:8, The Book of Mormon, p. 509.

[59]1 Corinthians 12:3, The Holy Bible p. 1452; Doctrine and Covenants 46:13-14, p. 86.

[60]Doctrine and Covenants 6:13, p. 11; Doctrine and Covenants 14:7-8, p. 25.

[61]Mosiah 8:15-16, The Book of Mormon, pp. 163-164.

Parents may not be seers, but they can see their children's behavior patterns, past and present. They know these patterns will occur in the future. This is why parents are to warn their children. We have to take the walk that the prophets and apostles do with our families toward the Savior. Fortunately, we won't have the burdens of the world on our shoulders while we do this. The burdens of a growing family will be enough to work through and endure. It would be very painful to be seers in our children's future and our own futures. We may cast someone out prematurely before they develop their gifts of the spirit after repentance. We would lose the normal spontaneity of families and lose hope.

The Lord has taught us to seek out the best gifts.[62] Parents have abilities that they have not discovered because parents are not willing to seek the best gifts for themselves and their families. Children do not have the best gifts because they are not willing to listen to the ones that gave them life. We also do not have the best gifts because we cast others away when they are struggling in their mistakes.[63] Naturally, the best gifts are gifts of the spirit.

With spiritual gifts, there are diversities of administrations. Diverse means different, but distinct. Administrations is a term meaning management or structure. Church and civic leaders, employers, and fathers are examples of administrators that we will come in contact with. We may find ourselves in an administrative position in these areas at various times of our lives. If so, we are to conduct ourselves in a manner pleasing to the Lord. Our administrations have to be done according to the Lord's will. The Lord wants our administrations to be suited to His mercies according to the conditions of men.[64] Remember. The Lord knows us best. He knows our hearts and our tender feelings. He is a seer, too.

With spiritual gifts, there is also a diversity of operations or functions. In many situations, we find ourselves in an operational position. This may be as a spouse, parent, child, sibling, employee, or staff member. We become doers. We are to carry out the Lord's will so that the spirit will be manifested in a manner that all men might profit from our calling.

Under the diversity of functions, we are given the responsibility to magnify our calling.[65] We do not just magnify our church calling. We must magnify our callings as parent, child, sibling, grandparent, grandchild, student, employee, employer, friend, and neighbor. This enlarges our spiritual borders within ourselves, and we have more to give others.[66] If we carry out the Lord's will, we will not be carrying around so many stones in our spirits. Spiritual stones cause us to serve stones and serpents to others. We lose our temper when we least expect it.

With these two spiritual gifts, the Lord is providing a balance between administration or management and ministration or service. Father and mother provide a balance between structure and function. This is why families work so well. Even the human body has a balance between

---

[62]Doctrine and Covenants 46:8, p. 85.

[63]Doctrine and Covenants 46:3-6, p. 85.

[64]1 Corinthians 12:4-6, The Holy Bible, pp. 1452-1453; Doctrine and Covenants 46:15-16, p. 86.

[65]Doctrine and Covenants 66:10-11, p. 123; Doctrine and Covenants 88:80, p. 170.

[66]Moroni 10:31, The Book of Mormon, p. 531.

structure and function. Some systems provide the structure. Some systems provide functions. Other systems stop or stimulate other functions. In other words, our service must have structure, and our structure must have service. They work best when they blend.

Spiritual gifts are different because we all are different. Fingerprints and the shape of our ears are different. Personalities and temperaments differ, too. With this diversity, we need a directory in our lives. The gifts of the spirit become our self-directory. Even computers have directories. We may be as many as the sands of the seas. However, we have things in common and are gathered under the same spirit and the same Lord.[67]

The Beatitudes become the service part in our directory. The Beatitudes nourish, develop, and renew the parts of our spirit that are willing to serve and follow instructions. This is how we again stay in balance between the administrator and ministrators in our spirits and personality. For example, it is easier to be meek and be peacemakers when we know how to interpret tongues and discern spirits. It is easier to be comforted when we mourn if we allow the ministering angels to comfort us.

We can have knowledge, and we can teach a Word of Wisdom.[68] The Glory of God really is intelligence. This is our glory, too. We are given the gift of knowledge that we may be wise.[69] Our knowledge and wisdom will come from study and experience. We can teach Words of Wisdom, not endless data, hearsay, and guesswork. This is how knowledge and wisdom bring peace to our souls. We are to teach by the same spirit that the other gifts are administered.

With the proper use of knowledge, we can council others in this life as well as the next life. Joseph Smith has said: "Whatever principle of intelligence that we attain in this life, it will rise with us to the spirit world." In other words, spiritual gifts work miracles in this temporal world. Our spiritual gifts will work wonders and miracles in the Spiritual world, too. However, we have to acquire our spiritual gifts in this world.

Spiritual gifts work by faith. The Lord has provided a way for us to learn all spiritual gifts. This way is by faith. To some, he has given exceeding great faith. With this great faith comes the ability to heal and the faith to be healed.[70] There have been mighty miracles worked with the Holy Ghost and faith. Of course, these individuals have asked often for this gift. They also make an effort to keep commandments and covenants after praying.

A Word of Caution. If you have asked for the benefit of a spiritual gift, you are going to be tempted to break a commandment immediately afterward. It may be something minor such as yelling at your children or breaking the speed limit. It can be something major. This causes the loss of the Spirit with you. Learning is difficult without the teacher. Without the Spirit, we have no Comforter. Satan is not going to sit idly by and watch you grow strong spiritually with successful growing spurts of faith and the aid of the Great Comforter.

---

[67]Doctrine and Covenants 27:13, p. 47.

[68]1 Corinthians 12:8, The Holy Bible, p. 1453; Doctrine and Covenants 46:17-18, p. 86.

[69]Doctrine and Covenants 46:18, p. 86.

[70]1 Corinthians 12:9-10, The Holy Bible, p. 1453; Moroni 10:11-12, The Book of Mormon, p. 530; Doctrine And Covenants 46:19-21, p. 86.

There is a spiritual gift of prophecy. In The Church of Jesus Christ of Latter-day Saints there are fifteen apostles, but there is one head.[71] He is known as our prophet or the President of the Church. A prophet has the gift of prophecy. A prophet also has all of the spiritual gifts to provide for all of the many members and future members of the Church. These future members are of all ages, status, abilities, and from every country. He has more than thirteen million of the Lord's children to take care of in different stages of development. Only a parent and step parent can fully appreciate this.

Like a prophet, there can only be one Head of the Household. In your home, the Head of the Household is the father or step father. In the absence of the father, it becomes the mother's responsibility to be the Head of her Household. It is not the eldest son or daughter's responsibility to be in charge of their parents and their children. One or both parents may have most of the spiritual gifts available to benefit their family and to fulfill the responsibility of being Head of Household. Their family is their stewardship. To benefit all of their children, parents have to be experienced in most of these spiritual gifts.

Mothers have been known to prophecy, too. It does not take rocket science theory to know that a child is going to get a cold if he does not bundle up in winter, gets wet, the finances are low, and all of the doctor's appointments are given out for the week. In addition, mother and father will get sick when the ward Relief Society President is out of town or has a baby.

We are given the gift of discerning of spirits. We can behold angels and ministering spirits.[72] We can know the difference between angels of our Heavenly Father's Kingdom versus workers for the adversary. This is also found in Doctrine and Covenants Section 129. One does not have to be dead to extend a hand in mock friendship. One does not feel anything.

The television sitcom families are not those ministering angels. Ministering angels are people who have lived upon this earth. They have been given the privilege to minister with the spirit of the Holy Ghost to their families.

This gift is one of the many reasons that families are under attack by the adversary. If someone has tormented or stonewalled a family member or their entire family's progress and peace of mind, it is not likely they will be allowed to be a ministering angel to their families when they die. If one cannot speak peace face to face in mortality, how can he or she speak peace to anyone's mind after they have left this life?

This is why the Savior taught us to teach our children not to quarrel with each other. We do not know when we are going to die. Someone will have to take our place as a ministering angel on the other side of the veil if we cannot speak peace to family members in mortality. Peace and discernment of spirits requires learning the gifts of the spirit. What we are discerning in spirits is the lack of spiritual gifts. This is painful for parents to discern in children.

We can have the ability of speaking with tongues and the ability to interpret tongues. If one is speaking in tongues, there has to be listeners in the audience who are able to interpret what the speaker is saying. This is not an oddity in The Church of Jesus Christ of Latter-day Saints. This happens all the time. It happens with you. It happens between mother and infant. Thus,

---

[71]Doctrine and Covenants 46:29, p. 86.

[72]1 Corinthians 12:10, The Holy Bible, p. 1453; Moroni 10:14, The Book of Mormon, p;. 530; Doctrine and Covenants 46:23, p. 86.

there are all kinds of gifts of tongues.[73] Some have several gifts of tongues. They can speak four or five languages. I have never spoke in a foreign language or been able to interpret a foreign language. I can feel their spirit. I have been given a gift of understanding and recognizing my children's and patients' different cries.

Even our child who is deaf has this ability. I will be looking for something. Without telling her what I am looking for, she finds what I am looking for. She has her own home. She is not used to where things are in my home, especially my piles of papers. I had to learn how to communicate with her in sign language. She had to learn how to communicate with someone who makes up their own signs. She would respond with the correct answer and the correct way to do it. She learned quickly when she peeled forty potatoes instead of four in my beginning years of learning some sign language or the interpretation of her tongue.

Everyone has to learn interpretation of tongues to know what their spouse, parent, children, grandchildren, friends, teachers, employers, employees, and co-workers are trying to tell them. Sometimes, it is plain. Sometimes, it is not so clear when they are angry, hurt, upset, and are trying to hide their feelings. Often, it is just a matter of taking the time to understand others' feelings. We are not the only ones with fears and concerns.

The Gift of the Holy Ghost is very important to us and our families. The Holy Ghost will guide us with large and small promptings. If we ask in spirit, we will receive in Spirit.[74] Remember. If you ask something of someone angrily, you receive an angry response, and they leave. The Holy Ghost will do the same. He will leave us to our own strength.

When we ask in the spirit, we should remember to ask for the will of God in the name of Christ.[75] Give thanks for every blessing that you receive.[76] Give thanks for things that you do not receive. The Lord may have spared you or your children some terrible headaches or your life.

How do I obtain a spiritual gift? All you have to do is ask.[77] Ask in prayer and express gratitude for what you receive.[78] Do this just as you would say grace over your food before you eat. Invited guests to a feast do not determine the type of refreshments served. The host does. When you ask for spiritual manna, be thankful for what you receive. The Savior is our host. He knows our hearts and knows what to serve. Gratitude is a very gracious gift. One cannot be hospitable and courteous without gratitude. Gratitude is the forerunner of respect and a forerunner of many things in our lives, especially accomplishments.

---

[73]Moroni 10:16, The Book of Mormon, p.530; Doctrine and Covenants 46:24-25, p. 86; 1 Corinthians 12:10, The Holy Bible, p. 1453.

[74]Doctrine and Covenants 46:30, pp. 86-87.

[75]Doctrine and Covenants 46:30-31, pp. 86-87.

[76]Doctrine and Covenants 46:32, p. 87.

[77]James 1:5, The Holy Bible, p. 1538; Doctrine and Covenants 46:7, p. 85; Doctrine and Covenants 6:14, pp. 11-12.

[78]Doctrine and Covenants 46:7, p. 85; Doctrine and Covenants 46:30-32, pp. 86-87.

Everyone has a gift or gifts of some kind.[79] The same spirit will divide to every man severally as he will.[80] These spiritual gifts will never be taken from the Earth. Spiritual gifts are only lost by our unbelief.[81] There are some habits that we have to give up.[82] We cannot procrastinate this work in ourselves and our families for the exciting things of this world.[83]

Don't be slothful in developing spiritual gifts.[84] *Thy gift shall deliver thee.*[85] However, the spirit that helps us cannot dwell in unholy temples.[86] There is no profit if spiritual gifts are not received.[87] Remember. We will do well or better if we will not neglect the gift that is in us.[88] Otherwise, there is no hope. A lack of hope leads to despair. Despair cometh from iniquities.[89]

Exercise your spiritual gifts.[90] Good spiritual tone is good and as necessary as good muscle tone. If you do not use it, you lose it. Your spiritual muscle experiences fatigue just like the muscles in our physical bodies. This is why we were given a Sabbath Day to rest. This why we were asked not to run faster than we can walk.

We will declare the gospel unto our families and the world by the spiritual gifts we have asked for and exercised. If we do not have spiritual gifts, it is not likely that we will be able to preach the gospel to others. We have to learn the gospel first ourselves. If we do not learn these gifts, the fear of man will overtake us and will overwhelm us. We probably will not have the desire to preach the gospel, the glad tidings from our Savior, to family and friends.

These spiritual gifts are so important that all meetings in The Church of Jesus Christ of Latter-day Saints are to be conducted by the guidance of the Holy Ghost.[91] The various bishops of our wards are to watch over us and discern whether there are any among the members of the

---

[79]Doctrine and Covenants 46:11-12, p. 86.

[80]1 Corinthians 12:11, The Holy Bible, p. 1453.

[81]Moroni 10:19, The Book of Mormon, p. 530.

[82]Mosiah 3:19, The Holy Bible, p. 153.

[83]Alma 34:35, The Book of Mormon, p. 295.

[84]Alma 37:43, The Book of Mormon, pp. 303-304.

[85]Doctrine and Covenants 8:4, p. 15.

[86]Helaman 4:24, The Book of Mormon, p. 376.

[87]Doctrine and Covenants 88:33, p. 167.

[88]1 Timothy 4:14, The Holy Bible, p. 1509.

[89]Moroni 10:21-22, The Book of Mormon, p. 530.

[90]Doctrine and Covenants 6:11, p.11.

[91]Doctrine and Covenants 46:2, p. 85.

church professing to have these gifts, but are not of God.[92] These individuals speak with their lips the things of God, but their hearts are far from God.

How do all these gifts work together for our good? Spiritual gifts work by listening to our Heavenly Father, His Son, Jesus Christ, the Holy Ghost, our spouses, children, grandchildren, friends, employees, employers, teachers, etc. They will tell you what they need and what will make them and you feel better. We can discover and recover the spirits of our children and ourselves simply by listening with love. Give your children the gifts of expression and understanding. They will not always speak in tongues that you can understand. "They may not remember what you say. They will remember how you made them feel."[93] Of course, the Lord will remember, too.

There are simple steps in the art of listening. Mothers and fathers can learn how to listen to the spirits of their children and interpret their language. In my communications class in nursing school, our group of student nurses were taught how to listen to our patients. Others teach similar methods. Listening is an excellent method for interpretation of all kinds of tongues. My instructor taught us to 1) Listen with your ears. 2) Listen with your eyes. 3) Identify the emotion. 4) Does their behavior match the emotion? 5) Identify their need, not your need. 6) Ask questions that cannot be answered by yes or no answers (or whatever). Use "Tell me," "Explain to me," or "Describe what you are feeling or doing'" This worked with my patients. It worked with my family. I could identify they just wanted something because there was no emotion. I could also tell they were not really sick.

The Lord knows parents are trying to make a mighty change in themselves and their children while parents are not feeling good, are working hard, or are experiencing catastrophes. These changes will mend broken spirits and be one of the many miracles of your life. Parents will know how to help if they identify the emotion and use the gifts of the spirit that is needed.

How do you apply spiritual gifts to families and children with attention deficit disorders? Here is what is available to the ones who seem dumbfounded or who are living in a consuming darkness: a testimony of Jesus Christ, two administrators (our Heavenly Father and Earthly Father), service operations (Mother), words of wisdom (the scriptures), knowledge (education, experience, and wisdom), the faith to be healed (mend), the faith to heal (restore), working of miracles, prophecies (experience and knowledge of fifteen or more prophets and two parents), the ability to discern spirits (discover), the ability to speak in tongues (expression), and interpretation of tongues (understanding). This is quite a resume' for us. However, they all must work in concert together. It takes time and repetition.

Do you spend time in the Lord's gift shop? This is a sacred shop. Set your pace in this world in the Lord's Gift Shop with His servants and with His principles. The experiences will be exciting, rewarding, and compensatory. Parent and child will have self-esteem–gifts of the spirit. There is no other way to achieve self-esteem. Do family members want to be administrators without learning functions? Do parent and child have enough gratitude to not be diagnosed with an attention deficit disorders? If your family members are low in gratitude, they will not have mercy for each other. We will always need the "Touch of the Master's Hand."

---

[92]Doctrine and Covenants 46:27, p. 86.

[93]Author unknown

67

Chapter Ten

"The Touch of the Master's Hand"

Sometimes, we feel like a lame duck because there are so many people trying to save us. We wonder: "What are they trying to tell me? Do I look like an idiot or appear incapable of making up my own mind?" We withdraw from our own potential and spiritual gifts.

The Mormons know how you feel. There are so many people trying to save the Mormons, members of The Church of Jesus Christ of Latter-day Saints. They almost have to take a numbered ticket and wait in line. When you stop and look at what the Mormons have, it really becomes ridiculous.

> 37...*how often would I have gathered thy children together, even as a hen gathereth her chickens under her wings, and ye would not!*
> 38 *Behold, your house is left unto you desolate.*

> *Matthew 23:37 - 38, The Holy Bible*

Here is how the Mormons are gathered. This is also what everyone is trying to save the Mormons from. There are many positions in The Church of Jesus Christ of Latter-day Saints where even the youngest and oldest of chicks can be gathered. How often does a hen gather her chicks? She does it at night for warmth and anytime during the day when that chick is cold or when the chicks are in danger.

Jesus Christ is the Head of His church. In daily prayer, we can gather anytime we feel the need. He is the Savior of the world. He atoned for my sins that make me look and act like a "lame duck" as well as others who have sins that make them look and act like a "lame duck." We do not need a "go-between" between ourselves and the Savior.

We do need men who have the proper authority to administer the saving ordinances and covenants to return to our Heavenly Father and become joint-heirs with Christ.[94] One cannot become an executor of a will without having the proper authority bestowed in a legal will. It does not work when anyone can do their own thing and change things according to popular opinion at the time. We need more than someone telling us that everything will be okay. Businesses have policies. So does the Lord and Creator of this world.

We have one prophet that holds all of the keys to the administration and ministering of Jesus Christ's church. Having the keys to administer sounds strange. It isn't. Many of you corrected papers for your teachers in school. Your teachers called the sheet of paper which had all of the correct answers neatly numbered in a row her "key." Through revelation from the Lord, prophets obtain answers to problems for the entire church. This is how prophets warn of problems. They have the Great Physician's key to all problems, the Plan of Salvation. We keep

---

[94]Romans 8:17, The Holy Bible, p. 1426.

pace with a changing world by keeping pace with the Lord's prophet who holds the Lord's Keys, the method of achieving things in this life.

We have fifteen prophets who teach the body of truth to the members of the church. They call us to repentance regularly at least twice a year.[95] This is done at General Conference and at monthly firesides. These men are dedicated men who bless or sanctify the ones they are in charge of. That is us. They just make that call of repentance such a "nice tongue lashing" that we thank them for it and request a ticket. Every mother wishes she could do this.

These fifteen men are seers. A seer sees the past, present, and future. This is helpful in determining where things will lead. A good idea on paper may not be so good when one person or thirteen million members tries to do it in real life.

The Book of Isaiah in the Old Testament is easier to understand if we read it with the understanding that Isaiah was a seer. Isaiah wrote of his past, his present, the Savior's present, our present, and the future which is often called the last days. Isaiah saw what it would be like combining all those "good ideas on paper" with the secret combinations of the world.

Parents and step parents can be seers for their family. Their children are their stewardship. They do not have to depend on intuition and luck. Parenting skills are refined with the Gift of the Holy Ghost which is given to you after you are baptized and confirmed a member of The Church of Jesus Christ of Latter-day Saints.

These same fifteen men are revelators. They reveal divine truths. It has been said that we will receive more light and knowledge as we are worthy and need it.[96] These men are the ones that receive more light and knowledge and reveal it to us in ways we can understand.

Parents and step parents can be revelators for their own family, too. They have to teach them. In order to teach more light and knowledge to one's family, parents have to receive the light and knowledge that we have had for centuries. Family Home Evening is a way to learn this light and knowledge with our children. It is also a great time to listen to the revelator of their family, their father or step father. This is why fathers are responsible for Family Home Evening. It a responsibility that should be taken seriously.

These same seers and revelators for the church are fifteen apostles. Apostles are special witnesses of Christ. Their testimony of Christ has opened doors for preaching the gospel in other lands. Christ tells them through prayer and fasting when countries or families are in need of help. These countries and families want more light and knowledge to bless their people and each family member. Fathers teach their family what they have been taught by these fifteen apostles. Every family member will be a disciple or follower of Christ.

Those fifteen apostles are also translators. A translator translates from ancient language to existing language. It is their responsibility to clarify existing language and its concepts. As more members join The Church of Jesus Christ of Latter-day Saints from foreign countries with many dialects, they need their own scriptures to read. A translator makes sure that everything is understandable, but accurate in a particular foreign language. Some concepts, because of foreign language, can be offensive when it is not meant to be if translations are not done correctly. Our ancestors' and descendants' languages of all times must agree for the Savior to remain the same.

---

[95]Doctrine and Covenants 121:43, p. 242.

[96]Ether 4:15-16, The Book of Mormon, pp. 495-496.

Members of The Church of Jesus Christ of Latter-day Saints are also led by a Presiding Bishopric, Seventies, Area Authorities, Temple Presidents, and Mission Presidents. These men lighten the administering or managing load of our fifteen prophets, seers, revelators, and apostles. Thus, our fifteen prophets, seers, revelators, and apostles can minister or give relief to those in need. [97]

In The Church of Jesus Christ of Latter-day Saints, we each belong to special districts called stakes and wards. The Church of Jesus Christ of Latter-day Saints does not have parishes or congregations of five thousand members. Too many people can be lost in the shuffle or politics of a large amount of people.

A stake president is in charge of the entire stake. He presides over all the Melchizedek and Aaronic Priesthood in the Stake, and the other organizations in the stake. There are approximately five to nine wards per stake. The stake president presides over a governing body of twelve men which has two or more members from each ward in the stake. This governing body is called a high council. There are many committees that work with the high council and stake president. Two of these committees are Bishop's Council and the Stake Council.

Bishops are the presiding officer in charge of the ward. The wards are approximately four hundred members. This includes men, women, and children. A ward has to have a certain amount of elders and high priests who attend church regularly and will accept assignments that have responsibility. This is to maintain a balance between administering to people and serving people. "Too many chiefs and not enough Indians who will work" does not work in any organization.

Bishops preside over the Aaronic Priesthood in their ward. This is the priesthood for boys, ages twelve through eighteen. Hopefully, they will take advantage of the opportunities to serve and learn while in their age group and will be ordained an elder at age nineteen and go on a mission. Some young men choose to attend college, marry, and go on missions when they retire.

Bishops also have committees called ward councils for the adults in the entire ward. There are youth councils with and for the youth. These committees are under the direction of the bishop who holds the Melchizedek Priesthood.

The local priesthood of the wards and stakes are gathered in quorums. Men over the age of nineteen are gathered in two kinds of quorums. One quorum is for all high priests of the stake, and the other quorum of Melchizedek Priesthood is for elders. All high priests are under the supervision of the stake president. They are presided over by a high priest group leader. The elders of a ward are under the direction of an elders quorum presidency and their bishop.

The lesser priesthood is called the Aaronic Priesthood. It is only lesser in age group. The things learned in this priesthood are important, too. This is for the young men in the wards. The young men are gathered in quorums, too. The deacons quorum is for young men who are twelve or thirteen years old. The teachers quorum gathers the young men who are ages fourteen to sixteen years old. The priests quorum gathers the young men who are ages seventeen to eighteen years of age. They are presided over by the bishop, but they have their own advisors or teachers. As the young men progress, they are given more responsibilities. They prepare and pass the sacrament to members of the church. The Aaronic Priesthood is called the Preparatory Priesthood because it prepares the boys to serve missions, others, and their families.

---

[97]James 1:27, The Holy Bible, p. 1539.

Male members who are worthy receive the Melchizedek Priesthood. Depending on the need, their age, their ability to cope with more responsibility, and cope with stress, they will be ordained an elder or high priest. The high priest is older usually. His family has a good start and can tolerate sharing their father with more people and responsibilities. High priests usually do the administering part of the gospel in their local neighborhood which is called a stake.

Elders also have a lot of responsibility, but the Lord remembers they are on missions and are raising young families. They are also receiving career training or are working in their communities. Elders do the ministering part of the gospel in the neighborhood. They are younger and can do the heavy service projects. They, hopefully, will retain and teach others what they have learned about ministering or serving their growing family and changing neighborhood.

We all love our bishops and stake presidents. We come in contact with them the most. As a step parent, I have much admiration and sympathies for these offices. It is an awesome responsibility to suddenly begin raising eight adults in varying stages of development. I can imagine what it is like for a bishop to take on the responsibility of three hundred adults and a stake president to take on three thousand adults in various stages of development.

Again, we are following the pattern the Lord has set up in apostles, prophets, seers, revelators, and families. The stake president administers and the bishops ministers for the stake president. In addition, the bishop administers over the members of his ward. He will preside at many meetings to maintain his ward. He is available for individual spiritual counseling as well.

The Church of Jesus Christ of Latter-day Saints does not have a paid ministry. These bishops and stake presidents have assumed these responsibilities while raising families and working at their own occupations. The Lord has asked for volunteers so that all of His tithing funds can be applied to ministering to the Saints in need. The efforts of the many volunteers with many responsibilities bring many blessings.

What about the women? There are many females in The Church of Jesus Christ of Latter-day Saints. They range from minutes old to over a hundred years of age. The women have many roles in the church.[98] They will be in primary for twelve years, a young women's organization for seven or eight years, and a relief society for over seventy years.

The men do the administering part of the priesthood. The women do the ministering part of the church. There is nothing like a ward relief society in action. Can women do the jobs that men do just as good? Yes, but there's one catch. Who would minister to the members? Who would minister to their families? Women have the emotional makeup to do this. Women are known to be the most faithful, best organizers, and the quickest to respond to a need with a list of others coming. This kind of love comes from their many sacrifices for their children. There is nothing like a functioning Relief Society. It is a great help to all.

How are the women gathered under the Lord's wing that seems so patriarchal? We have a beautiful example in our prophet's wife. She is not privy to many things that the prophet works on. It would be too much for her to bear. She would have to be comforted like the prophet is comforted. Instead, she allows her husband to administer without her opinion. She knows what her husband needs the most. He can just be himself with her. He can receive all the ministering from her he needs and an occasional administering from his wife. Naturally, that administering is so nice he thanks his wife for it. She learned from the best.

---

[98] 1 Corinthians 11:11, The Holy Bible, p. 1451.

We have stake president's wives and bishop's wives who are great examples. As expected, they do more ministering than administering to their husbands and ward and stakes. They are often called the mother of the stake or the mother of the ward.

The women gather under a General Relief Society, one Stake Relief Society Presidency, and their Ward Relief Society Presidency. The General Relief Society Presidency administers to the Stake Relief Societies of the church. The Stake Relief Society President administers to the Ward Relief Society President who ministers to the sisters in her relief society. The Stake Relief Society President has a representative on the high council to whom she reports any problems or concerns. This high council representative reports directly to the Stake President. The young women, young men, and primary age children are gathered in the same way.

Why does Relief Society work so many miracles? Women can organize under a banner that is not contrary to their own nature. At Relief Society, women do not have to call bitter things sweet and sweet things bitter to keep peace in their home. Women can include in their lives those things which women truly need and learn how to teach their children the things they will need in their lifetime.

Many teaching positions support the Primary, Sunday School, Young Men, Young Women, and adults. Though a parent has the ultimate responsibility of teaching their children right and wrong, parents and step parents have many organizations to support their families.

Each stake has one or two Stake Patriarchs. When one is sixteen or older, and shows developing maturity by being morally clean and attending church meetings regularly, he or she can ask to receive their patriarchal blessing. This blessing is our "coat of many colors." There are many blessings available for everyone, especially the youth if they are worthy and faithful.

We study four sets of scriptures called the Standard Works. Our church leaders recommend studying all four at the same time. We do this by the footnotes at the bottom of the page. The Standard Works that we study are: The Holy Bible, The Book of Mormon, The Doctrine and Covenants, and The Pearl of Great Price. In our Sunday School classes, we study one standard work each year and cross reference the other standard works.

Our prophet has asked us to read the scriptures daily for at least fifteen minutes. We could not go day after day without food in our physical bodies. Our spiritual bodies, our souls, cannot go without spiritual manna or food either. If we pray before we read the scriptures, we will receive inspiration from what we read. We can apply this inspiration to our problems. This inspiration will become our "daily bread."

The Church of Jesus Christ of Latter-day Saints are a temple-building people. We make covenants in these temples to unite and keep united families for all time and for eternity. We search out the names of our kindred dead. Those names are linked with us, as we are baptized for them in the temple. Our kindred dead will then have all the opportunities available to them, though they have passed beyond the veil. Of course, they have the right to reject any baptismal or marriage covenants made for them on their behalf.

We believe in ministering angels from the other side of the veil. This was discussed in the previous chapter. Those ministering angels possibly are our families who have passed on before us. All have experienced this phenomenon, especially at the time of death of a loved one. There is a special spirit in our homes when the Holy Ghost and ministering angels seems to be around to bear us up. At a death in our family, our retarded daughter even received this blessing of ministering angels. She was comforted as we were since she did not understand our emotions. We were able to control our emotions with her in her group home.

All families are gathered or ministered to by home teachers and visiting teachers. Ideally, a family has one home teacher holding the Melchizedek Priesthood and one home teacher from the Aaronic Priesthood. These two males "home teach" at least once a month with a monthly message and are on call for any emergencies for that family. They hold the same priesthood that a prophet, stake president, and bishop hold.

Women receive a visit from two visiting teachers at least once a month and on an as needed basis. They bring a spiritual message so the session will not lead to a gossip session.

Missionaries from all over the world are assigned to an area that includes many stakes, wards, branches, and districts. They have sacrificed two years of their life to teach people about the Lord's Health Care Plan for His children. They have given up educations, cars, television, movies, and dating. Missionaries are willing to serve anyone. Missionaries have fixed most anything. They have paid their way for two years to accomplish this task. They are among the most blessed volunteers in the world. They are only a phone call or a prayer away.

Who would want to be saved from this "touch of the Master's Hand?" As we can see in each of the Lord's organizations, He has a balance between administering (the manager) and ministering (service giver). There is a great warmth and strength in being gathered this way. Each calling has limits of administering and ministering. The calling presiding over that structure or function is within those limits. This is a great way to focus one's energy in the right direction. We do have our free agency to choose how we administer and how we minister.

Individuals may only want to be saved from the gossip that seems to come with large organizations. Gossip causes many doubts and leaves many mortally wounded souls lying in the ditches of our earth life. Each wonders: "What did I do to them to be picked apart by them? I must really be a lame duck if everyone feels like that about me. What chance do I have in this organization?"

In the battle of the Priesthood vs. Satan, gossip always seems to accompany this struggle. Gossip is Satan's way of destroying what the Priesthood and the Relief Society have tried to build up in a ward. After a large amount of gossip, people do not feel like serving anymore. They feel like a lot of administration is needed, and they want the job. A lot of administrators without anyone serving pulls everyone into living a law of mob justice. There is no mercy without service and sacrifice.

The Savior has taught us how to handle gossip. He taught us how to deal with mocking. Gossip is nothing but mocking. Gossip is an adversary's opinion. An adversary is someone who feels they have to work against others due to the gossip that they have heard about themselves. This gossip may be true. It may be false. Adversaries are not going to tell the truth about you or anyone else. They may be threatened by your efforts. Adversaries feel you are intruding on what they thought was their space, and they now consider you a rival. They have forgotten that a ward is built upon the precepts that each member knows and shares, not the gossip that each member hears and repeats.

Gossip can be idle chit-chat, meddling, hearsay, rumors, and slander as well as mocking. Our children view many gossipers in the media on television. People who rely on gossip may just be venting their feelings. They may be as frustrated as you are. People who gossip experience a panic attack after they have vented, slandered, or mocked someone. Someone else has to be blamed to remove the spotlight from them. Naturally, they do not want anyone imperfect around their children, as they try to make sense of things. They forget that one who is a gossip is imperfect, too. Gossip is the real tattletale.

We are all going to have a trial of faith.[99] Individuals may be going through their trial of faith. Some families have many trials of faith. There may be strain on their face. People do not understand what that strains means. People will assume the worst. Not all trials of faith are abuse or over sins. However, trials make excellent gossip. If someone continues with gossip, they are not going to have the strength they need to overcome their anger.

Do not leave the comfort of the Lord's wing. Learn the limits of the Lord's wing. There are reasons for the limits. Soft answers, saying nothing, agreeing with thine adversary, and kind thoughts will take the steam out of gossip.

"Tithing is too much for me." Giving the Lord ten percent of your income is a real test of faith. All organizations have fees. We trust that those who collect the fees will spend them wisely. In the Lord's organization, the fees are returned to you. However, let's look at tithing a little more closely.

All of us have had somewhere really important to arrive. We may have needed to arrive quickly. There is nothing more frustrating to get in the car, and our car only has one/eighth of a tank of gas or less. When we get to the gas station, there is a line, or we are short of money. Lives depend on fuel. Airplanes crash when they run out fuel. We all need a full tank physically. We need a full tank spiritually, intellectually, emotionally, morally, financially, etc. also.

All of us have family on the other side of the veil. Our deceased family members are continuing on with their patriarchal blessings, their "coat of many colors." They have assignments. They will work through us. They need us to have a full tank, or their efforts in our behalf and in others' behalf will be in vain. We are sealed to them. To keep that sealing in force, we need to pay our tithing.

The Savior needs a full tank, called a storehouse, too. He has places which He needs to go to be ready for the next generation. The Lord knows that you are trying to raise and provide for yourself, a spouse, and children. Our Heavenly Father also has a large family with many demands when money needs are at an all time high and climbing. To many of His children, our tithing can literally mean the difference between life and death.

The Savior knows that you have wants, desires, and fears. He knows that many manipulate your wants, desires, and fears to become rich. The Savior has wants, concerns, and desires, too. He appreciates the help that He receives for any member of His family through tithing. Everyone of these individuals is one of our Heavenly Father's children.

The Savior understands sacrifice. The Savior is also in control of this world. He knows what you need, when you need it, and how much you need before you can figure this out. Often, we do not know what we need. We just know that we are hurting and need something. Tithing will not impede your recovery. Tithing taps into the individualized storehouse that the Savior knows you need. The Savior will give back to you, as you would give to one who sacrifices for your little family. That's tithing. Tithing gathers the financial laws of the Lord's Kingdom for our benefit.

"The women of The Church of Jesus Christ of Latter-day Saints cannot have the priesthood." This is a concern and a great test of faith to many women. They feel women can do many of the jobs that men can do, just as good. Women are known to be more faithful and have great organizational skills. Women have sacrificed for their husbands, children, and homes.

---

[99] 1 Peter 1:7, The Holy Bible, p. 1544.

Women are eager and quick to develop charity for their families and friends. Yet, women have fought hard for equality and equal pay.

However, the Earth is in a war. It is a war for our families, their minds, their hearts, their spirits, their agencies, and their finances. The casualties of this war are known as sinners. Some sinners even become "sons of perdition."[100] Sons of perdition have been partakers of the Lord's power and have been overcome. They denied Jesus Christ, and they became defiant–even to truth. They knew the Lord's power, but they denied the Holy Ghost.

Power describes the Priesthood. Those holding the Priesthood have the power to act in God's name. They must make many judgements for and in behalf of God to help a sinner become a saint. By nature, men feel these things should be handled privately for the healing to take place. By nature, women want to help "sinners stop sinning." They often try to do this by making sinners a public example with gossip. After dealing with the sins and problems in my family, I do not want to deal or be hardened with the sins of my surrounding neighborhoods. My goal is to bring relief and softness to my family and community through service. The priesthood brings leadership, judgement, and firmness when needed to their family and neighborhood.

The responsibility and burdens of the family are shifting to women. Women are becoming hardened by faults and sins of their family, their neighborhood, and their community. Gossip is undoing the good that men are trying to do with their priesthood judgements. Only men having the Priesthood is not a stumbling block for women. It is a relief.

Why is this chapter included in a book about attention deficit disorder? We are all part of one large organization called the Lord's Kingdom. We are children of God. There is one God.[101] It is good to have experience in this organization. It is beneficial for us to be able to recognize the pattern that we lived with before we were born and the pattern that we shall live with when we shall die. Naturally, this pattern is beneficial to us in this existence, too.[102]

Individuals are not lame ducks because they are inexperienced in dealing with large organizations. Individuals can develop attention deficit disorders because they become overwhelmed with the gossip and politics of a large organization. We are all working out our own salvation. Unfortunately, feelings get hurt in this process. Individuals would not cancel their medical, car, or home insurance because of gossip and politics in these organizations. Do not leave the Lord's Health Care Plan because of gossip and politics in the Lord's Kingdom. No matter which church or organization that you belong to, there is a large organization behind it. It takes money to support a lot of little churches or organizations, their ministers, staff, programs, property, paperwork, utilities, cars, and causes.

A word of caution. It has been prophesied that the people who live this pattern of service and sacrifice are the Lord's people, and they will become the wealthiest people in the world. This is why Salt Lake City, Utah, is rumored to be the scam capitol of the world. Members of The Church of Jesus Christ of Latter-day Saints are trusting, frugal, and forgiving. They are also hard workers. People take advantage of the members of The Church of Jesus Christ of Latter-day

---

[100]Doctrine and Covenants 76:31-35, p. 139.

[101]John 10:16, The Holy Bible, p. 1345.

[102]Doctrine and Covenants 52:14, p. 96.

Saints because they think they are wealthy. Our wealth does not mean that we all will become millionaires. The vast majority will not have a large income. We are wealthy to the things that bring salvation, hope, and peace of mind. Because of tithing, our money seems to stretch farther.

There are many who will try to distract you from this pattern of living and these benefits. These individuals want to become wealthy from your hard work, frugal efforts, and fears. They want to become wealthy off your desire to be physically fit and enjoy quality time with your family. Do not let anyone take this harvest from you. You will be the one that will be diagnosed with attention deficit disorder or attention deficit disorder with hyperactivity if you are distracted from this pattern of life. The ones who are taking from you are very focused on what they want. *Keep hold of the Master's hand with your spiritual gifts.*

The Church of Jesus Christ of Latter-day Saints is an exciting church to belong to. You will have many harvests to reap. This church teaches one how to preserve and serve these harvests., too. It also teaches everyone how to play in concert with others. Approximately every two years, members get the privilege of learning how to play a new instrument. This process is known as a church calling.

The Church of Jesus Christ of Latter-day Saints is an easy church to belong to. It has so many tools for one to self-repair and self-renew with dignity. Just ask any Latter-day Saint intensive care nurse who has had to comfort a mother after her son is paralyzed or has died from a tragic accident. Many will feel this mother's child had an attention deficit disorder, and the mother does, too. This may be true. However, this family cannot be comforted with grace only. It will be a lot of work for this family to heal on both sides of the veil.[103] This family is going to have to be gathered under the healing wings of the Savior.[104]

Who is trying to save your family or step family? Who is the administrator, the manager of the family? Who is the ministrator, the caretaker of the family? Who has replaced father or step father, the revelator and administrator of the family, and mother or step mother, the caretaker of the family in your step family? Are they trying to save your family by isolation, intimidation, gossip, and stonewalling behavior or by gathering the family under the healing wings of the Savior?

What gossip continually rotates to keep others in charge of your step family instead of father and mother or step father and step mother? Is your family giving up the Touch of the Master's Hand to maintain control over father and mother? Is your step family covered under the financial laws of the Lord's Kingdom? Are you, your child, and step child covered under the Lord's Health Care Plan?

We need to remember. Satan did not want to share any keys with us, especially financial, health, and spiritual keys. He only wanted to force us to his side. If the Lord is going to share His keys of knowledge and salvation with us, we must first learn to follow instructions.

---

[103]James 2:17-18, The Holy Bible, p. 1540.

[104]Malachi 4:2, The Holy Bible, p. 1184; 3 Nephi 25:2, The Book of Mormon, p. 456.

Chapter Eleven

Following Instructions

Individuals will be diagnosed with an attention deficit disorder if they have not learned how to follow instructions. The ability to follow instructions is important. How well we follow instructions determines our ability to serve our family members and our fellow men. In this chapter, service is another name for following instructions.

Individuals also may viewed as one with an attention deficit disorder because they have different abilities and desires to serve their fellow man and family members. Individuals with one of the attention deficit disorders may seem like they only serve themselves or only serve others when it is convenient for them. They may not know how to serve themselves. Individuals may not have had the opportunities to learn to serve others. Unfortunately, there are those who refuse to serve or follow instructions under any circumstances.

There are many reasons why people do not follow instructions. There are many reasons why people do not serve each other. Here are a few. Stop and reflect about the times that you were not willing to serve or follow instructions. Children have fears and feelings about service which they must overcome, too.

First, our free agency is being manipulated by our lack of self-confidence. We can feel it. Children can feel it. We are so use to carrying heavy mental burdens. We do not recognize the burden of temptation or opposition when it happens. Actually, individuals are being tempted to not serve because they have other things to do or other interests that seems to have more pressing claims. It is easy to get out of the task by feeling not qualified to lead or serve.

Think about this now. If Satan thought that someone could not learn to do a task, he would not have to tempt them to not serve, to not learn, or to not follow instructions. Would he? This is why young children are not tempted with certain things. They cannot do the task.

Second, individuals are intimidated by over-achievers. Over-achievers may be able to learn things quickly. Do not feel inadequate around over-achievers. Over-achievers still have many things to learn, too. Many over-achievers are territorial and have their own agendas. They can be very manipulative for their own success at all costs. Otherwise, they would slow down and assist others. This is where everyone learns the most.

Many over-achievers cannot say no. They are afraid they will not be liked. Sadly, people do not let others say "no" gracefully with no grudges. Over-achieving parents do not spend quality or quantity time at home. They are always in a hurry. Children become angry at being left out all the time or waiting for parents to come home. Service becomes something to avoid or an impediment instead of a blessing.

Third, people do not follow instructions or serve when they are angry with someone. They do not want to be associated with that individual or his instructions. They may not feel worthy to serve because of their anger. They do not receive sudden spurts of wisdom when angry. This is why the Savior counseled us to go to those who have offended us and work it out. No one likes to work or serve in a critical environment. No one likes to work around someone who thinks they are the only ones that can do the job.

Fourth, people do not use soft answers. People do not listen to you when you use soft answers. Children can be labeled as having an attention deficit disorder and a learning disability simply because they refused to use manners, courtesy, and soft answers. Soft answers and manners are great services to mankind and our families.

Nothing turns someone off more quickly than a rude or abrupt request for service. This causes a lot of unnecessary hard feelings in families and in neighborhoods. Adults are guilty of this, especially when they are in a hurry or are worried about something. Children copy parents whether they are in a hurry or not. Children's stresses are not like an adult's stresses.

People do not use soft answers because they have not been thanked themselves. Soft answers are so out of habit. When we are around soft answers, they feel like a strange vocabulary. Children may not realize that people are not going to jump up and down every time they do something good. However, it is nice to be appreciated and thanked.

Fifth, children do not have a testimony of following instructions or service yet. They do not even have a testimony of learning. They do not have a testimony of too many things except mealtime, television, sports, Nintendo, and recess. This is where they spend all of their time.

Children have not built faith yet. Testimonies will come. Experience gratitude and emotion with your child so they will not be afraid of the various range of emotions which they will experience while they are learning the basics of reality and life.

Sixth, parents have to be home mentally and physically to begin the process of teaching children how to follow instructions. Parents have to be home mentally and physically to keep the process going, too. Too many times, children are expected to be home mentally and physically while parents are not. The ten-second rule does not apply to children. It only applies to dropped pieces of bread or cookies on the floor.

Seventh, children cannot learn to follow instructions well by cramming. Parents could not cram turning over, sitting, crawling, or walking into their child's brain. Parents cannot cram self-esteem, self-confidence, and the ability to follow instructions into their child's personality.

Though a child may have the intelligence to learn things quickly, cramming keeps children from learning precept by precept, step by step, and degree by degree. With cramming, the child misses those one-on-one experiences which build up his self-esteem to attempt harder instructions. These experiences of closeness give him feelings of trust as well as wisdom. This learning comes by doing and sharing experiences with his parents and others. Without them, his wisdom must come from reading, not experiencing. Movies and television have replaced reading and experiencing. Children are following the examples shown, not learning from these stories.

Eighth, adults cannot serve when their marriages and families are stressful. Neither can children. Marriages, families, and their activities are very stressful and fast-paced under the best of circumstances. Parents can become so involved in outside activities. They lose focus on just exactly who and what instructions they should be focusing on. Time goes by quickly when you are busy or having all that fun. If we let them, problems and activities can consume our time for our spouses and children.

Suddenly, parents realize their children are not where they should be in school. Parents and step parents forget that it is difficult for children to follow simple instructions for homework in an environment where everyone is fighting and walking on eggshells with each other. It is difficult to learn when children worry that both parents will be home when they get home from school. It is difficult to learn when children are hoping a parent will not be home when they come home from school.

Children become detached. Children may leave home mentally, too. In this environment, no one is allowed to develop their Gift of the Holy Ghost or the use of their free agency. These things are two important parts of learning how to follow instructions.

Ninth, adults cannot serve two masters.[105] *Neither can children.* A master is a boss, mentor, ruler, or our Lord. All of these things stand for the authority in your life. Children and adults cannot serve two authorities. We will always cleave to one and hate the other. The scriptures tell us this. We have to decide who is our Lord and whose instructions we will follow. Even God Himself gave the authority of this world to the Savior so we did not have two masters to choose between.

Battles between spouses and ex-spouses and between families and step families are raging and are very distracting and consuming. Children do not know which set of instructions to follow. There is very little energy left for following instructions anyway. Adults cannot concentrate and thrive in these atmospheres. We cannot expect children to thrive and serve all of these masters.

Many things and even people try to "master" a family. There is not enough time or money to serve all the masters of a family and receive a good education. A few might make it through life with all of these agendas. They cannot raise all the families of the world that need populating and raising. Parents cannot pay for the health care costs for the pace that they are setting for the world. There is another pace that the Lord wants us to take.[106]

Tenth, no one has taken the time to help children learn how to follow instructions. This gives children the idea that learning, following instructions, and serving are not important or can be procrastinated. Without a knowledge base or a desire to learn, how can children serve? They have nothing to serve.

Parents may not realize it, but school curriculums have changed. Children are not receiving in kindergarten what parents and grandparents received in their kindergarten curriculums. Our children and grandchildren are smarter and are bored with just coloring, pasting, and recess. If you think about it, parents and grandparents were smarter than what they received in kindergarten, too.

Kindergarten does not sound important, but it is. If a child waits till the third grade to receive help, he has missed three years of reading. He has also missed three years of learning how to follow instructions. Nevertheless, your child is expected to know certain basics, or he will be judged and condemned sharply.

Lastly, w*e do not follow instructions because we have received some lame instructions.* One knows how difficult it is to obtain directions for a particular destination from someone who has not been there, and they have no idea what they are talking about. We do not get to where we wanted to be and have to find someone else for instructions. Can you imagine a mother in a labor room at your local hospital trying to deliver a baby with many coaches screaming conflicting instructions? Breathe! No, don't breathe! I know more than the doctor or nurse. When the mother tries to follow one coach, the other coaches become indignant and begin persuading her to deliver her baby according to their experience and knowledge.

---

[105]Matthew 6:24, The Holy Bible, p. 1196.

[106]Mosiah 4:27, The Book of Mormon, p. 157; Doctrine and Covenants 10:4, p. 17.

One cannot give cardio-pulmonary resuscitation this way either. The true rescuers feel like a fifth wheel, or they feel they are just in the way. If adults cannot follow instructions in this manner, a child would not be able to follow instructions either. They would not be capable of making a decision. This happens with attention deficit disorder.

If one is unsure of the instructions, they can always trust following the instructions of ancient and modern prophets. The Lord will not lead us astray through prophets. For in the eternities, we will be led by prophets. The Son of God will delegate various aspects of His work to prophets. Adam, Abraham, Isaac, Joseph, Noah, Moses, John the Baptist, John the Revelator, etc., and all latter-day prophets are not going to be sitting idly by basking in the sunshine. They worked too hard in our behalf in mortality. They will be working in our behalf for eternity, too. If worthy, we may be under their direction at different times in our eternal life.

From experience with a living prophet, prophets are very comforting and soothing. They want only for our happiness. They know what will bring that happiness. Prophets have walked the road ahead of us. They had to follow instructions in order to testify of and warn us of many things. One cannot point out the way to another if he does not know the way himself from experience. Joseph F. Smith is a prime example.

Joseph F. Smith, nephew of Joseph Smith, is a prophet who has passed on, but he has pointed out many ways for us who would follow. He was President of The Church of Jesus Christ of Latter-day Saints during 1918. At this time, but on several different days, he received a revelation about the spirits of the dead. Many people feel he had been pondering the premature deaths of his children when they were young when he received this revelation. He did have many children die prematurely. A son did die before President Smith received this revelation.

However, at this time, World War I was in progress. There had been the sinking of the Lusitania in 1915. Many more ships and soldiers were lost afterward in this war. There was a flu epidemic going on. Deaths from starvation were occurring.

In May of 1918, the first proposals for an Armistice were made. There is always heavy fighting right before an armistice is signed. Each side wants to gain more territory before they give in or admit defeat until another day. This gives countries territory to bargain for without really having to give up something. Each side has to emphasize to the other side what they have done to their country.

Many people were dying. President Joseph F. Smith was concerned and grieved over the deaths of millions of Heavenly Father's children. They were so young. President Joseph F. Smith was experiencing deaths in his own family at this time. Families were eliminated or devastated. Individuals in these families did not have an opportunity to live their lives, raise families, receive an education, repent, change things in their lives, and experience the good from these things. In short, they were stuck with what they were at the time of their deaths.

Through this prophet's concern for the world, he prayed and received divine communications from the Lord. These divine communications are found in Doctrine and Covenants Section 138. President Joseph F. Smith could have kept this revelation to himself to comfort himself only. However, millions of people were suffering. They did not get to live to fulfill their "coat of many colors" in this life. Millions of people did not get a full chance to repent and refrain from their sins. They did not get a chance to make restitution. President Joseph F. Smith presented this revelation in General Conference in October of 1918. Here are a few excerpts from this section.

28 And I wondered at the words of Peter—wherein he said that the Son of God preached unto the spirits in prison, who sometime were disobedient, when once the long-suffering of God waited in the days of Noah—and how it was possible for him to preach to those spirits and perform the necessary labor among them in so short a time.

Doctrine and Covenants 138:28

36 Thus was it made known that our Redeemer spent his time during his sojourn in the world of spirits, instructing and preparing the faithful spirits of the prophets who had testified of him in the flesh;

37 That they might carry the message of redemption unto all the dead, unto whom he could not go personally, because of their rebellion and transgression, that they through the ministration of his servants might also hear his words.

Doctrine and Covenants 138:36 - 37

52 And continue thenceforth their labor as had been promised by the Lord, and be partakers of all blessings which were held in reserve for them that love him.

Doctrine and Covenants 138:52 - 53

About this time, this poem became popular. It expressed our feelings over the many war dead. Now, poppies even give us and our children grief.

IN FLANDERS FIELD

In Flanders fields the poppies blow
Between the crosses, row on row,
That mark our place; and in the sky
The larks, still bravely singing, fly
Scarce heard amid the guns below.

We are the dead. Short days ago
We lived, felt dawn, saw sunset glow,
Loved and were loved, and now we lie
In Flanders fields.

Take up our quarrel with the foe;
To you from failing hands we throw
The torch; be yours to hold it high.
If ye break faith with us who die
We shall not sleep, though poppies grow
In Flanders fields.

By Lieutenant Colonel John McCrae

81

The author of the poem, a member of the First Canadian Contingent, died in France on January 28, 1918, after four years of service on the Western Front.[107] Now, the poem, which many of us had to learn while in school, has more meaning and more comfort.

All the world had to comfort them and make sense of a world in chaos was this poem called "In Flanders Field." However, the world was prepared and comforted by our Heavenly Father through a prophet. Members of The Church of Jesus Christ received divine communications from the Lord through a prophet to comfort them and the world.

These divine communications can be applied to all wars and all catastrophes. This poem and this section in the Doctrine and Covenants can be applied to the war for our family and its remnants. Divine communications to prophets can be applied to the battle for your self-confidence and your ability to follow instructions or serve.

We cannot afford the luxury of being sidetracked and breaking faith with our war-dead through out the ages. They are the remnants of our family. We need to know how to follow instructions and the faith to be obedient when we do not understand.

Prophets will teach us how to do this. A prophet is one of the Lord's servants. Prophets follow instructions, too. Their instructions will help us to apply what we have learned to our lives. Prophets' words are not advice or opinions. Their words are instructions that we are to follow. The Lord would not give them instructions and inspiration to give to us if their instructions were not in our power to follow.

Reflect back on the times parents were asked to follow instructions. Was there grumbling from parents and step parents? How were you tempted to not lead or serve? Did it seem like parents and step parents were following two Masters? Was it the child within you or the adult? If children are trying to follow two masters instead of parents, the masters they have chosen to follow most likely will be childish. One childish master will be worse than the other.

Are you, the parent and step parent, available for your children? Are children available for parents and step parents? Does parent's and step parent's lack of availability to children and step children affect your children's self-confidence in your home and elsewhere? When children and step children are unavailable for parents and step parents, does this affect your self confidence? Could this be why you have parents, step parents, children, and step children who are angry and who are under-achievers and over-achievers?

How do you comfort your children and step children? Are you allowed to comfort them? Are step parents allowed to give step children instructions? Are your children and step children allowed to develop their free agency and the spiritual gifts given to them by a loving Heavenly Father? Are parents and children achieving only in sports and recreation? Thus, you feel instructions from prophets are lame.

Are you and your children and step children trying to make friends by not being friendly?[108] Do you and your children and step children have enough manners to not be diagnosed with an attention deficit disorder? As you mature, are you applying what you have learned in your life to your life?

---

[107]Http://buchanan.org/h-172.html

[108]Proverbs 18:24, The Holy Bible, p. 830.

Chapter Twelve

Applying What We Have Learned

Individuals will be diagnosed with an attention deficit disorder if they do not know how to apply what they have read or learned. Individuals may be too busy or too tired to even try to understand what they need to apply to their lives. For various reasons, the material may be confusing or boring. We may feel that others do not have much to teach us. We all have taken classes where we have learned things which we feel we will never live long enough to be able to apply in our lifetime.

Nevertheless, we have been admonished to learn wisdom in our youth in the scriptures.[109] Wisdom requires application or the commitment and utilization of our knowledge. No real understanding will occur without the application of things we have learned. We also cannot overcome things without the application of knowledge and wisdom. In other words, nothing compensates for experience, especially experience in truth.

There are scriptures giving parents instructions on what to teach their children. The Savior remembered to tell parents on both sides of the world what those things are. They must be important. Yet, these things have fallen by the wayside and are not considered important. Some of these things are now prohibited by law. Yet, we still expect our children to perform at a level that someone does when they use all of the tools needed to gain wisdom in their youth.

Elementary wisdom begins at home and in elementary school. Our education continues with junior high, high school, and college. Even in college, we study the basics that we learned at home and in elementary school. These basic things are reading, writing, arithmetic, language, history, and courtesy. Why are these things important? We will always be reading, writing, calculating, speaking in a language, affected by history, and affected by courtesy at all levels of learning. We will need to know how to communicate in these areas during our lifetime. We do not want to communicate that we know nothing, or we would not put forth an effort for even ourselves and our children.

Since children are to gain wisdom in their youth, there must be away for parents to teach their children how to apply truth to their lives. Logically, this must occur through the things that parents are instructed to teach their children. Like adults, children learn to enlarge their borders in wisdom and order. The Savior specifically instructed parents to teach these things to our children. If we want our children to have peace in their lives, we must follow instructions, too.

Our children are not to go hungry and naked. It takes food, clothing, and shelter to provide for children. It also takes food, clothing, and shelter to be able to think, ponder, and apply. We have seen pictures of children of all ages who were starving. They also had the barest of shelters to live in. These children could not accomplish much. Their energy was rapidly depleted because they had no resources. Their energy was consumed in looking or begging for a few necessities of life. Many children's and step children's energy was consumed because they

---

[109]Alma 37:35, <u>The Book of Mormon</u>, p. 303.

were constantly seeking a parent or step parent's attention. They needed spiritual food from parents and step parents. Unfortunately, they would not accept it from a parent or step parent.

There are many parents who have provided a lot of nourishing food, the best clothes, and very immaculate shelters for their children. Yet, their children, too, cannot apply what they have learned. Their children have gone out into the world hungry and naked emotionally, spiritually, socially, financially, morally, and intellectually. They are wanting in the areas of obedience, persistence, work, service, and sacrifice. Apparently, our children will not be naked and hungry if we teach and follow the other things that the Savior has asked us to teach our children.

*We are to teach faith in Christ, repentance, baptism, and the Gift of the Holy Ghost to our children, o*r their sins will be upon our heads.[110] What does faith in Christ, repentance, baptism, and the Gift of the Holy Ghost have to do with applying what we are learning. Repentance gives us the mental space to apply things that we have learned. Faith in Christ gives us the confidence to attempt new things. Faith also gives us the ability to change our heart as we change our borders and learn new things. Baptism is our launching or new beginning. The Holy Ghost blesses our endeavors. He reveals what to apply and what not to apply in our lives.

Christ is the one we are to follow. Christ is the pattern that we must learn to recognize in His world. He is the example of what to do when we do not know what things to apply. All measurements have a standard, but are not exactly correct. Christ is our standard of truth that is exact and reliable. We are to teach our children to follow the commandments of Christ.

Those commandments are not given to cumber us. Christ does not believe in that. He believes in liberty and free agency for all. His commandments are given to build and strengthen the body and spirit. He ought to know about that. He created our bodies. He knows the principles that the mind works under, too. He had to create a body that worked with the mind.

We are to teach our children to pray and walk uprightly.[111] Prayer is our foundation for mercy for ourselves and others. It is through our pleadings on the behalf of ourselves and others that we learn how to love one another as ourselves. If we do not pray, we must rely on justice only. There would be liberty for a few, not for all. Prayer fine tunes the strings of forgiveness, gratitude, sorrow, temptation, and wisdom on our instrument of choice.

Venting with the Savior and venting with others are different. Our children need to know this. The Savior blesses us with courage to persist through our trials. He has learned the ability to forgive and forget, and He knows our hearts. Others may give sympathy, but they have not learned how to forget. We cannot live on sympathy alone. We cannot live on the feelings of others who do not know who to believe. A discharge of steam emotionally on others usually inflicts more burdens than it solves.

There is a special wisdom that is gained through prayer over our experiences and our problems. Prayer gives us the ability to keep working when we are learning difficult things at the various stages of our lives. Thus, we will not have a mind to injure someone who is learning, or who does not do things as perfect and as fast as we think things should be done. The answers to our prayers give us helpful incites that we can share with others. Prayer changes us and makes us more flexible. However, we have to ask for these changes and the ability to be flexible in times

---

[110]Doctrine and Covenants 68:25, p. 127.

[111]Doctrine and Covenants 68:28, p. 127.

of change. With prayer, we do not have to resort to unrighteous dominion over another or wounding those who are already wounded.[112] This brings more wounds to our selves.

Parents are to teach their children to not transgress the laws of God, not to quarrel one with another, not to serve the devil, but to walk in truth and soberness, to love one another, and to administer to the poor.[113] Without these things in our life, we cannot impart of our substance. We learn most through service and sacrifice.[114]

The Savior tells us to impart of our substance, tells us how, shows us how by example, and tells us what to teach our children in order for them to learn how to impart of their substance. This is the measure of His love for us. If we omit or commit any one of these things in our lives, the only substances that we have to impart are gossip and hate. This is the measure of our love for Him.

It is important that children learn truth and walk in soberness. They must learn there will be a time to weep, a time to mourn, a time to laugh, a time to play, and a time to work.[115] There are things that we must approach with certain degrees of solemnity or seriousness in our life. Sober also refers to drunkenness. Alcohol and drugs are very harmful to children.

At our Earthly school, the Lord requires a willing mind and heart.[116] We must be willing to learn and to apply what we learn. Perfectionists and over-achievers have a tendency to rely on their ways and their strengths. Under-achievers rely on someone else's strengths. Eventually, everyone runs faster than they can walk, and they expect others to do the same. If they do not, they judge others very critically.

These are two examples of the carnal mind which the Lord tells us not to have. Those who do not have the desire to commit any sexual sins are not to have a carnal mind either. Carnal means worldly, as well as lustful. Carnal also means mundane which is tedious and boring. Perhaps, this is why people become so bored quickly with their carnal interests.

There are reasons that we are to teach these things to our children. I would rather have a home built on a deep foundation of many bricks than a shallow foundation of a few bricks. I am sure you would, too. If we do not teach children how to apply their knowledge, it is difficult to speak peace to their soul under trying circumstances, even for the Lord.[117] If we feel we have a perfect knowledge, then faith will become dormant in our lives.[118] If our faith will not sprout, it

---

[112]Jacob 2:9, The Book of Mormon, p. 120.

[113]Mosiah 4:14-16, The Book of Mormon, p. 156.

[114]Mosiah 4:16-21, The Book of Mormon, p. 156.

[115]Ecclesiastes 3:1-8, The Holy Bible, p. 848.

[116]Doctrine and Covenants 64:34-36, p. 121.

[117]Doctrine and Covenants 6:23, p. 12.

[118]Alma 32:34, The Book of Mormon, p. 290.

will also not root.[119] Roots are what plants depend on. Roots nourish plants. The plant, our life, becomes fruitful with good roots.

In other words, we are to rely on our spiritual knowledge, not just our worldly knowledge. By studying things out in our minds with scriptures and good books, we have a knowledge base to rely on for our foundation.[120]

All that we learn is not going to be used in just mortality. What we learn is going to be used for our eternity. In fact, we have space left in our brains for our eternity. It is going to be interesting to see how we are going to use those basics we learned from home, elementary school, junior high school, high school, college, and that college of hard knocks called parenting. It will be even more interesting as we apply our knowledge in the Lord's Kingdom without the buffetings of Satan.

Most children do not apply themselves because they are afraid to climb their "scaffold of life." Before children climb their scaffold of life, they must first build it. Otherwise, you will climb another's scaffold who may not have your best interests in mind. Though they may not know what to call it, even children are afraid of change. They do not like criticism. It is okay to change. It is okay to increase in wisdom and stature while young. People may expect more out of you and your children as you both increase in knowledge, wisdom, and stature. They will expect certain performance levels whether you have increased in wisdom and stature or not.

People do change as they add more knowledge, wisdom, and experience to their life. If this wisdom and experience are positive, they will enlarge their borders. If these changes are negative, their borders will diminish. Change is a natural course of enlarging one's borders and often feels awkward. Change enables us to do more, and life becomes more interesting.

Many individuals do not apply what they have learned. They will climb "their scaffold of life" when they are ready. Meanwhile, they will be judged as having an attention deficit disorder, and others will become very critical of their efforts. They will begin building an even more difficult scaffold for you to climb which is not the scaffold for your "coat of many colors."

Children are not learning to apply themselves because parents are doing homework for their children. For many years, I have watched parents do homework, science projects, and eagle scout projects for their children. I have been guilty of this myself. Our children and their projects had to be perfect, or their work was unacceptable.

Many parents have children who refuse to do their homework, and parents are weary of arguing with them. Parents become ashamed of their child's lack of effort. Their child's leadership skills become based on egos and bravados. They were playing while Mother or Father did their homework and their chores.

The projects get bigger, bolder, and more perfect. This child has amazing organizational skills and intelligence, and the child has the grades and yearbook information to prove it. This child will receive a scholarship based on these grades. Yet, the child reads poorly, cannot do simple mathematics, is insecure, and has very little organizational skills. He has poor language and writing skills. To accomplish the grades and yearbook projects, anyone would progress in all of these areas.

---

[119]Alma 32:42, The Book of Mormon, p. 291.

[120]Doctrine and Covenants 9:7-9, p. 16.

In the meantime, standards are formed, and many children are judged severely. These children must have attention deficit disorder because they cannot measure up to the standards, money, and efforts of adults who insist on doing everything in a one-hundred-and ten percent manner. These adults may have a college degree. Children are suppose to compete against peers within their age group not against an adult with a college degree.

Many parents are in a hurry to do something that is more fun than teaching an uncooperative child. However, these parents cannot stand to have their child criticized or be imperfect in any way. Even if their child is willing to do his or her homework, parents do not have the time and patience for them to learn. Both parent and child have schedules to keep. Naturally, their child still must have straight A's. Their child needs a scholarship. The parents have to do the homework.

Since parents are paying their children's debts intellectually, parents can easily slip into paying their children's financial debts. This can continue into adulthood. The practice of doing too much of children's homework can lead to parents trying to pay their children's debt's emotionally, morally, spiritually, socially, etc., and this cannot be done.

This dishonesty is as harmful to your child as doing nothing for your child. Doing your child's work is not family unity. It is a false sense of security. Anyone working with children knows what children can produce at their various age levels in a twenty-four hour period. Teachers know the quality of children's work versus the quality of work done by their parents. They also know children's vocabulary, sentence structure, and punctuation versus an adult's vocabulary and writing skills.

Your child is not immune. If your child has not done the work and has not learned basic wisdom from his experiences, he will be overwhelmed and hurt or will overwhelm and hurt others. It is easier to let your child fail at a young age instead of letting him realize he is a failing adult with straight A's. At some time in his life, the child has to do his own work. Your child or another child's life and mental health will depend on letting your child do the work

Children of all ages will always be applying knowledge to experience and gaining wisdom. As an example, at age fifty-five, I am still learning how to *follow instructions* better while doing my family history. I am learning this *step by step* and require some *one-on-one assistance* with my family history instructor. I still *jest* with the teacher, occasionally get *sidetracked*, and am *inconsistent* in my efforts with family history, but I am still learning. As expected, she knows when I have not done the assignment. I have nothing to contribute.

At age fifty-five, I am also still *learning to recognize patterns*. There are patterns to names, emigration, record keeping, and record destroying. There is even a pattern to my efforts. There is a pattern to my failures, too. I can see these patterns in my journal.

If I look for my family remnants, as I have been instructed, family history is not so overwhelming. It is easier to work on a list that has three hundred names versus a file that has three thousand names. I do not have a high risk of scrambling my computer disk as I gather families with the same name. It is easier to share information with someone who is interested in part of my family tree. If I follow the rules, I also will not be causing problems for others doing their family history. I cannot cram for this test or cram for tests in other areas of my life.

If I follow instructions, I can *focus* my searches. It is easier to find more information about a few than few information about a lot. My research does not sit in my filing cabinets for years because I do not have time to digest mountains of printed data. Most of all, my Heavenly Father blesses my efforts when I am *obedient*. I wished I would have recognized this pattern for learning earlier in my life. I would not have made some dumb mistakes. I would not have had depression over these mistakes.

When we apply ourselves, the adversary defeats our efforts and our parents' efforts. For example, very few like to learn history. Nevertheless, in the Doctrine and Covenants, we are asked to learn about the history of countries. Specifically, that verse reads:

> *53 And, verily I say unto you, that it is my will that you should hasten to translate my scriptures, and to obtain a knowledge of history, and of countries, and of kingdoms, of laws of God and man, and all this for the salvation of Zion. Amen.*

Doctrine and Covenants 93:53

From this verse, we can conclude that history is going to be an important class in our future. Yet, history seems to be one of those boring classes that most students dread sitting through. It is boring because we do not take time to make these people real. They are just names in a book. These names have been slandered so much in the news medias, we forget their sacrifices. We do not know who or what to believe.

Millions of people have had many unspeakable and unthinkable atrocities committed against them. They have had no voice in their destinies. They have been left to starve after being tortured. They have had their land and property seized as well as their lives taken. If they are able to recover, they feel that the only solution is to control others. They are stuck where they were when they died. Naturally, these individuals were told it was their fault for this treatment. The end justified the means. Are we going to tell these people which we are supposed to help that they have an attention deficit disorder, too?

The adversary began defeating our efforts as well as our teachers' efforts in our history classes in elementary, junior high, and high school. We did not want to learn about the history of our state as well as the history of our nation and other nations. We could not see the need for coloring all those blank maps and memorizing all those dates. Though the names of countries have changed, I see the need now. Thankfully, my sixth grade teacher didn't give up. We have similar experiences in language, literature, and courtesy.[121]

The adversary increases his intensity to counter growth spirts obtained by applying truth to our lives. The adversary's efforts prevent us from gathering our family remnants and the gathering of ourselves. He does not want any family to have any composure, self-control, or dignity. It is point and counterpoint, and families are the battlefield.

On this battlefield, the adversary also works from the principle that more soldiers will be removed from action trying to save one wounded soldier. A sniper can paralyze an army troop. One, two, or three family members experimenting in drugs, immorality, crime, gossip, and deceitful behavior can paralyze a family for many years. Many families paralyzed with drugs, immorality, crime, gossip, and deceitful behavior will paralyze a country.

Now, let's apply what we have learned over the years to the things the Savior has asked us to learn. We are to learn about the history of countries. We will be using mathematics,

---

[121]Doctrine and Covenants 90:15, p. 178.

language, and history to learn about the history of our ancestors. First, my instructor emphasized the rights of privacy and the rights of precedence while doing genealogy.[122] Though rules have changed since the first Genealogical Society was formed, individuals have a right to live in privacy and not have our beliefs inflicted on them.

As we read the documents and poetry of Civil War soldiers, there are so many people with the same name. If there are that many who died with the same name, how many people and soldiers really died during the American Civil War? How many really died in the other wars?

For family home evening, I calculated the rights of privacy and the rights of precedence for my ancestor soldiers who were married or had children born during the Civil War. From history, I have learned the Civil War broke out soon after Abraham Lincoln was elected president. President Lincoln was elected in 1860.

The rules for submission were different in this time period. They had the same goal in mind. I estimated that my rights of precedence and rights of privacy for my ancestors born during the Civil War would be around 1970. In other words, I could not unite these families until around 1970 without a documented death date. If someone married around 1860 and I did not have a death date, the rights of privacy and precedence would not end until 1955. I could not unite a husband and wife in my family who were divided in death by the many tragedies of the Civil War Era until after 1955. This time period would lengthen if I did not keep the commandments. If I remained unworthy and disloyal to the Savior so that I could not go to the temple, this period for my ancestors becomes indefinite.

I realized that the drug problem and morality problems of the 1960's were the adversary's way to defeat me and many others from gathering the remnants of our people. Families were so busy taking care of drug addicted family members. They did not have the mental and physical energy to do family history work or care for others in their family. I was curious about the other wars that I am slightly familiar with. I calculated rights of privacy for them, too.

There are lists of World War I soldiers being compiled. This war began around 1915 and ended on November 11, 1918 at 11 A.M. Calculating the rights of privacy by birth, I cannot do family history work until the year 2025 without a death date. If my ancestors married during the first World War, I cannot unite this family until 2010 without a death date.

The efforts to gather the families of World War I are being defeated by the adversary again. Many families have youth who are overtaken in secret combinations of drugs, alcohol, immorality, theft, and murder. The adversary has to intensify his efforts because we are better record keepers now and more educated. We are in better health, have better jobs, and can purchase the many things which are available to keep records. The adversary defeats these

---

[122]Members of The Church of Jesus Christ of Latter-day Saints are a temple-building people. They unite their families in these temples for eternity. Members cannot submit names for family history work which have been born less than one-hundred-and-ten-years after their birth or ninety-five years after their marriage date. To do so, they must have a documented death date and death place and be related directly to them. This is the rights of privacy.

The rights of precedence means members must be related closely to the family names that they submit for temple work. The closest living relative has permission to decide to do this work. The closest living relatives in order are: undivorced spouse, children, parents, and brothers and sisters. Ex-spouses, in-laws, steps, and cousins need permission from the closest living relative.

resources and efforts through doubt, depression, and concentration. It is difficult for children to concentrate in school with so many problems in the home.

Calculating the rights of privacy by birth for World War II soldiers, I discovered these families cannot be united until 2049. Calculating the rights of privacy by a marriage date for World War II soldiers, these families cannot be united until 2034.

The Korean War started June 25, 1950, when armed forces of the Communist North Korea invaded the Republic of Korea or South Korea at the 38th parallel of latitude. Soldiers and anyone born around this time and who is dead cannot be united with their families until 2060 without a death date. Spouses who married during the Korean War cannot be united until 2045.

The Vietnam War began over the struggle between the French and Communist Vietnamese for control of North and South Vietnam. The meeting that ended French rule occurred in 1954. Though Americans trained the armed forces of South Vietnam, Americans did not enter into conflict until June 1966. Calculating rights of privacy for this time period starts in 1954 and ends in 1975. Anyone born between 1954-1976 cannot be united until the years 2064-2085. Anyone married during the Vietnam Period cannot be united until the years of 2049-2070.

Now, we know why there are wars and rumors of wars and so much commotion in the last days. When the rights of precedence and the rights of privacy are up for these various wars, those years will be full of much commotion to keep us from gathering ourselves and our families.

I left one war until last–The Revolutionary War. The Revolutionary War began on April 19, 1775 when British Regulars fired on the Minutemen of Lexington, Massachusetts. This war ended on October 19, 1781 with the surrender of the British at Yorktown. In 1783, Great Britain signed the formal surrender recognizing the independence of the colonies. The arguments resurfaced in about 1807. Using the same quarrels, the United States became a pawn in the war between Great Britain and Napoleon of France. Each wanted control of the seas and the commerce of the United States to finance their war with each other. These families could not be reunited until around 1885 and 1907.

I am not a history expert, but I would hazard a guess the adversary was defeating the efforts of the framers of our Constitution in these years with contention in the land. Those men and their families not only applied themselves, but proved independence is better than dependence. We have much because of them. They are not the crooks that they have been painted.[123] Crooks do not pledge their lives, their faith, and their sacred honor. They have no faith and honor to pledge because they do not believe in sacrifice.

List the wisdom you learned in your youth. Are you using these wisdoms and learning more? Is your child and step child learning wisdom in their youth? What is the scaffold of life in your family? How are the growth spurts in each member of your family supported or countered by the actions of others inside and outside of the family? Does each member of the family have a mind willing to learn? Are you aware the Savior has left records of what we are to teach our children? Is your child or step child going out in his world spiritually and intellectually hungry and naked? If so, he os she will not be able to magnifying his or her calling. Your child will be diagnosed with attention deficit disorder.

---

[123]1 Nephi 13:11-19, The Book of Mormon, pp. 24-25.

Chapter Thirteen

Magnifying Your Calling

Individuals who do not magnify their various callings in their life will be accused of having an attention deficit disorder or an attention deficit disorder with hyperactivity. Individuals may not feel the need or desire to magnify their callings, especially when someone has hurt them. There are individuals who do not let others magnify their calling. Perhaps, you have no idea what I am talking about. Let me explain.

Think of a Magnifying Lens. When someone is looking through a magnifying lens, small things appear larger. Minute details can be examined with a strong magnifying lens. This small world is amazing. It is like a world within a world. We see things that we never noticed. We never dreamed those things were there. It is that way with people, too.

A magnifying glass gives one a deep respect for Father Adam who named all of the animals. He did this by grouping together those who had the same or similar characteristics. Size and shape did not matter. Perhaps, families have been grouped together in time frames by our Heavenly Father because family members have the same or similar characteristics, too.

The real amazing thing of a magnifying glass is that if you could look back through the magnifying glass, the one who holds the magnifying glass appears larger, too. The small animal or child that is looking back at you sees things they have never seen before in you, too. It can be frightening when the person does not understand or know what he or she is looking at.

This is what happens when one magnifies his or her calling. The one holding the magnifying glass, the administrator, takes a look at something or someone who needs some service, ministration. With magnification, someone is enhanced. Their field of vision has changed, and they notice things that seemed to not be there before. They notice things that need attention or things that could not be seen without magnification.

Correct principles are taught. Solutions are formed. Problems solved. Everyone grows, including both the receiver and the giver. Both receiver and giver learn to govern themselves with magnification.

We may not realize it, but we have several callings in our life that we have to magnify or enlarge. In short, we all have to learn our duties and show up for work. We will work at these callings or relationships for many years.

We have many relationships in which we need to improve or grow stronger the minute we are born. Those relationships are: son or daughter, brother or sister, step brother or step sister, boyfriend or girl friend, spouse or ex-spouse, mother or father, and step mother or step father, and grandparent. We must magnify our calling as a neighbor, friend, student, teacher, employee, and employer. Other relationships or callings may be added. We even magnify our calling as a consumer. We learn to shop wisely.

Last, but not least, we must magnify our calling as a son or daughter of God. Many think they do not have to magnify their calling as a son or daughter of God. They are busy trying to care for their families. Moreover, God loves us, and He will save us by grace no matter what we do or what we say to others. They do not realize that if they magnify their calling as a son or daughter of God, they will magnify their other callings in life automatically.

Many individuals are not sure that God exists. If He does exist, they are not sure about the form. Do radio waves exist? Yes, radio waves exist. Are we sure of their form? Yet, all of our communications work by radio waves and principles of circuitry.

Any amateur radio operator, formally known as a ham radio operator, will tell you that radio waves do exist. They have mapped their form in cycles and even measured bandwidth. There are regulations which determine how these radio waves will be used and who uses them. Give a ham operator a good sunspot, a power source, a few circuit components, a license, and a piece of piano wire, and he can hear plainly the results of a good radio wave. He can even talk and listen long distances around the world.

Would the Creator of this World have created radio waves if He didn't have two ears to hear the results of a radio wave or a sensory system to feel the results of a radio wave? He died to save us. Would He create radio waves blindly in a haphazard way, knowing they could be harmful to the very ones He was going to die to save?

No, radio waves are created in order. This order has a pattern. Do we understand those patterns and principles of circuitry in mortality? Not really. Some just know how to use them more than others. They have come prepared to learn and to work.

Our spirits are built on the same principles of circuitry. In other words, our spirits transmit as well as receive. We have to have a power source in order to magnify our calling as a daughter or son of God. We do not want to transmit false and deceptive signals or spurious signals? Wouldn't you rather transmit clear signals and receive clear, helpful messages? This will magnify ourselves as well as magnify others.

Our spiritual circuitry is not limited to prayer and fasting. Our spiritual circuitry operates through the Gift of the Holy Ghost and every principle we decide to learn. As a result, in the very hour that we need things, we can transmit and receive what we need and what others need.[124]

After we learn these principles and die, we will become perfected. In the meantime, the Creator of this world knew that we would have some static, picket-fencing, chirping, or have complete failures in our communications. Why?

We have become insulated from the very things that would conduct help and inspiration to our souls. From science class or chemistry in school, we know insulators maintain a tight grip on their electrons. This grip is so tight that an electric current cannot pass through the circuit within voltage limits. Likewise, we have seen people hold such a tight grip on others that they cannot learn or receive the things they need within normal limits. They must resort to outbursts. These people are the dictators and imitators in our world and in our families. These individuals will not let others make decisions without influencing (strong arm) others' decisions. They even decide who everyone can speak to or associate with.

Worldly interests hold tight grips on us, too. Can you imagine a worldly interest becoming a dictator to a family? I imagine this is why the Lord asked us not to have idols.

---

[124]Doctrine and Covenants 84:85, p. 159.

We are going to have many afflictions because of our family.[125] It is difficult for a ham operator to transmit or receive clearly when they are in a pit, especially an inexperienced ham operator. It is that way for family members, too. This includes step families. Family members and step families must come out of the pits they are in to magnify their callings.

Everyone is trying to learn the same things you are. When families are smitten with afflictions or various pits in their lives, it is everyone's duty to magnify their calling.[126] We must overcome the opposition in our lives, not avoid it, or ignore it. If you want to transmit and receive, abide by His correct laws, principles, and ordinances.[127]

After you have magnified one calling, you will be sent to another calling which you will need to magnify.[128] Individuals probably will be trying to magnify many callings at once. Don't be cumbered.[129] Even the Apostle Paul in prison stated he had to magnify his calling as a prophet.[130] One of the ways the Apostle Paul magnified his calling is that he let others learn and do their duty.[131] He also was always concerned about others less fortunate than he. To complete this circuit, Paul remained in contact with his power source by prayer.

We have been told to magnify our calling as the Savior magnified His calling. How did the Savior magnify His calling? He had twelve capacitors or twelve conducting plates for His force field. Jesus' twelve conducting plates which magnified himself and others are: faith, hope, charity, love, virtue, knowledge, temperance, patience, brotherly kindness, godliness, charity, humility, and diligence. This is why he told us to remember these things.[132]

The Savior also did not lay down and pick back up over and over weapons of rebellion. He, too, found His lost chord, His broken heart, and His contrite spirit. He developed the same "Gifts of the Spirit" that we can claim and develop. He followed the prophets before Him and after Him, too. He made a decision once about the commandments. In short, the Savior knew how to glean His fields. Now, He is teaching us how to glean our fields.

Are you willing to govern yourself by magnifying your various callings and relationships in your life? How is your family and step family being encumbered? Is it because you have not developed your spiritual circuitry? Do family members control their comfort zone by inclusion, exclusion, and intimidation? Are family members ready to glean new fields?

---

[125]Doctrine and Covenants 24:8-9, p. 43: Doctrine and Covenants 31:2, p. 55.

[126]Mosiah 1:17, The Book of Mormon, p. 147.

[127]Doctrine and Covenants 132:64, p. 273.

[128]Doctrine and Covenants 88:77-80, p. 170.

[129]Doctrine and Covenants 66:10-11, p. 123.

[130]Romans 11:13, The Holy Bible, p. 1431.

[131]Doctrine and Covenants 107:99, p. 221.

[132]Doctrine and Covenants 4:6, p. 7.

Chapter Fourteen

Gleaning Your Fields

Like Ruth and Noami, we will gean many fields in our life time. Glean means to collect, gather, acquire, or harvest. *Your child or you may not have an attention deficit disorder. You or your child may have a stupor of thought.* Not knowing what this is, you look for the easiest, neatest, quickest, brightest thing to entertain yourself and your family. This results in a person not gleaning the right field. Sadly, many individuals feel they do not have to glean any fields. The time is not right. Others will glean their fields for them if they stall long enough.

Stupor of Thought. The Lord has given His children a stupor of thought and a burning in our bosom to help us know which field to glean.[133] We are to use this when we make our decisions. It is our own personal light that stays with us to help determine what is right and what is wrong. Simply put, the Lord is not going to bless anyone's efforts which will intentionally or unintentionally harm His children. He died for these children. A mother can understand these feelings. She does not allow anyone to harm the children that she has sacrificed for.

We are directed with this stupor of thought. One time while working on a patient who was in cardiac arrest, I went to start Cardiopulmonary Resuscitation. I had a stupor of thought, and I could not remember how to do CPR. Naturally, I was very embarrassed. I could only function if I backed away from the patient. This patient had cardiomyopathy. When the rescuers and doctors arrived, I suddenly exclaimed the patient had cardiomyopathy. The firemen stated: "NO CPR!" They gave him heart medications to recover the heart beat.

I asked why no CPR. They explained: In cardiomyopathy, the heart is stretched paper thin and covers all most the entire chest cavity. I would have ruptured the patient's heart and killed him. No one had ever explained to me that the heart muscle was paper thin in cardiomyopathy. They just told my group of nursing students that in cardiomyopathy the heart becomes enlarged. I was grateful for this stupor of thought. So was my patient who is still alive.

Many have been protected by this stupor of thought. A classic example of a stupor of thought on a wide scale is the attack on Pearl Harbor. If one follows the various movie versions and books about the attack on Pearl Harbor, it appears that America not only was sleeping, but every Army, Naval, Air Force, and Intelligence officer was grossly incompetent and derelict in his duties. As a result, America has been the butt of many countries' jokes since 1941. America has been painted as a bunch of party animals and recreationists. Many conflicts have been incited with America as the incompetent bully. Yet, these countries make recreational, sports, and party products to sell to America. This is not the mind set of America.

After the attack, these officers and enlisted men came together under a common cause and fought heroically. They planned battles. Unfortunately, many officers were probably demoted or forced to retire because they were given a stupor of thought by the Creator of this

---

[133]Doctrine and Covenants 9:7-9, p. 16.

World. No officer or politician wanted to commit themselves to help the world offensively. The Lord put them in a position where they had to fight defensively.

After viewing the current release of "Pearl Harbor," my twelve-year old grandson thought Jesus did this to save the Jews. There were a lot of countries saved from the events of that day. Their Constitutions were saved by the men on the USS Arizona, the USS Utah, and the other ships that day. The Savior saved the world again with a stupor of thought and our sacrifice.

The Lord does not bless individuals who are involved in habitual lying, stealing, vandalism, adultery, fornication, homosexuality, smoking, alcohol, and drug addiction. He does not want you to rupture your spiritual hearts or the hearts of others.

There have been many thieves who have been caught in humorous circumstances. They had a stupor of thought. Many alcoholics had a stupor of thought and had to pull over. Many resisted this stupor of thought and drove to a destination on reflex and alcohol. Their consequences will be waiting for them when they return to their Heavenly Home.

Naturally, your health is affected by these activities. Poor mental and physical health causes stupor of thought. It is hard to think clearly when you are physically sick or facing bankruptcy because of someone's behavior, especially your own behavior.

There are people involved in habitual lying, stealing, vandalism, adultery, fornication, homosexuality, smoking, alcohol, and drug addiction. They appear to be very successful. They make more money than we do. They live in bigger homes than we do. These individuals usually have many people around them to build this vision of power over others.

They may be successful in their weapons of rebellion and secret combinations. Are they successful in their "coat of many colors?" Is this really success? One day, a day that is not known to you or them, their hearts will burst. They will have no way to eliminate spiritual waste. It is going to be very painful for them.

By gleaning your fields, you have a "coat of many colors" waiting for you, not weapons of rebellion and a genealogy of secret combinations. If weapons of rebellion are forced upon you as the tool of last resort, you just have to find two things–your broken heart and contrite spirit. This is done by repentance. As you go about your daily life, you will then not be cumbered or tangled with a stupor of thought.

There is a difference between stupor of thought and refusing to make an effort for yourself. Do you have an attention deficit disorder because you have not learned how to glean your fields? Do you or your child have an attention deficit disorder because you both refuse to glean your fields? Individuals will still reap what they sow even though they refuse to reap. Individuals who have not sown a crop will reap weeds or an empty, crusted field. Even farmers know if they want a better yield, they must rotate and harvest their crops. It is that way for successful spiritual crops, too.

Are you trying to glean your fields through lying, stealing, fornication, adultery, homosexuality, and chemicals? You will have a stupor of thought if you do. You will be diagnosed as one with an attention deficit disorder also. Stay close to your mortal home and your Heavenly Home when you have a stupor of thought. Do things to arouse your faculties not suppress them. Learn the difference between stupor of thought and lack of effort. There will be less contention and regret in your life.

Chapter Fifteen

The Spirit of Contention

Individuals may be diagnosed with an attention deficit disorder because they rely on the spirit of contention to resist evil in their lives. Many individuals also resist good with the spirit of contention. They cannot recognize the difference between good and evil. They may refuse to recognize the good in their life. Most usually, they want to control the good in their lives by calling evil good and good evil.

The spirit of contention seems to appear when we are magnifying our callings in life and are applying wisdom to the knowledge and experiences we are accumulating in life. Contention seems to appear when we lay down our weapons of rebellion and pride. Others are not ready to lay down their weapons of rebellion. They cannot control our physical growth spirts, but they can control our spiritual growth. Someone must not want us to have spiritual growth spurts.

The problems caused by contention are numerous and varied. It is impossible to mention them all in this book. One can be trapped with so many problems that it appears they have not learned from previous mistakes. Others may feel these individuals must have attention deficit disorder because they are impulsive. Naturally, we should pass them by. They will never change. They deserve what they get. We forget that if the storms of life are raging at our door, they are raging at others' doors, too.

This spirit of contention destroys families, friendships, marriages, and businesses. The spirit of contention destroys one's dreams, confidence, and aspirations. Who wants to be married to, work for, or be a friend to someone who digs a pit for you, whines about the pit, brags about the pit to others, blames you for the pit, and then denies that there is even a pit that both of you are in?[134] Acquaintances cannot take root and develop into lasting friendships. Engagements are broken, and divorces obtained. Contentious individuals are not viewed as prospective partners.

The Process of Contention. How does contention begin in one's life? Contention begins in our relationships with those in authority over us–parents and step parents. Children learn quickly that they can control parents and step parents with contentious behavior. Parents and step parents try to smooth things over with some very nice things. Children can stall with silence until the parent or step parent does the child's work for them. These tactics work so well that children use the same controlling tactics on teachers, policeman, employers, mayors, governors, presidents, and God. Simply put, children cannot accept the will of these authority figures over the things which they have control over. They create opposition to make sure that their will is done. It does not matter that their will is not good for the benefit of the family and ourselves.

When we become disobedient to parents and step parents and God and any authority figure over us, a spiritual decline occurs. In this spiritual decline, we want to make sure our rights are taken care of. I suspect this spiritual decline occurs until we almost experience

---

[134]Doctrine and Covenants 109:25, p. 224.

spiritual death. We experience the stages that one experiences in a physical death: shock, anger, denial, bargaining, etc. We never reach acceptance since we are always upset and angry with our own spirit of contention. In the process of contention, everyone's self-esteem has been attacked and destroyed, including the contender. Now, he has to force others to his will by destroying their reputation. Mankind has even tried to destroy God's reputation.

Shame, guilt, anger, defiance, and disobedience do not usher in dreams and successful relationships. The spirit of contention increases stress and aggravation in our lives. Your various retaliations and vengeance replaces your faith. It is faith that is the substance of things hoped for, but not seen.[135] Retaliations and vengeance will consume you and your family to the fourth generation.

The Aspects of Contention. Our marriage, family, and business lives are stressful and fast-paced. There are so many aspects to the spirit of contention in families that I have an entire book about the spirit of contention.[136] It is geared to step families, but all of the principles can be adapted and applied to biological families, too. The basic premise of my book is that there are twelve areas of our personality that we need to develop in order to have balance in our lives. Balance is important. It will lead to perfection and will give us temperance in our lives. If we do not learn how to balance these twelve aspects of personality, they become aspects of contention.

The amount of balance in our lives keeps us from the spirit of contention. Those aspects of our personality that we need to balance are: physical, emotional, social, intellectual, financial, moral, spiritual, work, persistence, obedience, service, and sacrifice. Just as we open files in our personal computers, we need to open these twelve files in our lives. If we do, the Lord will give us opportunities to learn more about these important aspects of our lives.

I discovered these twelve areas of our personality are mentioned by other names in the Doctrine and Covenants. Many have decided to regroup these areas into four, five, or seven aspects of our lives. We become severely out of balance when we do that. Our fears bring the spirit of contention into our lives, though we may not mean to be contentious.

> 5And faith, hope, charity and love, with an eye single to the glory of God,
> qualify him for the work.
> 6Remember faith, virtue, knowledge, temperance, patience, brotherly kindness,
> godliness, charity, humility, diligence.
> 7Ask, and ye shall receive; knock, and it shall be opened unto you. Amen.

Doctrine and Covenants 4:5 - 7

The Savior did not regroup or skim over these things. He said. "Remember." We cannot afford to forget them. This is how I have assigned the things which the Savior told us not to forget. With them, we have balance in our temporal life. Without, we have attention deficits.

---

[135]Hebrews 11:1-2, The Holy Bible, p. 1532.

[136]Mary Jane Grange, The Medicine Wheel for Step Parents, Trafford Publishing, 2008.

faith–work
hope–physical
charity–sacrifice
love–financial
virtue–moral
knowledge–intellectual
temperate–emotional
patience–social
brotherly kindness–service
Godliness–spiritual
charity–sacrifice
humility–obedience
diligence–persistence

Nine of the categories are obvious. For example, temperance is the emotional part of our personality. Temperance, a moderation in all things, is the opposite of depression, not happiness. If we do not want to be depressed, we must have moderation in all things and some prudent self-control. Knowledge is intellectual while virtue is moral. To be successful socially, we must be patient. We all need and love acts of brotherly kindness which is called service. We have all been taught that one who is teachable is humble. If we are teachable, we will be obedient. Lastly, we must be diligent, or persistent, and endure to the end.

There are three categories that were a little more difficult to follow the Savior's thinking. Following the words of previous prophets, specifically Apostle Paul, this is how I organized those three remaining categories. I find it very interesting that there are many in the temporal world who rely on just these three aspects of personality, the difficult ones to assign to a heavenly attribute.

hope–physical
love–financial
faith–work

By growing and building up our bodies, we hope we can endure. Our love for others and ourselves versus our love of money will determine how well we compete in the financial aspect of our lives.[137] Our love will also determine who and what we spend our money on and how we treat others.

Faith without works is dead.[138] This is why members of The Church of Jesus Christ of Latter-day Saints are encouraged to follow the admonitions of Paul.[139] We use this Article of Faith to help us decide when making our choices.

---

[137]1 Timothy 6:10, The Holy Bible, p. 1511.

[138]James 2:17, The Holy Bible, p. 1540.

[139]Philippians 4:8, The Holy Bible, p. 1492.

*13 We believe in being honest, true, chaste, benevolent, virtuous, and in
doing good to all men; indeed, we may say that we follow the admonition
of Paul—We believe all things, we hope all things, we have endured many
things, and hope to be able to endure all things. If there is anything virtuous,
lovely, or of good report or praiseworthy, we seek after these things.*

Articles of Faith 1:13, The Pearl of Great Price

    *Describe the contention in your home? Are contentious individuals resisting evil, or are
they resisting the good that parents and step parents are providing children and step children?
Watch your children and step children when they contend with one another. Are children
embracing contention or opposing contention in their home? Young children usually give you an
example of resisting evil. Older children usually give you an example of resisting good. Write
down your observations. This is how your children will contend with parents and step parents.*

    *Does the contention in your home come when family members have picked up a weapon
of rebellion or laid down a weapon of rebellion? Does someone want step parents and parents
to have weapons of rebellion in their home to take the spotlight off their children's and step
children's behavior? Who does not want you or your children to have growth spirts spiritually?*

    *Are you providing examples of the aspects of personality or the aspects of contention to
your children and step children? How are you balancing the twelve aspects of contention versus
the twelve aspects of personality and self-esteem. Are you temperate in all things?*

    *Here is a chart for you to begin on yourself and your children. This is what you need to
teach your children while they are in your home. Many times, children do not know there are
other alternatives to their behavior and consequences. Each area has its own way of handling
stress. Your child does not have to rely on one method of handling stress in all aspects of their
life–contention. These areas will become your coat or your child's coat of many colors.*

Savior Said: "Remember"	Aspects of Personality/Disputes	Symptoms of ADD in Your Children
Faith	*Work*	
Hope	*Physical*	
Charity	*Sacrifice (Childhood)*	
Love	*Financial*	
Virtue	*Moral*	
Knowledge	*Intellectual*	
Temperate	*Emotional*	
Patience	*Social*	
Brotherly Kindness	*Service*	
Godliness	*Spiritual*	
Charity	*Sacrifice (Adult)*	
Humility	*Obedience*	
Diligence	*Persistence*	

Chapter Sixteen

Your Lost Chord

In most cases, individuals do not have attention deficit disorder and attention deficit disorder with hyperactivity. Individual just have not found their lost chord. When individuals put away the childish things in their lives, lay down their particular "weapons of rebellion," and bandage their wounds correctly instead of repressing their wounds, individuals find something very special within themselves. They find their lost chord.

Keep in mind. A chord is a combination of at least three tones sounded together in harmony. There is a melody and harmony. Harmony has a mutual understanding with the melody. Balance occurs even though one plays major and minor keys in the chord.

Finding your lost chord requires one to stop existing on pride while he or she lays down their weapons of rebellion. Unfortunately, young children and many adults are not ready to put away the childish things in their life. They are also not ready to lay down their various weapons of rebellion. Childish things, pride, and weapons of rebellion have been too profitable for them to lay them aside.

What is our lost chord? Most people feel that faith in Christ, repentance, acceptance, forgiveness, gratitude, and courtesy are their lost chords which they will harmonize as best as they can. These attributes are great for us, but they are not our lost chord. These attributes are the tools that renew, repair, and tune our lost chord.

Your lost chord is a broken heart and a contrite spirit.[140] A broken heart and a contrite spirit are so important. Your parents and step parents agreed in the pre-existence to care for you while on Earth while you find your lost chord. Of course, parents and step parents cannot care for you indefinitely in your pursuit of your ego and hurt pride. Learning the difference is how we honor our parents.

Why is a broken heart and a contrite spirit so important? We cannot escape death. Is this the spirit that you want to enter your eternity with? Is this the spirit that you can spend eternity with and still be happy and productive? Is this the contrite spirit that your family can rely on for an eternity? Do parent and child have a spirit that both can learn with. Whatever principle we learn in this estate or lifetime, will rise with us.[141] These principles are what we will rely on for an eternity after our death.

It has been said: It is harder to change in the next life. Why? It is going to be so peaceful. There are not going to be wars, climbing prices, wage freezes or layoffs, sickness, death, infirmities, taxes, food bills, utility bills, insurances, increased gas prices, and car bills. The Lord is going to take care of the crooks of the world and their unrighteous or burdensome

---

[140]2 Nephi 2:7, <u>The Book of Mormon</u>, p. 57; <u>Doctrine and Covenants</u> 59:8, p. 108.

[141]<u>Doctrine and Covenants</u> 130:18-21, p. 265.

agendas. This all sounds good to me and probably you, too. Wait. There is not going to be any opposition.[142]

The scriptures tell us that it is difficult to change without opposition. Opposition causes us to get out of the chair and work. If we will not work and progress while enduring opposition, it is most likely we will not do anything without opposition. We will not have the principles within us to know how to work or what to do when there is not any opposition.

Opposition causes us to seek and ask our Father in Heaven. Opposition brings us to our knees to listen after we have prayed.[143] If we do not do the work in this life and have a habit of seeking righteousness and praying now, it is going to be difficult to develop these habits in the next life. Without opposition, the spirit will see or feel no need to change.

I know that parents and families are tired, frustrated, and overwhelmed. Many of you have chronic illnesses. Learn to deal with opposition in the Lord's way, not our way, the easiness of the way, or the court's way. Teach your children how to deal with opposition. Let them have their experiences with opposition. Remember. They do not have to be perfect adults at one, five, nine, and twelve years of age.

Ask yourself frequently: "Is this the spirit that you want you and your children to have when you and your family enter the Kingdom of God?" Make a list of things you want to change about yourself. Let children make their own list. Do not let them be too critical of themselves. This is a time to build up not tear down. Point out what they need to be doing each year. Include some fun things. Every year children do not do the work on themselves, they are behind. Work on one thing at a time. Add things as you and they are able.

We need another tone for a chord. The third tone that we will harmonize with our broken heart and contrite spirit is charity. Naturally, we want the best tone. The greatest of these is charity.[144] Now that you have found your lost chord, a broken heart, a contrite spirit, and charity, the world is open up to you. Contrite means apologetic and remorseful. Charity means love, the pure love of Christ.

Most people think that a broken heart is a shattered heart which is broken in pieces. This is not productive, even for the Lord. Broken means gentle or tame, not shattered. A tame horse follows instructions and can be used for many things. It is interesting to note. Indians tame their horses in water. It is the living water that tames or makes us gentle.

Our lost chord cannot be tuned with denial, repression, rationalization, regression, redirection, or redefinition. We tune or self-repair with faith, repentance, forgiveness, charity, and soft answers. Soft answers are: "May I help you," "Please," "Thank you," "No," or "Yes." Our patience, sacrifice, and persistence with these tuning forks will also tune others.

The Lost Chord. Sir Arthur Sullivan and Adelaide Proctor have written a beautiful song about our lost chord. Sir Arthur Sullivan wrote the music. Adelaide Proctor wrote the text.

---

[142]2 Nephi 2:11, The Book of Mormon, pp. 57-58, Doctrine and Covenants 136:31, p. 284.

[143]Helaman 3:35, The Book of Mormon, p. 374.

[144]1 Corinthians 13:13, The Holy Bible, p. 1454.

THE LOST CHORD

Seated one day at the organ,
I was weary and ill at ease,
And my fingers wander'd idly
Over the noisy keys.
I know not what I was playing,
Or what I was dreaming then,
But I struck one chord of music,
Like the sound of a great Amen.
Like the sound of a great Amen.
It flooded the crimson twilight,
Like the close of an angel's psalm,
And it lay on my fevered spirit,
With a touch of infinite calm,
It quieted pain and sorrow,
Like love over-coming strife.
It seemed the harmonious echo
From our discordant life,
It linked all perplexed meanings,
Into one perfect peace,
And trembled away into silence,
As if it were loathe to cease;
I have sought but I seek it vainly,
That one lost chord divine,
Which came from the soul of the organ,
And entered in to mine.
It may be that Death's bright Angel,
Will speak in that chord again;
It may be that only in heav'n,
I shall hear that grand Amen.
It may be that Death's bright Angel,
Will speak in that chord again
It may be that only in heav'n
I shall hear that grand amen.

Another great musician, but of our time, Dr. Michael Ballam, points out what Adelaide Proctor was telling us in her song, "The Lost Chord." Dr. Michael Ballam points out ten or eleven things which good music and The Lost Chord will do for everyone.[145] Good music,

---

[145]Dr. Michael Ballam, "The Lost Chord," <u>Building a Musical First Aid Kit</u>, Cassette One, Phoenix Productions, Logan, Utah, 1991.

harmony, turns fatigue into energy. The weary become at ease. Harmony turns idleness into work, depression into hope, fever into calm, pain into comfort, sorrow into joy, war into peace, hate into love, confusion into understanding, and death into life. This is just what happens when we harmonize our broken heart and contrite spirit with charity.

Now, we do not have to vacillate between victim and victimizer. Choose not to be a victim who is withdrawn and angry or a victimizer who is aggressive and angry. Both of these courses of action leave others with the impression that you have an attention deficit disorder.

Individuals who choose not to be a victim or a victimizer will need some assertiveness training.[146] Assertiveness gives you a positive outlook on things and confidence. Assertive individuals may appear aggressive and as a "know it all."

Assertiveness training costs about $1500.00 to $2000.00, depending on the course. I am going to give you some assertiveness training for the cost of this book. A patient's family member saved me $1500.00. He overheard the nurses discussing their assertiveness training. I did not have the money for the class. This professor gave me a course in assertiveness training at the bedside of his mother. This professor told me to pass it on. He was a professor at the University of Utah. I have always been sorry I did not remember this patient's name.

Here is your free assertiveness training. If one speaks up for themselves, it may seem aggressive, bold, and threaten people. This professor told me: "Anything that is positive in your life is assertive. Anything that is negative in your life is aggressive." I will always remember this professor's thoughtfulness to me. It has opened a new world to me.[147] All of us have room for improvement in our assertiveness training. When this fails, remember that we always have a perfect pattern to follow. There is repentance and Gifts of the Spirit. It is possible to follow Him with the Gifts of the Spirit. This is a much easier and happier way to live. Don't give up your self-confidence just because individuals are threatened with your self confidence.

List the things that you and your children and step children want to accomplish or experience in your lifetime. List what things that need taming in your life. How much time and money will these things take? Are there other things that have a more pressing need? Can you be tamed? Are you concerned that your child or step child cannot be tamed? How are you, your child, and step child trying to tame yourselves? Are you trying to tame yourselves with chemicals or with the Lord's living water? Are parents and step parents taming children and step children or are the children and step children trying to tame parents and step parents to children's needs, wants, and desires?

Are you able to lay down a life of pleasure to care for your family? Will you have to pick up a weapon of rebellion to accomplish your life of pleasure? If so, you will be viewed as one with an attention deficit disorder. Are you and your children and step children more aggressive or more assertive? By our actions, the world knows if we are a wild stallion or a wild mare which cannot be tamed. In spite of its beauty, what good is a wild stallion or a wild mare? A wild stallion or a wild mare may be used for breeding purposes. However, wild stallions and wild mares run away from others and drive others away, too.

---

[146]Doctrine and Covenants 101:97, p. 200.

[147]Matthew 7:14, The Holy Bible, p. 1198.

Chapter Seventeen

Charity

Many parents notice their children have lost the brightness about them which they had when their children were young. The following verse describes a mist of darkness. This mist of darkness occurs in individuals as well as our environment.   I suspect these mists are our attention deficit disorders.

23 And it came to pass that there arose a mist of darkness; yea, even an exceedingly great mist of darkness, insomuch that they who had commenced in the path did lose their way, that they wandered off and were lost.

1 Nephi 8:23, The Book of Mormon

Lehi's Vision. This verse is in a vision which a man named Lehi received. Lehi is a prophet from Jerusalem who is a descendent of Manasseh, son of Joseph of Egypt. Lehi experienced this vision on his journey to a promised land. He, his wife, and four sons left Jerusalem to preserve their lives because of religious persecution. On this journey, Lehi experienced a vision which Latter-Day Saint authors call the Tree of Life. This vision begins in 1 Nephi, Chapter 8 of The Book of Mormon. I am paraphrasing 1 Nephi 8:7 - 38 to save space and to make it easier to apply to families and step families. I urge you to read the vision yourself.

In this chapter of The Book of Mormon, Lehi has gathered his family and is telling them about his vision. Lehi rejoices in his sons, Nephi and Sam. He is afraid for his sons, Laman and Lemuel. They were a source of much contention and grief on this journey. Angels could not convince them of the errors of their ways. Lehi worries that his two oldest sons will be lost.

A Dark and Dreary Wilderness. Lehi sees in his dream a dark and dreary wilderness. A man dressed in a white robe spoke to him and told Lehi to follow him. Lehi followed him and found himself in a dark and dreary waste. He traveled for many hours in darkness and prayed to the Lord for mercy. After Lehi prayed to the Lord, he beheld a large and spacious field.

The Tree of Life. Lehi saw a tree which had fruit to make one happy. As Lehi partook of the fruit, he discovered that the fruit was sweeter than any fruit that he had ever tasted. The fruit was whiter that he had ever seen. As Lehi partook of the fruit, the fruit filled his soul with great joy. He desired his family to partake of this desirable fruit.

River of Water. Lehi looked for his family. He discovered a river of water near the tree with the white fruit. The head of the river was a little way from the Tree. His wife, Sariah, and sons, Sam and Nephi; stood at the head of the river, but they did not know which way to go. Lehi beckoned to them.. He told them to come to him and to eat of the desirable fruit that he was partaking. They did. Lehi looked for Laman and Lemuel. They were at the head of the river also. Lehi beckoned to them, but they would not come and partake of the desirable fruit.

A Rod of Iron. Lehi beheld a rod of iron which extended along the bank of the river. The rod of iron led to the tree by which Lehi stood. The term rod is not new to us. Moses carried a rod. The princes of Israel had rods, probably to denote a gathering place for their tribe. A rod is a measurement of five and one-half feet. Priests carried rods to denote power of their office.

A Straight and Narrow Path. Lehi saw a strait and narrow path. This straight and narrow path came along by the rod of iron to the tree by which Lehi stood.

A fountain. The path led by the head of the fountain to a large and spacious field as if it had been a world. A fountain is a point of origination or authority. [The current of the waters from the fountain in Lehi's dream seem to be traveling in an opposite direction from the Tree of Life which has the most delicious fruit.]

Numbers of People Pressing Forward. Lehi saw many numbers of people who were pressing forward to obtain the path which led to the tree by which Lehi stood. Lehi describes five kinds of groups in the many numbers of people

First, Those Lost in a Mist of Darkness. There arose a mist of darkness. It was so dark that they who had commenced in the path did lose their way. They wandered off and were lost.

Second, Those Ashamed Over Holding to the Rod of Iron and Partaking of the Sweetest Fruit. They caught hold of the end of the rod of iron, clung to the rod of iron through the mist of darkness, and were able to partake of the fruit of the tree. After they had partaken of the fruit of the tree they did cast their eyes about as if they were ashamed.

Third, Those in a Great and Spacious Building. Lehi looked around and saw a great and spacious building on the other side of the river of water. The building stood like it was in the air, high above the earth. The building was filled with people, old and young, male and female. Their manner of dress was exceedingly fine. They mocked and pointed their fingers at those who had come and partook of the fruit. After they had tasted of the fruit they were ashamed because of those that were scoffing at them. They fell away into forbidden paths and were lost.

Fourth, Those Who Caught Hold of The Iron Rod and Fell Down, and Partook of the Fruit. Lehi saw other multitudes pressing forward who caught hold of the end of the rod of iron. They pressed forward, continually holding fast to the rod of iron. They fell down and partook of the fruit of the tree.

Fifth, Those on the Way to the Great and Spacious Building. Other multitudes felt their way towards that great and spacious building. Many were drowned in the depths of the fountain; and many were lost from his view, wandering in strange roads. *I suspect this Great and Spacious building which has no foundation or no plan of salvation is The Church of the Devil.* Lehi's son, Nephi, mentions The Church of the Devil in his vision of the mists of darkness.

Great was the multitude that did enter into that strange building. After they entered into that building, they pointed the finger of scorn at Lehi and those partaking of the fruit; but Lehi and those partaking of the fruit heeded them not. Those who heeded the mockers fell away. Laman and Lemuel, Lehi's two oldest sons, did not partake of the fruit. As any parent would, Lehi greatly feared for Laman and Lemuel lest they should be cast off from the presence of the Lord. Lehi exhorted them with all the feeling of a tender parent, hoping they would listen to him, and the Lord would be merciful to them and not cast them off. Lehi prophesied to his sons.

Nephi's Vision of the Tree of Life. One of Lehi's sons desired to know the things that his father had seen. He believed the Lord was able to show these things to him. As he was pondering this vision, he was caught away in the spirit. He was caught away into an exceedingly high mountain which he had never seen. (1 Nephi 11:1, The Book of Mormon)

While Nephi was praying, the Spirit asked Nephi what he desired. Nephi told him that he wanted to see the things that his father saw. The Spirit asked him if he believed that his Father saw the tree which he had spoken of. Nephi replied "Yes." The Spirit rejoices because Nephi believes in the Son of God. The Spirit told him that he would see the things he desired and bore witness that the man descending out of Heaven was the Son of God. After he had seen the Son of God, Nephi was to bear witness of Him. (1 Nephi 11:1-8) Nephi does bear witness of the Son of God in later chapters of 1 Nephi and 2 Nephi.

After Nephi sees the tree which is precious above all, the Spirit asked Nephi what he desired. Nephi wanted to know the interpretation of this vision. Nephi points out that he spake to a Spirit who was in the form of a man and spoke like a man. Nephi knew he was the Spirit of the Lord. The Spirit of God then left him. (1 Nephi 11:9-12) At this point, I want to point out that the words Spirit of the Lord are capitalized indicating a specific individual.

Nephi sees the great cities of Jerusalem and Nazareth. In the city of Nazareth, he sees a fair and white virgin. The heavens open and an angel stands before Nephi. Nephi is told the virgin is the mother of the Son of God, and the child in her arms is the Lamb of God, the Son of the Eternal Father. (1 Nephi 11:13-21)

The Love of God. Nephi is asked by the angel if he knows the meaning of the tree which his father saw. Nephi tells the angel the tree is the love of God, which sheds *[or spreads itself]* abroad in the hearts of the children of men. This love is most desirable above all things and most joyous to the soul. Nephi saw the Son of God going among the children of men; and he saw many fall down at his feet and worship him. (1 Nephi 11:21-24)

The Rod of Iron. Nephi explains that the rod of iron which Nephi's father saw was the word of God which led to the fountain of living waters or to the tree of life. The living waters and the tree of life are representations of the love of God. (1 Nephi 11:21-24)

The Redeemer of the World. Nephi sees the events in the life of the Redeemer of the World, and he bears witness of them. He often teaches about them in 1 Nephi and 2 Nephi. Nephi saw the prophet who prepared the way and who baptized the Redeemer of the World. He saw the Holy Ghost abide upon the Redeemer in the form of a dove. The Lamb of God ministered to the people in power and great glory, but they cast him out. Nephi saw the Lamb of God healing multitudes of people who were sick and afflicted with all manner of diseases, devils, and unclean spirits. Nephi saw the Lamb of God, taken by the people, judged by the world, lifted upon the cross, and slain for the sins of the world. He saw twelve others following the Lamb of God. Nephi saw angels descending upon the children of men and ministering to them. I suspect that Nephi saw the graves opened and those who appeared to many at the time that Christ died. They would now be angels. (Matthew 27:52-53) Nephi saw the people fighting against the apostles of the Lamb. (1 Nephi 11:25-34)

A Large and Spacious Building. In his vision, Nephi saw that the multitudes of the earth gathered together in a large and spacious building. Nephi bears record that the great and spacious building is the pride of the world; and it fell, and the fall thereof was exceedingly great. The angel of the Lord told Nephi that this shall be the destruction of all nations, kindreds, tongues, and people that fight against the twelve apostles of the Lamb. (1 Nephi 11:35-36)

Wars and Rumors of Wars. Nephi saw many things such as his seed and the seed of his brethren, the land of promise, and multitudes of people. They had many battles and contentions. He saw so many cities that he could not number them. (1 Nephi 12:1-3)

A Mist of Darkness. Nephi saw a mist of darkness on the face of the land of promise. It appears lightning, thundering, earthquakes, and all manner of tumultuous noises accompanied this mist of darkness. He saw the earth and the rocks separate (rent); and mountains tumbling into pieces. The plains of the earth were broken up; many cities were sunk; burned with fire; and did tumble to the earth, because of the quakes. This is what happened at the time that Jesus Christ was crucified. We can see this phenomena in the earthquakes of our time.

The vapor of darkness passed from off the face of the earth. Nephi saw multitudes who had not fallen because of the great and terrible judgments of the Lord. The heavens opened, and the Lamb of God descended out of heaven. He came down and showed himself to them. Nephi bears record that the Holy Ghost fell upon twelve others. They were ordained of God, and chosen to minister to Nephi's seed. The angel of the Lord tells Nephi that the Twelve Apostles of the Lamb shall still judge the twelve tribes of Israel; and the twelve ministers of his seed shall be judged by them; for he is of the house of Israel. (1 Nephi 12:4-10) Nephi saw three generations and most of the fourth generation pass away in righteousness. He saw the multitudes of the earth gathered together. It was his seed and the seed of his brethren at battle again. (1 Nephi 12:11-15)

The Interpretation of the Two Dreams. The angel pointed out the fountain of filthy water and the river which his father, Lehi, saw. The depths of the filthy river are the depths of hell. The mists of darkness are the temptations of the devil which blinds the eyes, hardens the hearts of the children of men, and leads them away to broad roads where they perish and are lost. The large and spacious building represents the vain imaginations and the pride of the children of men.

Nephi beheld many nations and kingdoms. He sees the Gentiles who form the great and abominable church and which slays the saints of God, tortures them, binds them down, yokes them with a yoke of iron, and brings them down into captivity. For the praise of the world, the Gentiles destroy the saints of God and bring them into captivity. For the pride of the world, many contentions are among his seed. As a result, they are full of idleness and abominations. (1 Nephi 12:18-23)

Nephi sees a man that probably is Columbus coming to this continent. These Gentiles prospered and obtain the land for their inheritance. They were white like his people before they were slain. He saw them fighting their Mother Country, probably the American Revolution. He saw a book, probably The Bible, a record of the Jews, carried among the Gentiles. Plain and precious things are taken away as The Bible goes forth to all the nations of the Gentiles in this land and across many waters. (1 Nephi 13:1-42)

A great and a marvelous work is done among the children to convince them to peace and life eternal, to deliver them from the hardness of their hearts and the blindness of their minds to prevent their captivity and destruction, both temporally and spiritually. (1 Nephi 14:7) I suspect that Nephi's vision is till the end of time. Many things which both Nephi and Lehi saw in their visions are in John the Revelator's great vision in Revelation. The angel tells Nephi that one of the twelve apostles shall see and write the remainder of these things and many things concerning the end of the world.

The Great Gulf. Nephi sees an awful gulf which separates the wicked from the tree of life and the saints of God. (1 Nephi 15:28) Remember. Lehi and Nephi saw five groups or kinds of people in their vision. In all the things that Nephi and Lehi saw, they had to see the behavior that is now described as attention deficit disorders. I suspect these behaviors create the great gulfs that exists in families, step families, our communities, and between nations.

Lehi and Nephi describe these behaviors as lost, hard-heartedness, blind, pride, shame, loathsome, idleness, and all manner of abominations. In Chapter Two, we learned the symptoms of attention deficit disorders. If you recall, everyone does not experience the same symptoms all the time. I suspect that the severity of attention deficit disorders depend on how lost, how hard-hearted, how blind, how idle, and how prideful we are. I also believe there is another common denominator that keeps us from the Tree of Life, the Love of God. I suspect that common denominator is charity, specifically our level of charity for ourselves and others. We begin learning charity in families and step families. Many siblings do not allow this learning to occur.

Application of these two visions to families and step families. We learned in these two visions that the rod of iron is the word of God, our scriptures. We are to hold to this rod. This is not a new concept for families, step families, and individuals to learn. The rod of iron of the Lord has provided families a system of standards to live by. Many wars have been fought over the interpretations of the iron rod. Somewhere in the history of the Jews and the world, a rod became a tool to hit someone. Nevertheless, we still hear this standard most often at funerals.

4 Yea, though I walk through the valley of the shadow of death, I will fear no evil: for thou art with me; thy rod and thy staff they comfort me.

Psalms 23:4, <u>The Holy Bible</u>

John the Revelator writes about a rod of iron when recording his miraculous vision of the events of the history of the world. Other prophets such as Isaiah write about a rod of iron.

5 And she brought forth a man child, who was to rule all nations with a rod of iron: and her child was caught up unto God, and to his throne.

Revelation 12:5, <u>The Holy Bible</u>

Lehi and Nephi describe a straight and narrow path along the rod of iron. This straight and narrow path is needed so the word of God will not become polluted like the water from the fountain near the path. With the rod of iron, the word of God can remain the word of God yesterday, today, and forever instead of the word of God changing to suit everyone's beliefs. Everyone and their families and step families will be judged by the same rod or word of God.

The Word of God will always restore peace and order to the world. The straight and narrow path is not a new concept for us. John the Baptist told us about the straight and narrow path that we must prepare for the Lord. (John 1:23; <u>The Holy Bible</u>) The Savior taught us about the straight and narrow path in the New Testament and mentions those broad roads that lead to destruction.

13 Enter ye in at the strait gate: for wide is the gate, and broad is the way,
that leadeth to destruction, and many there be which go in thereat:
14 Because strait is the gate, and narrow is the way, which leadeth unto life,
and few there be that find it.

Matthew 7:13 - 14, The Holy Bible

Nephi's Vision. Every parent and step parent wishes all of their children would retire to a private place and pray about what their parents have tried to teach their children and step children. I suspect that most children do not even think of doing this. Most children and step children cannot take criticism. A power struggle begins with a mountain of pouting and anger.

Both Lehi and Nephi describe people pressing forward in their dreams. All of God's children are pressing forward–in families and step families. They are waiting to be born, grow up, be educated, married, or waiting to die. We all want the joy and fullness that Lehi, Nephi, The Apostle Paul, the Angel Moroni, and other prophets have told us that life could bring. We just have different ideas on how to achieve it. We do not like to give up something we want for things that have a more pressing claim.

A Great Gulf. Nephi sees a gulf between the wicked and the saints of God. Parents and step parents have experienced this great gulf with a spouse or with their children and step children. There is a great gulf between wayward siblings and siblings who are trying to do right. We have witnessed gulfs between people at work and between our families, and step families. Let's simplify these gulfs and two visions like one would simplify an equation in algebra. First, let's place like terms with like terms. Like in Algebra, the terms in families and step families will be positive, negative, or zero. Let's combine like terms in these great gulfs in our children instead of just overlooking them.

Contention. If one reads The Book of Mormon, he will read about many of the contentions that Lehi experienced with his two oldest sons, Laman and Lemuel, and the contention between Nephi and his brothers, Laman and Lemuel. It did not matter what Lehi and his wife, Sariah did. Their efforts never stopped Laman and Lemuel from contending with Nephi. Laman and Lemuel could not accept their father and his teachings. They could not accept their younger brother, Nephi, as spiritual ruler over them. By contending with Nephi who believed in the same things that Lehi did, Laman and Lemuel opposed their parents' authority over them. They always retreated to the "bossy younger brother defense." After Lehi died, the contentions grew worse. Nephi had to separate from Laman and Lemuel to preserve Nephi's life.

The people who stayed with Laman and Lemuel had no protector. No one could make decisions without the approval of Laman and Lemuel. No one could disagree with Laman and Lemuel. Everyone had to walk on egg shells with them. I suspect everyone feared that Laman and Lemuel would turn on them. Lemuel even followed Laman.

Even if one decides to side with wayward children, wayward siblings, or a wayward spouse, there is always a distance when someone coerces another individual. Its an involuntary response of our spirits. There is no confidence in those who compel others to their side. They know the difference between contrived issues and real issues or problems in a family. Family members cannot trust wayward individuals, especially when one is aware what a wayward spouse or child is capable of doing. Contention always destroys every one's self-confidence.

Distance. Families may not be in physical danger. However, no one knows who to believe,. Family members often widen the spiritual gulf in our homes and families with physical distance to separate ourselves from the problems, agitation, and hurt feelings. They create a scapegoat. Nephi was a scapegoat. No one can visit or trust the scapegoat of the family.

Family members have been designated as loathsome because of their age, weight, skin color, the clothes they wear, the money they make, the job they have, the person they married, and the religion they follow. Most usually, they disagree with someone who now creates a scapegoat. Scapegpats are usually nice people. However, it is easier to move away from family than to constantly deal with hurt feelings. The people judging you and your family as underachievers usually are guilty of many abominations and poor performances themselves.

Religion. Even after seeing angels, Laman and Lemuel did not believe in the God that Lehi and Nephi did. Our children and step children do not believe in the God that parents and step parents believe in. They are just learning about God. They are being cared for by parents. They will not learn about God and the special blessings until they are caretakers. Often, our children and step children complain about being forced to go to church where they will learn about the nature of God and the Tree of Life for them, the love of God for His children. They do not want to learn what blessings God has in store for those who keep His commandments and follow His Son, Jesus Christ. They are content to take the blessings which parents and step parents have received. They are entitled to them. Children will not bend to the will of their parents let alone the will of their Heavenly Father. They want to do what they want to do when they want. They are distancing themselves from God.

When children mock a parent or step parent for being religious or holding to the rod, a gulf or impassable separation develops between parent and child, step parent and step child. Those who are doing the mocking receive all kinds of stumbling blocks in their life, but they always blame these stumbling blocks on the ones they are mocking or trying to control. They refuse to acknowledge that their waywardness and mocking are causing their stumbling blocks.

Unwilling to Change. Parents become very concerned with gulfs or great differences between their children and their siblings and their friends. A mother or father always worry about mental retardation. Parents spend a lot of money on well-child check ups to make sure their child is doing what he is supposed to be doing for his age. Gulfs are tragic when the root cause is an unwillingness to change not the loss of physical ability to change.

Parents expect change in their children. They see these physical changes as their children press forward from infant to toddler to preschooler, and through the school age, teenage, young adult, and adult years. Parents may not look forward to it, but they expect emotional changes as the child matures. Parents and step parents have been through these changes themselves. They know the child needs these changes of growth as they press forward. Sometimes, children need to be allowed to make changes on their own schedule.

When these changes do not happen, children remain at the junior high level emotionally. Parents notice when a younger child is maturing faster than older siblings. It is very difficult to accept that your wayward child is not willing to change or benefit from parents and step parents' love and experience. Your child would rather intimidate, control, and manipulate his parents and step parents, and do what they want. He succumbs to the temptations of the world. Children even try to manipulate God. Mists of darkness hang over their family or step family.

Parents Cannot Rejoice in Their Children. Like Lehi, the parents and step parents of today have dreams and visions for their family. Parents and step parents usually have several children who are progressing and bring a lot of joy and comfort in the home. Parents and step parents also have several children who are regressing and bring a lot of grief and embarrassment to their family. It seems that the whole family exists to support these wayward children. Parents and step parents still love and worry about their wayward children. They often go to bed in tears over them and have many sleepless nights over their children. Parents and step parents do not want their children lost to the Lord and lost in the cracks of the world.

Parents and step parents always glory in their children and step children. Its what parents do. Just ask a mother of a retarded child how hard it is to glory in that child when he should be in school or married instead of living in a wheelchair. When children do not progress and only cause contention and heartache as they press forward, parents and step parents, no matter how much they love their children, do not rejoice in their children.

Children know when parents and step parents do not rejoice in their children and step children. They notice when the smiles and the glimmer in a parent's eye is different with them. This happened to Jacob and ten of his sons in the Old Testament. This has happened to many parents and step parents. A great gulf and a mist of darkness appears in the family when a child feels that his parents love their other children more than him or her. Children will not accept the fact that any good can come from a parent who seem to love their siblings more than them. Some wayward children like to brag that their parent loves them more than the other children in the family. They have the stories to prove it. This gulf is very dangerous in a family. Joseph of Egypt and Nephi can tell you about this dangerous gulf.

Our Heavenly Father was also caught in the contention caused by one of His sons, Satan. Satan was jealous of His older Brother, Jesus Christ. Heavenly Father lost one third of his children before they were ever born. Even He cannot rejoice in the loss of so many members of his family. Our Heavenly Father has accumulated vast knowledge and experience in the trials of His large family. He has shared His knowledge and experience through prophets with us.

Shame. Lehi and Nephi mention people pressing forward who become ashamed after they have partaken of the Tree of Life. It is hard to imagine that someone would be ashamed of understanding and partaking of the word of God. It is hard to understand why people allow themselves to be chased away from joy and happiness by the pointed finger. They are mocked because they are partaking of God's love, mercy, faith, forgiveness, acceptance, and repentance for themselves. I know that it is very difficult to receive scoffing and mocking from family and friends over religious beliefs or anything that you do. You will find as many has. The ones who are mocking you experience shame over your religious beliefs, but they do not experience shame over their own mocking of others and all of their abominations to which they have succumbed.

We cannot absorb another's lack of vision, pride, anger, hard-heartedness, blindness, idleness, and all manner of abominations to make others comfortable in their sins. This only enables others to manipulate, intimidate, and isolate us. When we combine our anger, pride, etc. with others' pride, anger, blindness, hard-heartedness, this gives us an anger and a hard-heartedness that we cannot control. We act out and become ashamed of our actions and feelings. We become past feeling or without charity. As we do so, we receive an attention deficit disorder. Things are not well with us. We can feel it, and others can, too.

Pride. When children sense that their parents do not rejoice in them or their posterity, children experience shame and anger. They cover their shame with pride. When our pride is hurt, we tend to like to hurt the pride of others. Wayward children and spouses like to control the positive feelings that we have for others and ourselves. They easily shift blame to you with the pointing fingers and mocking words.

Attention Deficit Disorders. Laman and Lemuel seem to have the same symptoms of attention deficit disorders that we discussed in Chapter Two. They now suffer from adult attention deficit disorder. Remember. Not all people with ADD have all of the difficulties noticed in Attention Deficit Disorders at the same time.

Laman and Lemuel were experiencing shameful behavior, pride, an unwillingness to change, and procrastination. They mocked their parents, siblings, and God. There was a great gulf or separation in their family because of their behavior. Because of their behavior, their parents and siblings did not rejoice in them anymore. It is very difficult to concentrate under these circumstances. If this happens in your family, your children will act like Laman and Lemuel. Your children and step children are not going to follow through with the instructions of their parents or the ones who believes in parents and in whom their parents rejoice. Neither believes in each other anymore. They hate the parent for the misery they brought to them. They cannot see the good their parents and step parents have done for them.

Laman and Lemuel were lost among the distractions in the mists of darkness. They went down some strange roads. The distractions of the world do not require *long term planning, change, and physical effort.* Since Laman and Lemuel *chose not to pay attention* to what their father told them to do, they *missed important details* in their progress. They became *idle, disorganized, rebellious, and loathsome* as they fell behind their younger siblings and friends emotionally and spiritually. They "*over focused,*" on something that was highly stimulating *to them–getting even with their visionary father and brother who were really the ones causing all the problems. Laman and Lemuel mocked their parents, siblings, and God.* They become *verbally impulsive* when confronted. They were *unable to wait their turn for leadership, or they put the burden of their turn on Nephi.* Laman and Lemuel *acted on impulse* regardless of consequences. They were *forgetful* even about consequences. When working *one-on-one* with their father or with Nephi, Laman and Lemuel were able to pay attention and asked some deep questions about their teachings. They could not or refused to make the same efforts on their own. Nephi was *blamed* for all of these stumbling blocks that they placed in their own paths.

Laman and Lemuel and the twelve sons of Jacob are not the only ones going to be tried and tested in the mists of darkness (depths of hell) or the vain imaginations of this world (pride). We all are being tested. Even the Son of God was tested. If we are always on the way to the building that has no foundation instead of the straight and narrow, our unhappiness is not going to be an inherited disorder. We will not be able to blame our sins on another. We will follow the example that we choose to follow. If our example is living in the spacious building and mocking the saints of God, and this can be our parents and step parents, we will be mockers of those that partake of the blessings of the Lord instead of partaking of these blessings ourselves. There will not be much room for the tree of life, charity, in our disorganization, stalling, and mocking. We will be forced to manipulate, stonewall, and isolate to preserve our feelings. These are poor substitutes for the supports from God in your life.

There are many people pressing forward. These are not classes of people pressing forward. We have our free agency to choose which path we will follow–lost, ashamed of good efforts, mocking, vain imaginations, or the straight and narrow. The Lord's path may be straight and narrow, but there is room for all of God's children and many blessings therein. This is the beauty of His Plan of Salvation.

From my own experience in each of these categories of the people pressing forward, I know that I concentrate better on the straight and narrow path. I have better memory. I am not verbally abusive even when I have things weighing down my spirit. The Lord assists me with the things weigh me down. I understand "the weightier matters of the law" better. I can press forward in meekness and love instead of mocking and anger toward the fruits of the tree of life.

There are many distractions and temptations in that mist of darkness that everyone is tried and tested in. Most children caught in prideful behavior refuse to acknowledge that their behavior is a problem to themselves and their family members. When children allow the mists of darkness to control their lives, it is as painful to them as it is their parents and step parents. They just will not admit they need to change. Children cannot concentrate or ponder for long periods of time on things that have substance. This is what increases the gulf and darkness in their lives. Children can concentrate on things that have no substance and require very little effort. They seem to fight every step a parent tries when trying to teach their children. Parents quickly notice their teenager is losing the abilities they once had as a child. The child views learning as too hard or a punishment. They even claim they cannot learn, but they can learn to do new acts of mischievousness. Their acts of mischief range from annoyance to inflicting great loss and great pain on others and themselves. They are not concerned with learning how to do their personal duties at the proper time. They cannot take constructive criticism. Their hearts have become hardened to progress.

The Tree of Life for Families and Step Families. Lehi and Nephi and our Father in Heaven taught us about the Tree of Life for everyone. All of us exist in families or step families. A lone person is a family and head of household of one. The Tree of Life for everyone is the love of God. Nephi understood that the Love of God spreading itself abroad in the hearts of God's children was most desirable above all things. (1 Nephi 11:22 - 23) The world teaches us and our children that money is our Tree of Life. Money, no matter how we obtain it, will buy our happiness. If we do not have much money, then power and passions are our Tree of Life.

The Love of God is not a new concept for us. Since Christ did nothing but the will of His Father, the Love of God would also be the same as the pure love of Christ–charity. Other prophets have taught us about the love of Christ such as the Apostle Paul and the Angel Moroni.

46 Wherefore, my beloved brethren, if ye have not charity, ye are nothing,
for charity never faileth. Wherefore, cleave unto charity, which is the greatest
of all, for all things must fail—
47 But charity is the pure love of Christ, and it endureth forever; and whoso
is found possessed of it at the last day, it shall be well with him.

Moroni 7:46 - 47, The Book of Mormon

13 And now abideth faith, hope, charity, these three; but the greatest
of these is charity.

1 Corinthians 13:13, <u>The Holy Bible</u>

The Fruits of Charity. Since the time of Adam, we have heard about fruit. Some fruit is forbidden, and some fruit is encouraged. Our Father in Heaven who is a Heavenly Parent was not anxious for Adam and Eve to taste the fruit of the Knowledge of Good and Evil. Most parents are not anxious for this to happen with their children or step children. They know they are going to have unpleasant experiences in the acquisition of this knowledge. They prefer to keep them young and under their wing. Parents and step parents wonder if they have the ability to keep up with many children learning about good and evil. It's the evil part that weighs everyone down.

The fruit that Lehi saw and tasted is fruit for the soul because it brought great joy to Lehi's soul. I suspect this sweet fruit is faith in Jesus Christ, repentance, baptism, the Gift of the Holy Ghost, keeping the Lord's Commandments–and there are more than ten of them–prayer, love, acceptance, mercy, order, forgiveness, tithing, sacrifice, gratitude, peace, work, etc. Why are these fruits so sweet that they bring joy to the soul? With these kinds of fruits there are increases in our stature. Our identity forms, and we have an identity and a self-esteem built on substance.

Forbidden fruit has a negative impact on our soul. Waywardness, disobedience to parents, step parents, and the law of the land, lies, smoking, stubbornness, fornication, adultery, theft, addictions, excessive spending, and excessive hours in sports, vacations, pride, and excessive hobbies, (idleness) bring decreases to our soul and our health. Our self-esteem is built on pride, anger, shame, power, humiliation, intimidation, isolation, and manipulation. One bitter or forbidden fruit leads to the next. Our money that we have gained is not for the support of ourselves and our family. It is to obtain the next vacation, next drug, or next drink of alcohol, etc. Our family, self-confidence, identity, education and the Savior's blessings are replaced with these things. Things are not well with us because we have lost the things that we learned with fruits that have substance.

Jesus taught us about fruits in His ministry on Earth. We have been given agency to choose between sweet fruit, charity, and fruit of a thistle, hate and pride, both forbidden fruits.

16 Ye shall know them by their fruits. Do men gather grapes of thorns,
or figs of thistles?
17 Even so every good tree bringeth forth good fruit; but a corrupt tree
bringeth forth evil fruit.
18 A good tree cannot bring forth evil fruit, neither can a corrupt tree bring
forth good fruit.
19 Every tree that bringeth not forth good fruit is hewn down, and cast into
the fire.
20 Wherefore by their fruits ye shall know them.

Matthew 7:16 - 20, <u>The Holy Bible</u>

The Examples of Charity in Your Home. Children need an example of charity to follow in their home. Parents and step parents are supposed to be the examples of charity. Hopefully, grandparents can be a second witness of charity to their grandchildren. Many times, children follow the examples of charity provided by older siblings and peers. Older siblings may love their younger siblings, but they do not have the unconditional love of parents, the obedience to parents and step parents, and the willingness to change even in the face of opposition which form the proper example of charity. Your children's older siblings may say they believe in Christ, but they do not believe in following His commandments. His commandments are too hard, too inconvenient, or too outdated. Your young children want the acceptance of the older, very brisk siblings. Older children control younger siblings in this manner to control your estate and control parents and step parents.

Older siblings do teach their younger siblings about lies, theft, smoking, fornication, adultery, abortion, homosexuality, alcoholism, and drugs. Minor children can experience these things. If parents and step parents do take their children and step children to church, minor children must wait until they are over age eighteen or twenty-one to make a decision about religion. Siblings or children are not mature enough to make a decision about religion. They are mature enough to decide if they want to be sexually active, drink, smoke, use drugs, etc.

Parents and step parents, provide an example of charity to your children and step children, even when you are victimized by children and step children. Remember. Anti-depressants and street drugs will not replace charity in your life or your child's life. These drugs take more from you and your children than they give.

Your younger children probably have discovered they are intimidated, manipulated, and isolated if they follow their parent's and step parent's rules. Younger children receive the stumbling blocks of those they substitute for parents, usually their older siblings. Naturally, it must be the parent or step parent's fault. A great gulf forms between parent and child, step parent and step children. Step children like to create a gulf between parent and step parent. This is how they control the finances of the family, their idea of the Tree of life for this world. Parents and step parents, children and step children are devoured in this power struggle.

Without charity, young children are not allowed to choose the first fruits of the Love of God which form their identity–faith, trust, security, and mercy from parents and step parents. If children are not allowed to experience these things from parents and step parents, they will not be allowed to experience the first fruits of charity from their Heavenly Father–faith in Jesus Christ, repentance, baptism, and the Gift of the Holy Ghost. Without charity, children are not allowed to experience the benefits of mercy, forgiveness, justice, prayer, service to parents, peace, and, order. Parents and step parents may become so protective that children cannot experience work and sacrifice for others. Without charity, children cannot distinguish the difference between mercy and leniency.

Attention Deficit Disorders. At the beginning of this chapter I stated that I thought attention deficit disorders were the mists of darkness in ourselves. Let's look at this further. I have defined charity with some scriptures. I pointed out the fruits of charity to ourselves and to others. Notice the behavior in the opposite of charity. List the definition of charity either by the dictionary or in the scriptures. Scriptures will give deeper meanings. List the opposites. I have started an example of how to do this.

1 THOUGH I speak with the tongues of men and of angels, and have not charity, I am become as sounding brass, or a tinkling cymbal.
2 And though I have the gift of prophecy, and understand all mysteries, and all knowledge; and though I have all faith, so that I could remove mountains, and have not charity, I am nothing.
3 And though I bestow all my goods to feed the poor, and though I give my body to be burned, and have not charity, it profiteth me nothing.
4 Charity suffereth long, and is kind; charity envieth not; charity vaunteth not itself, is not puffed up,
5 Doth not behave itself unseemly, seeketh not her own, is not easily provoked, thinketh no evil;
6 Rejoiceth not in iniquity, but rejoiceth in the truth;
7 Beareth all things, believeth all things, hopeth all things, endureth all things.
8 Charity never faileth: but whether there be prophecies, they shall fail; whether there be tongues, they shall cease; whether there be knowledge, it shall vanish away.

1 Corinthians 13:1 - 8, <u>The Holy Bible</u>

Charity

1. Speak many languages, including angels' tongue–spiritual understanding

2. Gift of prophecy, understand all mysteries, all knowledge, & all faith
3. Feed poor and needy.

4. Suffers long and is kind. Envies not, & not prideful
5. Does not behave unseemly (behavior matches circumstances, laws, and mores.)
6. Seeks not own, and is not easily provoked.
7. Thinks no evil.

8. Rejoices in truth, not iniquity.

9. Bears all things, believes all things, hope in all things, endures all things.
10. Able to stay on task even in sorrow. pain. and stress.

Mist of Darkness–No Charity

1. Sound like brass–Become tinkling cymbal–hollow sound; repetitive sound is a source of agitation; impudent sounds
2. I am nothing and feels this way.

3. Have money, but will not feed poor & needy. Willing to burn own body to show sacrifice (Cut it, also)
4. Impatient, cannot endure trials, and is not kind. Full of envy and pride, arrogant
5. Behavior is unseemly. Behavior does not match circumstances, laws, and mores.
6. Constantly seeking own glory and is easily provoked. Follows strange roads.
7. Thinks a lot about evil things. Does not think evil things are evil anymore.
8. Rejoices in iniquity, Avoids truth or rewrites truth.
9. No belief or hope in anything or anyone. Will not try so cannot endure all things; idle; disorganized, careless; impulsive.
10. Great gulfs in individuals who are not on task.

There are many forbidden fruits on the strange roads in the mist of darkness which we experience in this life. These forbidden fruits are a result of a life without charity, the Tree of Life–the pure love of God and Christ–for others and ourselves. If you refer back to Chapter Two, many of the symptoms of Attention Deficit Disorder can be seen in our uncharitable behaviors. Forbidden fruits cause great gulfs in individuals. This is why they were forbidden by our Heavenly Father. I suspect the Lord gives your uncharitable child stumbling blocks to protect charitable adults and charitable children. Only the Lord can take these stumbling blocks away from us.

1 AND it shall come to pass, that if the Gentiles shall hearken unto the Lamb of God in that day that he shall manifest himself unto them in word, and also in power, in very deed, unto the taking away of their stumbling blocks—

1 Nephi 14:1, The Book of Mormon

What is the Tree of Life for your family? How does this compare with the Tree of Life or the Love of God? Describe the fountain of living water in your family and step family. Has this water become polluted? If so, who are the polluters inside your home and outside of the home? Are their pollutions separating you and your children from the love of God and the love of parents and step parents? Are parents and step parents ashamed and defensive because they have partaken of the many fruits of the love of God? Are children and step children ashamed of partaking of the fruits of the love of their parent and step parents? Are children and step children ashamed of having parents, step parents, and siblings who partake of the love of God?

What is the rod of iron in your family? Who determines what the rod of iron will be for your family? As everyone presses forward in your family, what kind of paths are they on? Do you have children and step children in each kind of path mentioned in Lehi and Nephi's dream? Those paths would be: lost on strange roads, on the way to the great and spacious building (pride), in the great and spacious building (more pride), ashamed of partaking of the love of God, or the straight and narrow way. What paths are parents and step parents in?

How do you handle the mockers in your family and step family? How do you redirect your children to the straight and narrow path? Are you re-routing them to another strange road or another scapegoat instead of to the straight and narrow way?

Describe the mist of darkness that hangs over your family or step family. Describe the separations or gulfs in your family. If family and step family has separated, who is the leader of the individuals who have regrouped themselves from parents and step parents? How is this controlling you, your emotions, your estate, and your finances? How do the leaders keep this separate circulation going? Is the family able to keep up with the separate groups in the family.

Do you rejoice in all of your children and step children? If you cannot rejoice in your children, how will you change this? You cannot change children. You can only change yourself. Are there examples of charity in your home? Does each family member of your family or step family have enough charity for their lives to be well for them in the last days and forever? Do you and your family members have enough charity within yourselves to not be labeled as one with an attention deficit disorder in mortality?

Chapter Eighteen

"Nurse, It Wasn't Supposed to Be Like This!"

Individuals, no matter how old, may be diagnosed with an attention deficit disorder because somebody wants to play "This Little Piggy" while the storms of life are raging at their doors. This is how a parent and child play "This Little Piggy." Parents start with their child's big toe and state the following nursery rhyme. Of course, they tickle their children and grandchildren. They love to hear their children and grandchildren laugh. Children giggle clear down to their precious little toes. This is what they recite.

> *"This little piggy went to market.*
> *This little piggy stayed home.*
> *This little piggy had roast beef.*
> *This little piggy had none.*
> *This little piggy cried: 'wee, wee, wee.'*
> *I am going to tell mama when she gets home."*[148]

Of course, when you play with your children and grandchildren, they give a precious giggle and say: "Do again, Momma or Gramma." When I was playing this with one of my grandchildren, I wondered why this nursery rhyme was ever written and became part of our folklore. I suddenly realized this is the way we respond to the many trials in our life. Only this time and at this age, it is not a game and very few are laughing. Of course, no one thinks that anything will happen to them.

In the game of "Nothing will ever happen to me," this is how individuals play "This Little Piggy." Individuals become shopaholics. They overindulge in something. They retreat into their homes and overeat, becoming bullimic or anorexic. They do not feel they are worthy of an equal portion. Individuals cry and whine and tell on others or threaten to tell on them to have power over them. This is going to make them and everyone in their family feel better.

Of course, the ones who threaten to tell on others do tell others. They have to vent their feelings. Everyone makes fun of these individuals. They have to have a good laugh. This is a hard environment for anyone to concentrate and learn in under these circumstances.

There are many mothers and fathers who are severely anxious and depressed over their teenage and adult children. Their children are caught in the deadly game of "This Little Piggy" with abusive spouses, various addictions, crime, sexual promiscuity, and homosexuality.

"Nurse, it wasn't supposed to happen this way." One of the most saddest of comments stated to me in my nursing career is this statement. This comment has been expressed to me by accident victims who are now paralyzed, abused spouses, patients who attempted suicide for

---

[148] Author unknown.

various reasons, families dealing with terminal cancer, families who had babies out of wedlock, homosexual patients who now had AIDS, patients who had herpes or hepatitis, and criminals in chains. These patients had become severely depressed and now no longer wanted to live. Naturally, everyone concludes these patients are suffering from an attention deficit disorder.

These patients came from different ethnic, social, and religious backgrounds. Their financial status' were as varied as their ages. However, all of these patients had something in common. All of these patients and the society which they came from blamed their parents, particularly their mother, for the catastrophe that had befallen them.[149] Surely, their mother had done something wrong in their life, or she could have done something to prevent this from happening to them while they were just experimenting with some fun.

Mothers are very ingenious. They have a lot of capabilities. However, even Mother cannot compensate when the Holy Ghost, the Spirit of Christ, or the minute remnants of a conscience have left an individual or her child.

Mother and father, let's discuss these things which you have been blamed for and are now blaming yourself. From experiences in the hospitals and doctors' offices that I have worked in, I know there are some very anxious mothers around the world. Health statistics prove it, too. Mothers are sitting and waiting for their beautiful daughters to come home from various dates. Unfortunately, mothers are also waiting for their children to come home with AIDS, herpes, hepatitis, and pregnant. Mothers are aware that children will be tempted because of her experiences with temptation. At least with syphilis and gonorrhea, these diseases of promiscuity were treatable in their first and second stages.

Mothers are also waiting for their beautiful sons to come home from many evenings of crime, passion, drugs, and alcohol. They usually have a girlfriend with them. They, too, may come home with a deadly disease or a pregnant girlfriend.

There are parents who are waiting for a gay son or daughter to come home with AIDS, herpes, or hepatitis. Some parents wait days, months, or years for teenagers or adult children to come home with these deadly diseases of promiscuity. Some parents have several children participating in harmful activities without restraint.

These parents, particularly mothers, know their children are playing Russian Roulette with a loaded gun. Only this time, there is a cartridge in every chamber. There is a cartridge for each member of the family. There is a cartridge for the family of the children who date her children. All will be affected.

If their beautiful child survives, parents wonder if they can financially and emotionally meet the demands of these senseless illnesses, especially when there is more than one child in the family that mother is worried over. It is no wonder that Mother gets angry with her family. Is it any wonder, there is an increase in heart disease, diabetes, cancer and autoimmune diseases, particularly in women?

Naturally, all of these parents have something in common, too. These parents have been ordered to cut their children some slack, or they will not get to see their children or their grandchildren again. Their children have the right to act out their fantasies, find themselves, and to relieve their stress. All this will be accomplished without any restraint. It does not matter

---

[149]Doctrine and Covenants 121:16-20, p. 240.

how their behavior affects the family. Parents have to call bitter things sweet and sweet things bitter to try and maintain some integrity in their home. This will not work.

Parents become severely depressed and begin to pick themselves apart with grief, doubt, guilt, anger, shame, and envy. It is difficult for mother to relax and be even-tempered with her family. This leads to depression and thoughts of suicide. Children who grow up with a depressed mother view this as a normal solution to problems. This is not what parents had in mind for themselves and their children. This is not what the Lord had in mind for His children.

From sexual promiscuity to crime, drugs, alcohol, and homosexuality, parents have been the focal point and the cause of these things in their children. For example, children become alcoholics and smoke cigarettes because parents did not give them adequate oral satisfaction (a baby bottle). Thus, children were not able to build trust. If parents fed their children or toilet trained them, they were too strict or stern. Parents learned this from their ancestors.

Our forefathers built up a nation on hardly anything, do you think they were stupid? If they had food, the baby got it first. They ground food with a stone and mixed it with water to give it to their infants–first. Our ancestors did not have television and game systems to babysit their children. They were not going to scream at a baby that was ready to go to sleep. They did not enjoy listening to a screaming, fussy baby anymore than this generation does. Furthermore, our ancestors did not have washers, dryers, and a closet of extra bedding. One child wetting the bed usually affected four other children who were sleeping in the same bed. I am sure that our ancestors scolded the offending child and so did everyone else. What would you do in the winter with a child who wet the bed, and you only had one or two blankets for five children?

However, how many of these children who are now adult alcoholics, drug addicts, criminals, and homosexuals feed and clothe their children first? Yet, all of these children who are now alcoholics, addicts, criminals, and homosexuals thrived in the most vulnerable parts of their life–their infancy, toddler, and preschool years. There are doctors' records to prove it. There are laws requiring doctors to notify law enforcement when they suspect abuse.

First, parents are you feeling guilty for punishing your children, slapping them, and yelling at them? I am sure you do. No parent likes to resort to these matters. If you feel there is a problem that needs discussing with your religious leader, do it. Do not carry these burdens around indefinitely. Parents will only punish, slap, and yell at children and your spouse more frequently and intensely.

However, many religious leaders do not have children with these problems and cannot relate to your pain. Unfortunately, there are many religious leaders who can. Their children have a severe form of "preacher's kid syndrome." Many preachers in a family or community results in many kids with "preachers kid syndrome."

Second, parents are you extremely depressed and worried over a child who is in an abusive marriage? It is not rocket science to know that marriage is hard enough under the best of circumstances. Marriage is impossible in an abusive relationship.

At a time when parents thought they could relax and prepare for retirement, they are afraid for their child and grandchildren's safety. They know that criminal acts are being done to their child and in front of their grandchildren. If parents interfere, they will never see their child and grandchildren again. Their interference could even bring death to them.

Parents do not have an attention deficit disorder. They have become Isaacs.[150] Mother and father are bound and gagged by abusers of spouse and child. Abusive relationships are not a random occurrence. This is happening more than we realize. So much that children believe that violence is the answer to everything. Mother cannot even send her children out to play without other children expressing violence in some way. Let's unbind father and mother.

Abusive friends and spouses like to play "The Hitler Game." If you remember the films from history class, Adolph Hitler had cruel doctors who did various experiments on Jewish families. The doctors claim they wanted to gather psychological information for science.

A father or mother would be positioned in front of their children. Electric wires would run from a power source to parent, from parent to child, child to parent, and from both parent and child to the doctors and their assistants. The doctors and their assistants could throw a master switch that would cause an electric shock to run on these various pathways.

Parents were forced to give electric shocks to their child in increasing amounts or the doctor's assistants would give their child a shock. The parents would receive a shock if they did not shock their child. This was cruelty at its highest. These doctors wanted to see if a parent would shock their child and how far parents or children would go before they killed each other.

With other experiments, the children were ordered to shock their parents, or they would get a shock. Naturally, in most cases parents did not shock their children all the time, but children would shock their parents. Children did not know that parents were taking many shocks to keep their child from receiving shocks.

Abusive spouses, and this includes abusive boyfriends, like to "shock" the parents of their spouse or girlfriend, as well as their children, your grandchildren. They want to see how long it takes for the parent of a spouse to respond. Because they know the child desperately wants any relationship, they know that the child will argue with the parent. Parents have always interfered where they were not wanted anyway. The child will not argue with the abuser of your child because they may fear them, though they will not admit it.

The abuser knows the parents desperately want to have a relationship with their child and protect them. Naturally, parents try to help any way they can. They buy food, clothes, furniture, and make rent and car payments. Soon, it is a power struggle between in-laws and your child's spouse. Your child and grandchildren are the cannon fodder, as well as the target. The abusive spouse has to keep your family hurting, or starving, or helpless for parents to continue these monetarial payoffs. They want your money more than they want a healthy, happy family for themselves. They can spend their money and your money on themselves.

Now, the abuser is in control of both parent and child. Abusers always have a few heart-rendering stories and apologies to keep the process going. This is how they controlled their parents and teachers. They had to remain delinquent to keep the bribes coming. It worked for them then. They can control others the same way in marriage. No one is going to control them.

It will take an average of eight to twelve times for your child to leave this abusive relationship. Abuse has become addicting because your child feels guilty and scared. You, the parent, always fed them when they were guilty and scared. They have to stay in an abusive relationship to be provided for one way or another.

---

[150]Genesis 22:1-13, The Holy Bible, pp. 30-31.

It is time for your child to learn how to provide for themselves. However, when your child comes out of this relationship, he or she will have much sorrow and pain that you can see and feel. They will have thoughts of suicide and may even attempt suicide. This may be to attract your attention and begin the same power struggle again. This is the only way they can express the kind of emotion that they are feeling. Their baskets are empty. (Doctrine and Covenants 121:16) They have been robbed of many things.

Remember. Your child has been in an abusive environment. This abusive relationship has replaced all of your love and efforts over the years with your child. Parents have to begin again. However, your child has learned how to manipulate abusers to survive. Unfortunately, they will view you as an abuser over the slightest provocation–just like they have witnessed for several years. Your grandchildren will see this behavior of the abuser as normal behavior.

Your child will try to manipulate you until they learn differently. When they cannot win at this relationship either, they attempt suicide. People spring into action. Parents don't. Do everything you can to save your child's life physically. Stay calm for this is your window of opportunity to reteach your child.

Parent's will begin with some spiritual algebra. Your child's self-esteem is in the negative column. In fractions, it can be difficult to distinguish which fraction is higher or lower. Thus, when anyone tries to add or subtract fractions in algebra, they must first convert the fractions to the same denominator. It is that way with fractured people, too. Otherwise, parents do not know where to start. This is why we will be gathered under one Lord and one baptism.

Remember. If one subtracts negative with negative, there will be no gain. Parents must begin subtracting with the positive to have any gain. It will be awhile before this child reaches the positive. Do not give up. Begin the conversion of your child and grandchildren the way the Savior converts or restores people–soft answers.

The Savior restores a person by restoring their dignity. Dignity is restored in a combination of several principles found in the scriptures. Those principles are: agreement with thine adversary, forgiveness, gratitude, repentance, reproof softly followed by love, saying nothing, and soft answers. Prayer and fasting will help parents decide the combination of these principles. The Savior has not left parents without any tools to do something for their families. *There are many scriptures, prescriptions of the Great Physician, to help you.*

Third, parents have always been accused of causing homosexuality in their children. Yet, the Apostle Paul states that is not so. The love of money is the root of all evil.[151] Therefore, the root of homosexuality is not comfort with one's own gender, but it is the love of money. Paul also wrote about avoiding unnatural affection. He did not write: "Parents do not yell at your children, or you will cause unnatural affection in them." I wonder if he witnessed this unnatural affection while in prison in Rome.

I know that there are those who disagree that homosexuality is wrong. If it is not wrong, why does homosexuality cause Mother to fear for the life of her child who is gay? Why do homosexuals have a hard time telling their parents? Why does a parent of a gay child have an immune disorder, particularly the mother or grandmother, even though Mother and Grandmother have decided to accept her child or grandchild in the gender they want to be?

---

[151] 1 Timothy 6:10, The Holy Bible, p. 1511.

122

Homosexuals are trying to tell us something. Homosexuals are trying to tell us that they cannot stand severe kinds of hurt anymore. They would rather give up everything, including their gender, than be hurt anymore. What hurt are they talking about? They are talking about the pain of isolation and being severely criticized for not having a perfect body. Where does this criticism come from? Extremely critical peers and siblings.

Children are notorious for being cruel. Brothers and sisters have not bonded with your children and are extremely critical, jealous, and territorial, especially over their younger brothers and sisters. Some siblings are so critical. Their brothers and sisters cannot make a decision on their own, even about their own gender. This is one of the reasons that mother should be staying home and raising her children with whom she has bonded with. Yes, the family will have to give up some pleasures of this world. If families don't, they are taking a great risk with their family, considering the degree of the love of money that is now in the world.

Your child may have the love of money. They want to spend their money on themselves instead of a family. They may be mixed up with people who have the love of money and who have to have a perfect body to earn more money. These individuals experiment with prescription steroids and diet pills and the over-the-counter steroids and diet pills so much that their secondary sexual characteristics are affected. They also have very angry, controlling, hair-trigger-tempers, a steroid side effect.

However, the desire to mate is still within them, too. They still want their sexual experiences which they are entitled to have. There are many waiting to make anyone's children a concubine, no matter what gender they decide they are. After your child has experimented with the ways of the streets and prisons, someone who has the love of money will decide that your child must remain a concubine instead of becoming a future mother or father.

Fourth, are you severely depressed over a child who has become a drug addict or an alcoholic? Drug addicts and alcoholics like to play "the Hitler game," too. Only they have connected another electric wire. These controllers or dictators have connected a wire and switch to themselves. If parents do not give into their many childish requests, they will shock themselves. The shocks increase in intensity. It is common for a boyfriend or girlfriend or spouse to assist your child in shocking themselves. This keeps your child and you dependent on these abusers. Father and mother become bound and gagged again because of the love for their child.

It wasn't supposed to happen this way. Children were supposed to grow up with good friends, want an education, get a job, find a spouse, and have children. We were supposed to have many family reunions in our retirement and discuss the sad times as well as the good times.

As you remember the first time you held your baby in your arms, you had so many high hopes and dreams. Parents had a lot of faith for their family, the things hoped for, and the substance of things not seen.[152] Faith is going to get you through these unseen trials. It will be tough, but you have to learn your child's cry all over again. Parents will even have to learn their child's cry when he or she is an adult. They may have to learn what their own cry really means.

A wise diploma nurse taught me to learn the cries of pain like a mother would know the difference in her child's cry. As a student nurse I did not understand, but I remembered this

---

[152]Hebrews 11:1-2, The Holy Bible, p. 1532.

advice. To my surprise, I have used this wisdom much as a nurse, as a mother, as a step mother, and as a grandmother. I first had to learn it within myself. I had to learn there are not always tears shed when people are crying.

A nurse and a mother deals with many types of pain. A nurse and a mother will deal with dull pains, sharp pains, acute pains, chronic pains, cramping or squeezing pains, headaches, foot pains, and back pains. There is referred pain or localized pain. Some patients and children have several types of pain at the same time. It is hard to know where to start.

There are also emotional, social, moral, spiritual, intellectual, financial, as well as physical pains. There are pains due to lack of persistence and the pain of disobedience. Contention, addictions, weapons of rebellion, and pride cause regression which causes one to fear and to cry. Speaking against the Lord's anointed which causes one to have an empty basket and causes a darkened countenance is very painful. These things make it difficult to listen and to learn. This is where attention deficit disorder and attention deficit disorder with hyperactivity roots. Work, service, and sacrifice will help these pains.

It is hard to learn with pain. Identify your child's cries. Work on the different layers of pain. It is easier to find the solutions. Be aware. The depression that occurs with these pains can be as addicting as drugs and abuse.

There is a method to treat your own depression. First, I am not telling you to not seek counseling or to stop taking antidepressants if you need them. This method is a way to shoulder the responsibility for your depression and feelings. As you become skilled in the many layers of attention deficit disorder and depression, you will not need your counselor or antidepressants.

I discovered this method through much prayer and fasting. My requests were simple. I did not want my life to be in vain. I did not want a psychiatrist to be the only one who would respond to my needs as long as I paid his bill. I prayed earnestly for help.

I was impressed to go immediately to the Jordan River Temple. In the Celestial Room, I was impressed to make a covenant with Jesus Christ that I will no longer have thoughts of depression and suicide to solve my problems. I was skeptical, but I did it. I felt a peace immediately. I expected the feelings of depression to return as soon as I left the temple. The peace stayed with me. I had more composure and dignity, and I began building from there.

With the burdens of step parenting, I worried that I would lose this peace. I was impressed to renew this covenant with Doctrine and Covenants 121:43. The Holy Ghost taught me that day. If I speak sharply to myself, I was under the same obligation to speak kindly of myself. Lest, I become my own worst enemy.

This has worked. It was awkward. At first, I had to speak kind thoughts to a personal photograph of me. I can now accept compliments from others. I learned a lot from this experience. I learned there is more to our covenants with the Savior than just making and keeping promises. Since depression and thoughts of suicide are not solutions, my mind has space to seek other solutions in the scriptures, at Relief Society, Sunday School, and at Sacrament Meeting. I also learned how to seek my children sorrowing.

Do you know your step child's cry? Do parents and step parents attend church regularly? Does your step child have "preacher's kid syndrome?" How does your step child play "Russian Roulette" with his present and future family and then blames step parents? How are step parents trying to compensate when the spirit of Christ has left their child or step child?

Chapter Nineteen

We Have Sought Thee Sorrowing.

As a former obstetric nurse at LDS Hospital in Salt Lake City, Utah, I know how excited parents are about their babies. As their children join their family, each baby is so beautiful, so perfect, and so trusting. Parents have great hopes for their children.

All parents want their child to have tremendous ability and beauty who will achieve greatness. Then reality hits. Parents discover their children do not have the same abilities and potentials that parents want them to have. Some children will only be able to achieve a small amount. Some children will achieve on the average scales, and some will always achieve on the above average scales. Step parents experience this reality with many children at once.

As a former intensive care nurse, I also know that it is very hard when parents discover their child is not so perfect. They realize that perfection is not so easy in children. However, their child is still beautiful and very precious to parents, and parents love them very much. Parents experience what Mary, the mother of Jesus, experienced.

Parents seek their children sorrowing. Since time began, there probably has not been so many ways and so many places for parents to seek their children sorrowing. Parents have sought their children sorrowing over attempts to love, educate, and instill some values within their children. Parents have sought their child sorrowing in places that were not safe or good for parents as well as children.

Mother especially seeks seven days a week and every waking moment. She wonders: If Mary was sorrowing over her lost child, Jesus, in the temple, how am I going to find and save my children in their various places of refuge?

Sorrowing over children is even harder when parents compare their child to someone else's child who seems so perfect. Those parents seem so perfect, too. Mother wonders, where did I go wrong? What happened to my beautiful baby? Mother longs for that perfection that was placed in her arms on the day of her child's birth.

Parents have sought their children sorrowing so much. Their children's behavior has affected parents' health, their children's health, their pocketbook, and their retirement. Parents' behavior has affected their children's health and their children's pocketbook, too. Everyone's behavior has affected everyone's marriage and their peace of mind so much. Parents and children doubt themselves greatly. Worrying over children affects parents' abilities. When one child is lost, it is difficult for parents to do the things they use to do or want to do for family.

Parents may take upon themselves extra jobs to pay for the sorrow in their children and themselves. They add jobs to pay for those comparisons of their family with others. They avoid conflict by calling bitter things sweet. These things will be bitter to the fourth generation. In spite of parents' best efforts, their child only finds other crisis' and other places of refuge.

While seeking their children sorrowing, parents receive much criticism. Parents are shunned for many reasons. They should not have done this, or they should have done that.

Parents do not wear designer clothes or have designer habits. Others even complain that your house is dirty. The storms of life are raging at your family. Others can only acknowledge your dust. Your dust will keep, your babies won't. Someone wrote a beautiful poem about that. Nonetheless, both parents, especially mother, are very discouraged, and may become depressed.

The *Savior and our Heavenly Father seek us sorrowing, too.* The Savior and our Heavenly Father has sought us sorrowing in so many ways. They could write many poems like Elizabeth Barrett Browning. Her poem was titled: "How do I Love Thee?" Our Savior and our Heavenly Father love us to the height, and width, and depth, too. (Romans 8:38-39)

One may wonder, "How could the Savior and our Heavenly Father love so many fractured people?" His children have made so many mistakes, attention deficit disorder and attention deficit disorder with hyperactivity seems the least of our problems that Heavenly and Earthly parents would help us with– or are these disorders the cause of our problems?

Our Heavenly Father and the Savior has sought us sorrowing through the Atonement of Jesus Christ. Nothing could compare with this. However, the Savior's work was not finished after He died for us. Our Heavenly Father and the Savior seek us two thousand years after the Atonement was completed. They will always seek us. They know that everyone needs help, guidance, instructions, and some good examples on a daily basis.

The Savior and our Heavenly Father seek us by teaching us how to organize our time, talents, and possessions. This is called the United Order. In the early years of The Church of Jesus Christ of Latter-day Saints, members of His Kingdom were asked to consecrate their time, talents, and possessions to building up the Lord's Kingdom. Consecration means to bless and honor by giving. These funds help build meetinghouses, temples, and care for the poor.

The United Order includes other things. When I hear and read about the United Order, I have always been intrigued that the United Order includes things such as listening, the Ten Commandments, loving our neighbor, laying of hands on the sick, covenants, cleanliness, idleness, our death, knowledge, and wisdom. All of these things do affect how our time, money, and possessions are organized. However, these things are how people are organized and increased. Money and property are not organized and increased by the United Order. In fact, this is how we are to organize our families. Step families are allowed order in this Kingdom.

People, particularly families, have always been the Lord's talent or value. This leads me to believe that the story of the talents means something other than the pursuit of fortunes, possessions, resumes', hobbies, and special interests. If one reads the story of the talents, it says: "For the kingdom of heaven is *as* a man traveling into a far country, who called his own servants, and delivered unto them his goods."[153]

We have all been called and been given at least one talent. We have been endowed with life. We have been given stewardship over that life. We are the caretakers and can use our free agency to manage the time and possessions that we will accumulate in our talent. With our one major talent, we have been endowed with other talents known as parents, siblings, spouse, and children. Our neighbors are a talent. We have to learn how to play them in concert with each other, not against each other. We do not have to bury our talents or the talents in others for us to succeed or be noticed.

---

[153]Matthew 25:14, The Holy Bible, p. 1232.

15 And unto one he gave five talents, to another two, and to another one;
to every man according to his several ability; and straightway took his journey.
16 Then he that had received the five talents went and traded with the same, and
made them other five talents.
17 And likewise he that had received two, he also gained other two.
18 But he that had received one went and digged in the earth, and hid his lord's money.

Matthew 25:15 - 18, The Holy Bible

24 Then he which had received the one talent came and said, Lord, I knew thee that thou art an hard man, reaping where thou hast not sown, and gathering where thou hast not strawed:
25 And I was afraid, and went and hid thy talent in the earth: lo, there thou hast that is thine.

Matthew 25:24 - 25, The Holy Bible

With one life and at the appropriate age, we trade our parents, brothers and sisters, and neighbors for a spouse and children. We are given according to our ability. Whatever principles that we learn with them will rise with us. How much more could our parents do for us if we just listened to them? How much more could we do for our spouse and children if we organized our talents, our families, under the principles of the United Order?

The more we live the principles of the United Order with our families, particularly our parents, spouse, and children, we will double our talents in them and ourselves. The Lord has said He would make us a ruler over many things if we have faith in following the United Order with our time, talents, our parents, spouses, and children, and our possessions in a few things. When we become a ruler over many things, departure from the United Order or natural pattern of our lives creates chaos.

The Lord is not pleased with the ones who hide their talents or bury their talents.[154] If we do not have charity because of our weaknesses toward our talents, ourselves, parents, children, spouses, and neighbors, the Lord will prove us and take away our talents.[155] Idleness with our talents does not work. Waiting to organize ourselves when we become a millionaire does not work either. This will never happen, except to a few. Abuse or neglect buries our talents deeply.

Remember. Our talents are equal with others and will increase if our wants are just.[156] In other words, The United Order builds and bears us up in times of trial and gives us increase. We do not have to accumulate possessions to have an increase. We receive an increase by organizing our time, our talents, and possessions in the Lord's way. With success, He gives us

---

[154]Doctrine and Covenants 60:2-3, p. 110.

[155]Ether 12:35, The Book of Mormon, p. 511.

[156]Doctrine and Covenants 82:17-19, p. 152.

more to organize. This is how their sorrow for us does not overwhelm our Savior and our Heavenly Father. This builds up the Lord's Kingdom more so than titles or ownership of property. Unfortunately, there are conflicts that arise as we apply the principles of the United Order to our lives. Conflicts come because we are not living the United Order. Couples are to be united.

"First, my husband does not cleave to me." This has been a complaint from many wives and the subject of many columns in "Dear Abbey" and "Ann Landers." This is how husbands bury their talent. Husbands, are you cleaving to your wife and children? Are you looking back to your parental family for support when you have difficulties? When you cannot go home, are you looking to other things for comfort?

Remember. Your wife is a talent that you have traded for with the Lord. If you remember the story of the talents, after being faithful in a few things, the servant was made ruler over many things. It is now the husband's turn to be ruler over his own family. It is his turn to discover what it is like to rule people who do not want to be ruled or who want to be ruled in their own way. This includes your wife. It is your turn to deal with opposition. Husbands, you learned or were supposed to learn how to be a good follower with your parents. Husbands, it is now your turn to learn how to be a good leader with your wife. In this day, we have this reversed. Husbands led parents every which way they could as children, and follow wives as an adult. They think the Lord does not notice this spiritual dyslexia.

Husbands, if you do not cleave to your wife, there will be much contention in your home. All children know when there is trouble between Mother and Father. Contention is a difficult environment for children to learn in. No one, especially children, can function in a "needles and pins" environment. It is difficult to concentrate when children are hurting and concerned their father will not be in the home forever when they come home.

Remember. If the ruler does not obey rules, the ruled feel they do not have to obey rules either. The ruled can go their own way, too. This is how so much damage is inflicted by wayward spouses, wayward parents, wayward siblings, and wayward older children.

Second, extended families cause a lot of emotional pain to families. Friends and neighbors can, too. So much, that fathers begin seeking them sorrowing. This pain thrives on jealousy, gossip, intimidation, manipulation, and idleness. It starts with borrowing money.

Extended family feel they have the privilege and obligation to treat a sibling like they have always treated them. It does not matter if their siblings are not children anymore, and they are married and have children. Extended families take every advantage like they took advantage in childhood. They know the right buttons to push. Who is watching? Your children.

Children notice when parents defend themselves and when they do not. Children will treat the teachers in their lives, beginning with mother and father, the same way extended family treat their parents. Children will treat their spouses the same way their parents treat each other. They will also treat their spouses the same way parents allow themselves to be treated.

Wives especially do not like their husbands and children being treated in a manner that extended family have become accustomed to treating their siblings. For anyone not conforming or submitting to their pattern or will or whims, extended family feel obligated to tell everyone how your family really is. Wives and husbands are not going to be accepting of this kind of treatment of his or her family.

Third, husbands, it seems that you are in a power struggle between wife and family. Each wants you to wash your hands of your family, your talents, as Pontius Pilate tried to wash his hands of blame in the Savior's death. It cannot be done. If feelings proceed on a downward course, you may decide to wash your hands of your wife and children through divorce. However, you are still responsible for this family through civil law and through spiritual law.

Husbands, you are actually in a power struggle between you and your wallet. Wives and children are an extension of you. Most wives and children have the same interests as fathers. They have been together along time. Wives and husbands usually think alike. This is why they married. Now, if someone is picking at your wife, think about what is going on. If your wife cannot do anything good, and she is always mean. She is the stingy one of the family. She is similar in taste to you. Who are they really picking at? Your extended family knows you. Your extended family knows that you will give in after so much picking. They even know how much to pick. They have had practice for several years.

Fourth, picking at someone's spouse has become an acceptable form of venting feelings and blaming others for personal problems and family manipulations. This is nothing but scapegoating. Naturally, the scapegoat of your family, your talents, must pay and pay and pay for all these problems which they have caused over the years.

Most usually, the spouse can see through these manipulations and personal agendas of the "survivors" of the family. Survivors always have the next coop to fly to. Wives do not understand why their husband cannot see how they are being manipulated. Wives feel that others' needs are more important than your family's needs, bills, and peace of mind. Your family sacrifices for extended family members to have season tickets to their favorite basketball, baseball, football, hockey, soccer, and rugby teams, many vacations, and every adult toy.

Wives do become the barrier for achieving extended family's personal agendas. Husbands, you are supposed to be the barrier to those who harm your family, physically and emotionally to achieve their goals–even if they are your personal childhood family or friends.

Husbands, there are twenty pits in this struggle.[157] Let me name a few. One, you are aware when you are being manipulated and are caught in a pit. It is painful when you have to admit that your childhood family, whom you love very much, is willing to cheat you and blame you for every minor and major crisis in their life. Two, you do not have to be a member of The Church of Jesus Christ to know that you are to pray and bless those who despitefully use you.[158] Three, you are trying to honor parents and honor your wife. No one can serve two masters. This is why the Savior told you to cleave unto your wife. Four, your childhood family will not "cut you any slack."

Husbands feel their wife should cut them some slack. Wives would cut you some slack. There is no slack to cut. The money for your home has to come from somewhere. If husbands cannot support their family, her family, and his family, wives cannot support his family, her family, and your children either.

---

[157]Mary Jane Grange, R.N., The Medicine Wheel for Step Parent, Trafford Publishing, Victoria, British Columbia, Canada, 2001 & 2008, pp. 44-70.

[158]Matthew 5:44, The Holy Bible, p. 1194.

Husbands, if you are having this problem with your extended family, the greatest blessing for them is for you to tell them "No." A very loving Heavenly Father tells us "No." It has not changed His love for us, but has directed His love and made it productive. Are you trying to take the Savior's place because you do not like to be mocked and want acceptance in your family? To keep on the receiving end, family members have to keep you and your family distant and not accepted–just like extended families treated their parents, peers, and teachers.

Handle mocking like the Savior did. The Savior handled mocking by leaving, soft answers, and agreement with thine adversary. Agreement means "have kind thoughts for" not bank-roll relatives who have some very convincing stories for their extravagant ways. There are other ways to seek your family after they recognize your family is first in your life

Wives, do you cleave to your husbands? Wives your husbands may be trying to handle mocking as the Savior did. He is trying to have kind thoughts for individuals who have hurt him. He is praying for ones who have despitefully used him. He does not want to speak against the Lord's anointed or be idle. Husbands bear many burdens silently so that we can be wives and mothers without panic attacks. Husbands do this by not talking. Husbands are entitled to find their own answers and talents. Keep the lines of communication open.

We must seek one of our lost talents like we would seek a lost piece of silver.[159] The Savior has provided many scriptures for all of his sheep, especially the lost sheep, in order that they may reorganize themselves and their families. One of the many ways that we seek our lost sheep is through the Welfare Program of The Church of Jesus Christ of Latter-day Saints. It is based on scripture. Many books have been written on the subject.

This welfare program causes conflict within the priesthood holders of the home. Priesthood holders are taught to care for their families, their childhood family, and their nuclear family, the family with their spouse. Before coming to The Church of Jesus Christ of Latter-day Saints for monetarial help, families are to seek help from family members. Hopefully, in a time of crisis, families do not have to ask. However, it is not a crisis when one does not have sports tickets, a new outfit, and a monthly vacation.

Seeking our talents has to be done with a Word of Wisdom and order. The Lord does not require families to sacrifice their health to the point of cancer, arthritis, diabetes, fibromyalgia, bankruptcy, emotional depression, divorce, etc., in order to assist others when they cannot pay their bills from living beyond their means. Many family members ask for assistance, but they have season tickets to many sports teams, a $300,000 home, two or three cars, campers, boats, skidoos, multiple cell phones, computers, several charge cards, vacations, jewelry, etc. Let them downsize so they can become a successful ruler of a few things.

Charge cards cannot compete with this kind of spending. They have limits. The principle of tithing cannot compensate for these overdrafts. Husbands cannot either, nor can wives. If a family is trying to do this for their extended family, their nuclear families will fall to last place. Husbands and wives become unavailable to their children and spouses because of multiple jobs. Fathers will be breaking multiple commandments which I will let you look up.

In the welfare program, bishops and stake presidents have rules to follow. They have heard every excuse. They can say "No" and do. The person leaves, and except for hearing

---

[159]Luke 15:8-9, The Holy Bible, p. 1305.

130

about how mean and stingy he was for five years, it is over. The bishop never tells. However, the one who was turned down because there is a bottom to everyone's well, has a duty to tell everyone how the bishop really is. They have a right to vent their anger, too.

Most problems in wards are caused by someone who has been turned away monetarialy from the church's welfare program. These individuals may or may not pay tithing, but have elaborate homes, cars, charge cards, tickets to sports teams, vacations, jewelry, etc. They also have elaborate stories on why they need church welfare and cannot work.

Can you see the pattern? The priesthood holder and father of the home is being treated the same way the bishop or father of the ward is treated. The same problems that occur in churches or wards occur in families. A family member has been turned down with money. No matter how diplomatically done, family members can hear and feel the results of temper tantrums from their "No's," seven days a week for years and at every family gathering. When nuclear families feel deprived, they become angry with Mother for being so mean to them like they are to extended family. They become disrespectful to Father for not stopping the problem.

Some people must learn the hard way. The greatest blessing and service for them is for you, the Priesthood holder of the home, to let them learn. "Pull the bandage off quickly, not slowly." Better yet, do not put this sticky bandage on. In other words, do not get this abuse started. It harms everyone. This is not service or sacrifice. Service and sacrifice bring blessings, seen and unseen, not burdens, seen and unseen. This is how you tell the difference.

I know that you do not want to see your family lose their home, fortunes, and experience bankruptcy. Your families will be spiritually bankrupt when they need that income the most if you do not allow your families to learn from the opposition in their lives. It hurts to see others suffering from their mistakes. Now, you know why your wife is so stressed. She gets to deal with everyone plus you in your distress. Who supports your wife when she is stressed?

Fifth, fathers and mothers may have a parent who is declining in mental status. The elderly are forgetful and forgiving, but they can be stirred up because they are forgetful. This is not a selective process. If your parent is forgetful about everyone and their spouse's behavior, but your spouse and your behavior, be suspicious. Your parents are being manipulated because of their age. Wills can be changed. Things disappear from your parents' home. You or your wife are blamed. Decreasing the numbers of heirs increases the amount of inheritance that others receive when your parents die. This hurts. This is not how it is in the Lord's Kingdom.

My teachers use to say "stick to your task, till your task sticks to you." Father, stay on task. Your wife and children are your task. They need to stick to you. Wayward spouses, wayward siblings, or wayward child can take you from your task. Children need your example of how someone stays on task in spite of heavy opposition. It may save their life someday.

List how you maintain order in your home. What do spouses and the family need to work on? If there is no order, notice how you treat your spouse and parents. Children will treat you in the same manner. To what and whom does each member of your step family cleave to? How do you seek your children and step children and their lost talents while sorrowing? Parents, are you staying on task? If not, you will be diagnosed with an attention deficit disorder. Become familiar with the pattern of behavior of each member of your family and step family when you tell them "no." Does everyone fall like dominoes fall when you say no to a particular child?

Chapter Twenty

The Dominoes in Our Lives

In a previous chapter, I mentioned that our problems with children seem so overwhelming, parents feel like they are bound and gagged like Isaac, son of Abraham. There are reasons for this unpredictable, irregular, inconsistent, and wandering behavior in being a modern-day Isaac. Let's start with the first thing that everyone automatically assumes or seems to always complain about your child.

First, your child does not listen. Why doesn't your child listen? Do their examples in their lives listen? Whether parents listen or not to good examples, many children view their parents, or any adult in their life, as people who have nothing to offer them, but work. Your child does not listen because he does not want to work at what you want him to work at.

Your child may be daydreaming about what is going on around him, what he is going to do after school, or what parents have planned for after school. He may be tired from things he did late after school the night before. He may not be interested in the subject you are teaching. He may be bored, hungry, or sick. Parents cannot leave their jobs to care for sick children.

What happens when either a child or an adult does not listen? They are not paying attention when they need to listen. Your child missed important details as they were given instructions. With only part or no instructions at all, your child cannot follow instructions, nor can he follow through on the tasks for which the instructions were given.

Your child now has difficulty remembering simple things because he did not follow through on simple instructions. We learn by doing. His task must be performed by guess work. Since he is not prepared, he will have trouble starting tasks or with completing tasks that require planning or long term effort. If your child chooses not to do the task that is asked of him, he appears lazy and disorganized. His parents and others become angry and impatient with him.

Second, your child becomes impulsive. He becomes verbally impulsive and insubordinate with adults and peers. He can attack physically, especially siblings and peers. He has a fight or flight mechanism built within his or her body. Your child will act on these impulses regardless of consequences because he feels he has a right to defend himself.

Your child becomes angry with you for being angry with him. Because of a guilty conscious, he becomes fidgety. He appears to be easily distracted because he seems to be angry and unprepared for no reason at all. He will do anything for acceptance or entertainment.

Third, his needs are more important than others. Rules do not apply to him or her. They are unable to wait their turn. No one notices him or her or meets his or her needs. When questioned, "I forgot" is his or her excuse for not listening. Doing things on impulse and being impatient becomes a habit. With all of the shoes, backpacks, etc. that your child has misplaced, he does seems forgetful.

Naturally, his not listening, impulsive behavior, and the feeling that his needs are more important than others affect everything. He cannot organize, plan, and manage the most important areas of one's life. He may be too young to be expected to manage his life. These things affect children's relationships with others, running a home, and keeping track of finances. The dominoes in their life fall rapidly.

Others can take advantage because this person can be stirred up so easily with anger. Others naturally do not want to trust these individuals with anything important. Many people feel individuals cannot learn because they have attention deficit disorder or attention deficit disorder with hyperactivity. Instead of learning to control their environment by listening and following instructions, adults and children with attention deficit disorders learn to control their environment with manipulation, stonewalling, or intimidation of others. Positive experiences becomes limited. Daydreaming increases. Very few people take time with an impulsive child.

Your child becomes restricted in some way. He has to work one-on-one with someone to help him make up his work. When parents and teachers really notice this child with the quality time that we have been talking about, they see this child has great ability and potential. Not only is your child able to pay attention while working one-on-one with someone, he has "steel trap" memories for complex issues. Your child can even focus on something that is not of great interest or highly stimulating to your child.

Your child does not have all or any of these difficulties all of the time. However, when your child is left to his own devices, is in a hurry, is impatient, or he is tired, your child returns to the same behavior. His learning becomes inconsistent. He may or may not be listening again. He also may be tired of being victimized. This leads to outbursts of temper.

My child has outbursts. Parents must distinguish between temper tantrums or a child's indignation over how he is being treated. Individuals with attention deficit disorder have feelings and have freedom of speech to express their anger in appropriate ways. Often, it is a game to stonewall or pick on individuals, especially ones that have the following disabilities: wearing the wrong brand or color of clothes, not giving up one's seat to another, having the wrong skin color, weight, or shape of eyes, or having something that someone else wants, etc. These individuals may have a chronic illness, birth defect, or may not be an A-student.

Adults know when they are being stonewalled and intimidated, and they leave. Though children do not know what to call it, they can sense when they are being stonewalled and bullied. They cannot tell anyone because they become a "snitch," the lowest form of tattle tale. Children do not have the freedom or sense to leave. Their feelings boil like a boiling tea kettle.

Emotions build up because they are not allowed to express their feelings. These individuals have to take the mistreatment they are receiving. They know no one intends to do anything about the problem anyway. They do not want to overstep their bounds of authority. These conflicts lead to outbursts that seem like this individual has a hair-trigger temper when they actually do not. They have endured a lot before their outbursts.

They endure a lot after their outbursts. Outbursts are embarrassing to all. Outbursts only bring more accusations and mistreatment. They also bring the silent treatment. Friendships are lost. Of course, if friends are treating each other this way, they are not friends.

However, individuals who have all of the above disabilities are expected to give, not make demands, or express any displeasure. Essentially, they are to serve others from an empty plate and not complain. What is the answer? Are there any answers? The answers are found in Matthew 5.

133

*38 Ye have heard that it hath been said, An eye for an eye, and a
tooth for a tooth:*
*39 But I say unto you, That ye resist not evil: but whosoever shall
smite thee on thy right cheek, turn to him the other also.*
*40 And if any man will sue thee at the law, and take away thy coat,
let him have thy cloke also.*
41 And whosoever shall compel thee to go a mile, go with him twain.
*42 Give to him that asketh thee, and from him that would borrow of
thee turn not thou away.*

Matthew 5:38 - 42, The Holy Bible

In this scripture, some of the symptoms of attention deficit disorder can be found. The Savior is also teaching us how to deal with the problems when someone has an attention deficit disorder. First, let's list the symptoms.

ATTENTION DEFICIT DISORDER FROM THE SCRIPTURES

resist evil–retaliation
smite–hitting, agitate, afflict (eye for an eye)
sue thee–won't compromise, want something for nothing
take away thy coat–stealing
compel to go a mile–insist on doing things their way. If it is not their idea, it is not a good idea.
borrow–forget to pay back, forget what has promised to lend, ignore pleas for help, beg

The Savior listed the problems. He taught us what to do when these things occur. The Savior taught us to turn the other cheek. He taught us to give to those what they have stolen from you. Give life back to people even though it seems they have taken life from you. We are to even give more. We are to give when someone wants to borrow from us. When we are compelled, Jesus told us to go the extra mile.

How can these things help when your child will not listen? How can these things help when children are impulsive? How can these things help when children feel their needs are more important than others and when children feel rules and common sense do not apply to them? It seems like we cannot say "No" to the offenders in this world. We cannot set limits for our children. Yet, the Savior has told us to obey the laws of the land. Can a parent teach a child not to steal by not only giving to your child what he has stolen, but give him more?

I do not believe "turning the other check" means to stand there and let yourself be beaten. There is no dignity, and this is extremely dangerous. I believe this scripture means to leave. When the Savior was mocked, He got lost in the crowd. When you are afflicted or smitten, turn the other cheek. It also means to forgive. Jacob turned the other cheek many times with his sons' behavior.

When someone steals from you such as your coat, make it a gift. The thief is now indebted to you. Of course, we are to forgive our debtors. Remember. The thief is indebted to the Savior also. Don't let the offenders aggravate you so much that they keep repeating offenses against you. I know that you do not want to go the direction that these individuals are trying to take you. The key to this scripture is: How much are you willing to resist evil? There is more dignity if you do not resist evil.

What does going that extra mile really mean? Often, it means listening and hearing the emotion or feeling. Friends and parents may not be able to fulfill all of their child's requests. He just wants to know if he is being heard. This is why we were given the gift of revelation.

Give the gift of turning the other cheek or going the extra mile. Leave if necessary. Give as a gift the things that have been stolen from you. If you give your gift grudgingly, it is the same as not giving it. The Savior gave His coat and His life at the time of His crucifixion. This is how His gift of life for us was not given grudgingly. There are many who steal to the point of rape, murder, and premeditated robbery and theft. There are commandments against these things. These things are not gifts that we give quietly. We cannot even forgive this kind of debt. We do not have the authority to forgive rape, robbery, or murder.

The Savior would not give a commandment and then give us conflicting instructions to accept this behavior from others. It is okay to defend ourselves and our families and seek solutions. We can do this with soft answers most of the time. We do not have to accept this kind of treatment to be popular. There is no dignity this way either. We must turn the other cheek and leave dangerous situations.

I am aware that individuals like to resist evil when evil is done to them. It becomes point and counterpoint. Accusations bring more mistreatment. When one is baptized, he is stating that he will not live the law of Moses anymore. The law of Moses is an eye for an eye, tooth for a tooth justice. This type of justice caused a lot of problems for Moses. Eventually, the Israelites went to judges to keep up with this justice. Baptized individuals are stating they can live the law of Christ, the law of mercy. This is how we take the name of Christ upon us.

Attention deficit disorder is a result of being overtaken in a fault.[160] When individuals are overtaken in a fault we are to restore that person in meekness, lest we be tempted by the same fault. We are also not to find fault with one another.[161] If someone trespasses against us, we are to tell him his fault in private.[162] If he listens to you, you will have gained a friend. This is an example of going that extra mile with each other.

Resisting evil, smiting, stealing, suing, compelling others with behavior, and excessive borrowing, faults, and fault-finding–is this attention deficit disorder or attention deficit disorder with hyperactivity in a nutshell? However, there still seems to be some loose ends. It describes the individuals that I know that have been told they have an attention deficit disorder. These individuals fought back when they were picked on, but they had poor handwriting.

My child has poor handwriting. If the child has not done the work in writing, he will have poor handwriting. However, computers have replaced writing. Calculators have replaced mathematical skills. These are important areas of learning. Writing and mathematics

---

[160]Galations 6:1, The Holy Bible, p. 1479.

[161]Doctrine and Covenants 88:124, p. 174.

[162]Matthew 18:15, The Holy Bible, p. 1219.

coordinate concepts with other skills. There is hope. Every doctor that I have ever worked with has had terrible writing, except one. They must have had an attention deficit disorder.

Is attention deficit disorder the result of a chemical imbalance? There is much debate about chemical imbalances in the brain. Other psychiatric disorders are believed to be caused by chemical imbalance. The most common chemical believed to be out of balance is serotonin.

Chemical imbalances in the brain are hard to measure. We are talking about measurements that are so small that we cannot conceive of the amount of these chemicals in the brain. Yet, they have great impact on the mind and body. There are chemicals that we are not aware of. We do not really know or understand how the brain communicates to and stores information in a neuron, a brain cell, by way of an axon which has gaps.

Do our emotions cause a chemical imbalance which affects our ability to focus, sustain attention, and affect recall? Maybe. I am skeptical. I have seen doctors prescribe multiple anti-depressants, anti-anxiety, and mood elevators for their patients. These medications require sleeping pills, antacids, muscle relaxants, and pain pills. The doctors claim they are restoring the balance of an absent chemical in the brain. Their patient is stoned, pale, has slurred speech, no memory, no sexual desire, sleeps all the time, and cannot function without tremors or expensive antacids. This is not balance. This is expensive over-medication suppressing body and mind.

We do not achieve balance by denying we have a problem. One achieves balance in his life by admitting they have a problem, repentance, praying and studying their problems, finding solutions, playing wholesome music, laughing, or receiving a hug and acceptance. Our moods and emotions are also changed by these methods.

If all of our problems were caused by a chemical imbalance, there would be too much of a yo-yo effect on the brain and the entire body. There would be no way to achieve a balance or temperance in our spirits and our thoughts. We would not be able to stand up physically or emotionally. Procreation or reproduction would be drastically effected. Birth defects would occur. All systems of the body would be affected. Our immune system would be effected. These things would be taking free agency from us. We do have choices in our behavior. There are other sources for this answer.

Are our problems a chemical disorder or a disorder of the spirit? The scriptures tell us that we will be resurrected with a perfected body, and there shall be no sorrow.[163] Things that were wrong with the physical body will be laid to rest with our mortal body and will be corrected when it is our turn to be resurrected. Our turn of resurrection depends on how we lived our life and if we were valiant in overcoming opposition.

Things that are wrong with the soul will not be corrected. Whatever principle of intelligence that we learn in this life will rise with us. The more we learn, the more advantage we will have in this life and the life to come.[164] Learning and retaining are systems within the soul. There are physical abnormalities which affect how much we can learn in mortal life. These physical disabilities do not affect our spiritual self. Learning and retaining are a matter of choice in most people. Healthy bodies with no desire to learn cannot be saved in ignorance.

---

[163]Revelation 21:4, The Holy Bible, p. 1587.

[164]Doctrine and Covenants 130:18, p. 265.

Why is my child able to pay attention and work better in a one-to-one relationship? When children experience emotional and social shock, they experience shock in the same manner as a person who is hemorrhaging physical blood. There may not be any blood, but their spirits seem to bleed right out. They become combative, argumentative, and do not follow instructions well. Instructions may have to be repeated over and over for them to register with a child. Their spirit comes right back in when there is a comfortable, attentive, and stable environment. This is why children do well in a one-to-one relationship.

This is exactly why the Savior gave us the tenth method of learning, the Holy Ghost. We will always have someone to work with on a one-on-one basis in mortal life. We do not have to rely on pride, childish behavior, contention, or weapons of rebellion. The Holy Ghost, once he is bestowed to us, is there in our failures, our inconsistencies, our sorrows, and our successes. He is the great Miracle Worker. However, the Holy Ghost will never encumber any teachings of any prophets of any dispensation or period of time.

The Holy Ghost will not bless us in our vain ambitions, our contentions, our childish behavior, our pride, and our weapons of rebellion. The Holy Ghost would be speaking against the Heavenly Father's Anointed if he condoned our behavior. We would seek more vain ambitions, contentions, pride, and weapons of rebellion if he blessed our efforts in these areas. This would effect many people. Everyone would have a decrease, not an increase in our lives. The Holy Ghost will withdraw from us, if he has to, for the words of God's Anointed and the words of the prophets to be fulfilled in everyone's life.

Do your children have the Miracle Worker in their lives? Do parents have the Miracle Worker in their lives? Parents, in our exuberance to provide for ourselves and our children the necessities of life and recreation to the point of indulgence, have you created Helen Kellers of your sighted children?

To refresh your memory, Helen Keller is a woman who became deaf as a young child. In their grief for her, her parents could not tell her "No." The servants who cared for her were not allowed to tell her "No." As a result, she behaved terribly to others. She screamed. and she hit and kicked everyone she came in contact with when she did not get her own way. Helen would not sit at the dinner table. She took other people's food off their plates at the dinner table. She locked her mother and her teacher, Annie Sullivan, in rooms.

The world has many, many sighted and hearing children doing the same things as Helen Keller did in her rage at not being able to see, hear, or speak in a stable environment. Parents are treating their children the same way as Helen Keller's parents treated her. Have parents taken their children's voice, hearing ability, and vision for past, present, and future? Parents are trying to create perfect children without the principles of deity, their Heavenly Father, in the face of much opposition, and by not telling their children "No." Parents could not accomplish much under these circumstances. How can we expect our children to learn things this way?

Parents are constantly being told that their children are the brightest children that have been born on this Earth. The world can only take them so far. Our children can only go so far with excessive possessions and excessive recreation. Our children want to see, hear, and speak. They want to learn things that can only be taught by the principles of deity. They want to learn those principles by doing, not by reading about them. Children want to be accepted while they are learning and making their mistakes. Children want to learn together as a family.

Don't bury or encumber your talents, your children, in your grief, wants, and desires. Don't encumber your children with frequent breaks from them. Parents, don't bury or encumber the talents, their children, belonging to your neighbors because of your fears or jealousies. Don't bury your talents, your family, with evil-speaking of the Lord's anointed in your home. Otherwise, the great Miracle Worker and Great Tutor in your life leaves your home and presence.

> *26 But the Comforter, which is the Holy Ghost, whom the Father will send in my name, he shall teach you all things, and bring all things to your remembrance, whatsoever I have said unto you.*

John 14:26, <u>The Holy Bible</u>

Most children do not have attention deficit disorder. They do not have the gift of tongues. Keep in mind that a gift is an ability as well as a present. Most religions teach that the gift of tongues is speaking in a foreign dialect, and someone in the audience, listening to the speaker, understands miraculously. This is such a small part to the gift of tongues. Most people decide not to learn the gift of tongues. They will not need the gift of tongues in their life time.

We use the gift of tongues all the time. We can ask for this spiritual gift in prayer, and we learn this in school. Another name for gift of tongues is language skills. My language skill is English. This was predetermined by my parents for me. Your gift of tongues may be Spanish, Indian, French, German, Scandinavian, Russian, Norwegian, Chinese, Japanese, Hebrew, African, Polynesian, etc.

How do we learn our various language skills or gifts of tongues? First, it is a marvelous gift to be able to speak at all. There are many people who are deaf or autistic, and they cannot speak. Their fingers, hands, and a computer are their voice box.

Those first sounds from your baby are not happanstance. Breathing, seeing others form words with their mouth, hearing those sounds, structure of the mouth, teeth, tongue, moisture in the mouth, a voice box, emotion, understanding, and a desire to communicate are all working in concert together. For this to be a smooth concert, it takes time, practice, and patience. Sound needs to be a pleasant experience. Even the absence or presence of hormones changes the pitch of your baby or teenager's tones.

Second, it is a gift for a combination of sounds to be able to convey words, ideas, and groups of ideas. It is a gift to be able to convey thoughts through sentences. The gift of tongues allows us to express thoughts that we do understand, concepts that we do not understand, and the ability to tell the difference. Third, it is a gift to be able to read and write and study what an individual or others have expressed on paper. Raised dots or Braille is the gift of tongues for the blind. Fourth, it is a gift to convey sounds in an intelligible manner that is not offensive. Fifth, it is a great gift to be able to convey peace and love instead of hate and frustration as we learn to communicate with others.

There is a key or a first step to the gift of tongues. The key to your gift of tongues and attention deficit disorders is the ability to recognize that there is no one listening to us or can be benefitted by our speech and behavior, especially ourselves. We must learn to recognize that our outbursts and behavior are not cute or an expression of our rights. Our behavior is just agitation and hurtful. When we learn this, our gift of tongues gives us a wisdom which combines the art of speech, reading, writing, studying, soft answers, intelligence, and peacemaking with our ability to see, hear, touch, taste, and smell. Our gift of tongues will be limited if we do not continue with steps three, four, and five.

We learn the five steps of the gifts of tongues by seeing, hearing, tasting, touching, and smelling. Naturally, these steps are a process which requires a one-to-one teaching relationship with children. Smooth concerts will not occur by the ten-second rule in children of any age. These expressions could be scrambled after they are expressed to us for a number of reasons.

We store information by the five areas of senses: seeing, hearing, tasting, touch, and smell. We comprehend or learn by what we store by the five aspects of our senses. The aspects of our personality are determined by how much we decide to store. In other words, seeing, hearing, tasting, touching, and smelling are not just for the physical sense of our lives. We will use them in all aspects of our lives, such as financial, social, emotional, spiritual, moral, etc.

Seeing and hearing are self-explanatory. There is nothing so quick for learning as seeing a bad example in a child's life. We can tell if something is sound by listening or hearing. Tasting is not just sampling a food item.

Tasting is discernment through trying. Babies explore their world through taste. Babies do not explore their world with no taste and then suddenly develop taste. We have experiences in regards to taste to apply taste to other things. As a result of our experiences, we learn to discriminate between good and bad experiences. We learn to know what we like and dislike and what helps and what does not help us through taste.

Now, how do children of all ages decide what is bad and what is good taste. Bad taste encumbers us. When we are encumbered, we are burdened; hindered, or obstructed in some way. Sometimes it is with many things. High prices encumber us. Weapons of rebellion and an attitude of "anything goes" encumbers good taste.

Smelling is learning discrimination by odors, good as well as bad. Everything leaves a trail that can be discerned by smell. A poor sense of smell in infants and toddlers leaves them without learning the rudimentary skill of discernment between good and bad when they are too young to know about good and bad. Our sense of smell teaches us that by their fruits ye shall know them.

Touch is not learning by contact. We learn *to communicate influence by touch.* This kind of touch touches the soul. We can also learn texture, power, and organization by touch.

There is a handicap to what we can learn and how we will learn when any of these five senses are absent. The absence of sight, sound, and touch has terrible impacts on our bodies and minds. The absence of taste and smell has very large impacts in our lives, too. The absence of language skills or gift of tongues has a severe impact on our lives. We need to know how to express ourselves–what we see, hear, taste, smell, and what touches our soul.

Children with attention deficit disorder and learning disabilities have difficulty learning patterns in their life. Patterns are important. In order to express sounds, words, sentences, and ideas, we must learn the patterns of speech. This includes sounds as well as nouns, verbs, adjectives, adverbs, participles, phrases, clauses, sentences, and punctuation.

Children begin with the alphabet and learn the sounds of consonants and vowels. We cannot express ourselves effectively with half of an alphabet learned. We cannot do arithmetic with a little bit of addition, subtraction, and a few multiplication tables learned. Children of any age cannot recognize a pattern if they have only been given or learned part of the pattern. Learning is difficult when learning is not interesting, too hard, or is not a positive experience.

This is why it seems children do not learn from previous experiences, especially negative experiences in their life. They do not recognize a pattern because they have only experienced half the pattern in their own senses.

What is the other half of the pattern? It is not a matter of what. It is a matter of who the pattern is. The Savior is the pattern. Parents are important parts of the pattern. If parents are absent or functioning below their level, children are missing patterns which they were supposed to be taught to recognize by a parent.

Naturally, if the Savior is missing in their parents' lives, children are missing most all of some very important patterns for their life. If neither the Savior nor parent is involved in a child's life, the child is missing all of the patterns he was supposed to follow. Friends and teachers can help some, but not if they do not have the correct patterns in their life. At best, they will not be able to help on a regular basis. They have their own lives to live.

With half the pattern, plaids become stripes, or just a few lines here and there. Stripes become plain. If a pattern requires stripes, faded colors or a few lines will not work. Of course, no one needs or can use patterns which do not work or fit.

However, your children still have minds that have storage facilities available. They will store anything that comes along. Most usually, this is in a very unorganized pattern. It can be an unethical pattern. If children of all ages do not have the Great Example and the Great Organizer in their lives, many people can take advantage of your children. Your children will become distracted from the things that will give them a better quality of life and an increase in time, talents, and possessions.

The Savior has told us through James the Apostle to not be hearers only.[165] If hearing is the only sense we rely on, and we are not listening, we will have a tremendous disability in our lives. We can deceive ourselves. We also can talk ourselves out of doing what we do not want to do so easily. We will not become hearers only if we have developed all of our senses– sight, sound, touch, taste, and smell–and by developing our gift of speaking in tongues and our ability of interpreting tongues with the assistance of the Holy Ghost.

Notice how you and your children are restricted by parent and child's actions, needs, outbursts, and time with friends. Can you speak comfort, peace, and love in your native tongue? Are parents complaining about a pattern of behavior they set for their children? Are children copying the patterns set by parents and step parents or are they copying the patterns shown in the movies they watch? What faults are you and your children relying on to overcome opposition? Will your method of overcoming opposition and mocking cause you to be diagnosed with an attention deficit disorder?

It sounds like we have no choice in the matter if we have an attention deficit disorder. We are stuck with what our body decrees for us. We may be at different levels of intelligence and performance. Humans are not stuck with impulses or reflex and their consequences. We have our free agency, the ability or choice to stay on task.

---

[165]James 1:22, The Holy Bible, p. 1539.

Chapter Twenty-One

Free Agency

Many parents have children with severe attention deficit disorder with hyperactivity. Their children never stop. They are in constant motion. Their children have sudden periods of rage. Some parents are afraid to go to sleep or leave these children alone with their siblings. Parents are afraid to leave these teenagers home alone. Things are stolen or damaged. These children are too disruptive to maintain in a school setting.

Sometimes, medications work with these children. Often, they do not, and psychiatrists, pediatricians, and social workers do not know why. A child can become a walking pharmacy. Parents cannot achieve any sense of order in their marriage or homes or meet the needs of other members in their family? Parents cannot relieve this nightmare in their home?

First, parents need to find out if their child is taking the medication they give their children. To be effective, medications have to be at a therapeutic level for the size and age of your child. This means that the medication must be at a certain concentration in your child's blood before it works. This concentration varies according to drug. A blood draw can determine if a child is taking their medication or if their medication is at therapeutic level.

All medications have side effects. Adults stop taking drugs because they do not like the side effects. Children stop taking the medications because they do not like side effects, too. Street drugs and alcohol increase side effects and decrease effectiveness of any prescription.

Unfortunately, teenagers stop taking their medication for other reasons, too. Teenagers can hide pills in their cheeks, back of a tooth, and under the tongue. They can palm medication expertly. Medications that have been palmed can be sold to other teenagers or exchanged for other drugs. They can be used to make other drugs. Watch and see if your child pretends to adjust his clothing or scratch somewhere when taking his or her medication. Teenagers can deposit pills in their hair, ears, nose, between their breasts, pockets, or in folds of clothing or folds of skin. Those buying drugs do not care if a tablet has been partially dissolved by sweat and saliva. They are going to mix the pills with other chemicals anyway.

Parents may not give medication regularly because of the cost of the medication. The medication will never reach a therapeutic level when only taken during outbursts. Parents might as well save their money. Parents forget to give medication regularly. Obtain a pill calendar box to maintain a schedule. This pill container has to be placed in an area that is away from small children because it does not have a child protective lid on it.

Many individuals with attention deficit disorder with hyperactivity complain of racing thoughts that drive them crazy. Think back to when you have been overtired to the point of exhaustion. If anyone has worked a graveyard shift, they can identify with this behavior. After that last graveyard shift, individuals usually have one or two hours of sleep, thinking they will not sleep well that night if they have more sleep. At bedtime, they are exhausted mentally and physically, but cannot sleep. Their mind races, and they cannot relax. This is a frustrating situation. It would be devastating to live with these racing thoughts everyday of your life. Many drug addicts want to be relieved of these racing thoughts.

Inconsistent and violent behavior can be caused by not enough sleep. Children with attention deficit disorder with hyperactivity may need sleep studies to see if they are having sleep apnea. They may also need a simple adenoidectomy. Swollen adenoids may interfere with breathing during sleep.

However, children stay up on their own. My generation read books by flashlight. This generation uses headphones to watch television all night or listen to the stereo. They can talk with their friends by phone or by text messages and play video games.

Unfortunately, the generations since the sixties have experimented with drugs which can keep them up for days, too. Children are not honest with their parents anymore. They can obtain these drugs at elementary school. They feel it is their life, and they can experiment with any drug they chose. Drugs for attention deficit disorders can cause insomnia.

Children are very body conscious and use steroids and diet pills. They use steroids and diet pills while drinking many cans of soda pop which has caffeine. To party all night, teenagers purchase twenty ounces of flavored drinks of caffeine or eight ounce cans of a drink which have extremely high doses of caffeine. They use these drinks in combination with over-the-counter caffeine pills. This all combines with medications for attention deficit disorder, lack of sleep, and lack of self-control. Is it any wonder these children have periods of violence and rage. They do not care who the violence is directed at.

It is difficult for a mother to deal with an infant who needs a nap. Mother gets to deal with a teenager who has not had any sleep in days and who has steroids, diet pills, large doses of caffeine in their body, and any other drug they are taking to keep them awake. Anything minor sets these teenagers off. I have wondered if this is how kids kill kids and their parents.

Could this behavior be a form of a seizure? I have cared for the parents and spouses of children who had severe hair-trigger tempers. These tempers leave as quickly as they come. Doctors are now calling this rage childhood bipolar disorder and are prescribing seizure medications. I wondered if this could be a form of a seizure that we have not recognized yet. Perhaps this electrical misfire is not enough to cause unconsciousness or tremors, but is enough to cause sudden rage. If medications for attention deficit disorder do not work for your child, consider a seizure medication. Remember. Seizures can occur because of inadequate sleep. Caffeinated drinks counteract many medications. Children do not need any energy boosters.

Parents have an ungovernable child. Their teenager can hold the entire family hostage because the teenager can get away with it. These teenagers can manipulate, stonewall, intimidate, and bully anyone in their family. Everyone is so concerned with the child's free agency and rights. They have forgot about fixing the problem. Everyone hovers over this child so much. It is profitable to be ungovernable. Since it is profitable to be ungovernable, other children in the home feel it is profitable for them to do the same behavior.

Parents need to consider the welfare, rights, and free agency of others living in their home. This includes parents and step parents as well as siblings of ungovernable children. Ungovernable teenagers cause severe doubt and hate in other siblings. Siblings will deliberately set your ungovernable teenager off to give them the advantage for a change. They know what buttons to push. They have had to walk on egg shells with them long enough.

Since parents are liable for the ungovernable child and his behavior until age eighteen, parents may have to consider a boys or a girls school to maintain the integrity of their home. They may have to declare their teenager disabled to help pay for this school.

Do not be tempted to let ungovernable teenagers live with relatives, friends, or coaches. Relatives, friends, and coaches have a tendency to cut parents out of the picture. They have heard many stories about parents and do not know who to believe. Relatives, friends, and coaches cannot provide the counseling your child needs. Relatives, friends, and coaches will not be able to do anymore for your child than you, the parents, and their doctors and counselors can. They will let your child run without restraint. They will not send your child home where he belongs because they become attached to your child's disability, child support, or social security check.

Seek counseling for your child and yourself. If you cannot tolerate this behavior from a child or teenager, a future spouse and future children cannot tolerate this behavior from an adult. A future spouse and future children will appreciate your efforts in their behalf. Counseling can show you where you are dependent on your child or spouse being dependent on you. You may have heard of the old wives' tale that familiarity breeds contempt. Dependency breeds hostility, too. If you want your child or spouse to change, you must change. Your independence will reveal others' dependence. This is why there is opposition to positive changes in your life.

It would be nice if a parent did not have to walk on egg shells with their children anymore. Try the many suggestions in this book. However, begin by controlling the number of outbursts. Reward as the outbursts decrease. It is hard not to punish. Allow children to have consequences instead.

Lastly, your child may be given a gift to think quickly to help others in some way. He has to slow down and control the speed of his thoughts as well as the quality of his thoughts. The person he needs to help may not have the ability to think quickly.

Quit trying to prove that you are a good parent. Once started, this will continue until the child is fifty years old or more. Your child does not have to be an eagle scout, a missionary, an accomplished musician, an A-student, and a valedictorian for you to be good parents. You do not have to prove you are good parents by being another source of income for your children. Parents do not have to prove they were good parents though their child has an addiction.

Parents may have to cope with a violent child who is an alcoholic or drug addict. Many have chosen to live with various addictions in their lives. Addictions have become a lifestyle. This can range from substance addiction to coveting anything one sees. This lifestyle causes a large amount of stress in one's life and for those with whom they associate. When individuals have excessive stress in their lives, mortal beings resort to various defense mechanisms to relieve that stress. Remember. Defensive mechanisms distort stress and reality in our lives. They also magnify our distress, not our personal callings in life.

The Savior called this the natural man or carnal man. He did not call it attention deficit disorder. Members of The Church of Jesus Christ of Latter-day Saints call these ways "The Pride Cycle." The pride cycle is dangerous because it leads to idols or addictions. The Savior has said to have no other idols before me.[166]

---

[166]Alma 1:32, <u>The Book of Mormon</u>, p. 210; Exodus 20:3-5, <u>The Holy Bible</u>, p. 109.

As a nurse, I cared for teenagers and adults with many addictions or idols in their lives. I nursed or recovered these patients from drug and alcohol overdoses and severe accidents in the intensive care unit where I worked. Many of these patients went on to drug or alcohol rehabilitation centers. They also went to physical rehabilitation centers so they could learn how to talk, feed themselves, walk, and care for their own bodily functions again. Family members had to learn how to care for family members who could not learn to do these things anymore. They had to cope with feelings of doubt about their ability to parent, too.

The sad thing is, friends and family would sneak alcohol or marijuana to their very sick or injured friend or family member who was on other medications, including some pain medication. They would sneak the same substances by which patients were going to be limited the rest of their lives.

Parents gave these substances to their children. Siblings gave these things to older or younger siblings. Boyfriends gave these things to girlfriends. Husbands, and in some cases wives, gave these things to their spouse. They could not work in concert with parents nor with a doctor or nurse for the benefit of family, spouse, or friend. They had no respect for order. To have any peace or association, friends, family and spouses had to settle for no order in their lives. However, they all had something in common. After years of giving harmful substances or participating together in partaking of harmful substances, they complained bitterly about the poor performances of their family member, friend, spouse–and parent. They even "jumped ship" with friends, parents, and spouses. They had divorce papers delivered to the hospital. Naturally, they sought others to blame for their behavior and predicaments.

This lack of respect for the order in our bodies and our relationships is more than just being a prodigal son or a prodigal daughter. This lack of order results in addictions to various things and various substances. Addictions are not just sowing some wild oats. Addictions take control over everyone. Addictions oppress one's family and one's self similar to the plagues of Egypt. Addictions take away everyone's free agency.

The father of the prodigal son recognized the order of things. If you remember the story of The Prodigal Son, the son wasted his own inheritance. He did not waste the inheritances of his entire family. His father did not consume the fortunes and inheritances of the entire family, begging the prodigal son to come back. As a result, he only had one prodigal son. The father had some very painful waiting. He most likely had to endure murmuring about his lost child. In the story of The Prodigal Son, it was not more profitable to be a prodigal son or daughter.

I have often wondered what it would be like to be on medical rounds with the Great Physician over a prodigal son or daughter who had various idols or addictions in their lives. Where would he start? What physician's orders would he write?

This physician, the Savior, knew the great difficulties that families would experience. He experienced the same kind of opposition with the same kind of energy drain. The Savior knew that weapons of rebellion and pride would replace our talents–our families. He knew we would withdraw from our talents and become addicted to harmful substances. How did the Great Physician provide for those with harmful addictions in the scriptures?

First, overcoming ANY addiction requires fasting. The Savior said, this kind will not come about except by prayer and fasting about some medical conditions. It is that way with addictions, too. Become familiar with the fast found in Isaiah 58:6-12. I recommend a family fast. I call this the Heimlich Maneuver found in Isaiah. Write the steps to this Heimlich Maneuver on a card. Learn those steps and carry that card with you. Read it often.

Second, you will need help during the withdrawal period. Turn off the television!! Avoid R-rated movies. The bands that television has been assigned to broadcast on is a band that is similar to meditative thought. However, the material that is being broadcasted is irritating and contrary to order. You cannot build up while tearing down at the same time.[167] Individuals trying to withdraw from addicting substances cannot do so while irritated and watching others doing the very things that they are trying to withdraw from.

Individuals trying to withdraw from addicting substances do not need a lot of irritation at this time. Substitute television with music. Dr. Michael Ballam suggests Handel's "Water Music for difficult times." I do, too. It is very soothing. It is relaxing to individuals who are learning new ways and are frightened. If you do not want to listen, play it just out of earshot. Those working for the adversary like to create havoc around us and do not like order.

Third, avoid sugar as an energy substitute. During withdrawal, you will be jittery, nervous, and lacking energy. Sugar will accentuate this. Use fresh fruits and fresh or steamed vegetables. Members of The Church of Jesus Christ of Latter-day Saints follow a health code that is found in Doctrine and Covenants Section 89. Eat this way. If your body is satisfied with good, nourishing food, it is not so easy to tempt you. Fatigue will not be accentuated either.

Fourth, seek medical care. Hallucinations, disturbances in heart rhythms, and seizures can occur during the withdrawal period. There are qualified medical people who can help you over this rough period. It is also good to be away from children at this painful period of your life. Their innocence has been taken away enough with your addictions. Children do not understand your suffering and do not need to view you as a helpless, hopeless individual.

Fifth, buy some note cards. Write on your first card the following statement. Put it where you can see it every day. Read it often. Say it to yourself frequently. Pray to this end. This is what you ask for in prayer.

OUR GREATEST GLORY COMES NOT IN NEVER FALLING,
BUT IN RISING EVERY TIME WE FALL.

AUTHOR UNKNOWN

List the problems that you, your family, or your children are having. List the addictions in which everyone takes refuge while having their problems. List the addictions that you resort to for energy boosts or to sleep. There may be many things on your list. The aggravations in your family may seem to concentrate with one individual.

Work on one thing at a time. Remember. Individuals will be learning precept by precept, here a little, there a little, and degree by degree. Each individual can control the depth of those precepts and degrees. Each individual has to become sick and tired of being sick and tired before they are ready to learn a new precept.

---

[167]Dr. Michael Ballam, Building a Musical First Aid Kit, Cassette Two, Phoenix Productions, Logan, Utah, 1991.

List what is making you depressed. I know what you are thinking. There is nothing that makes me more depressed and angry than for someone to tell me that my depression comes from sin, especially when I am trying very hard, and there are many to try my patience. I have to admit depression comes from sin and faults. Repent of using depression and repression for your sins instead of remission of sins. Repression and depression are great sins of omission. These two things cause us to omit repentance from our life. We seek other things for relief.

Sixth, open the scriptures. Seek new answers or solutions in the scriptures. Use them like an open book exam. Find your problem. Pick out the principle that solves the problem. Learn the principle and the promise that always accompanies the principle. Begin learning about you and your problems with that principle and faith. Soon you will want other principles. Everyone will know when to go on. Practice what you are teaching yourself. Keep a journal of the new things you are learning about you. A little more dignity will come with every principle you learn and practice in your life–and so will energy.

The scriptures will be your boat for you to cross your "Red Sea." You decide how many timbers and how many nails go in your boat. You also get to decide how water-tight your boat will be and if you take any spiritual repair kits or spiritual food storage on your boat ride. Thus, this will be a life-long pursuit. Read the scriptures for at least fifteen minutes a day. The Lord knows we are in a fast-paced society. Read more if you want or feel the need.

Keep in mind that there are more than one text of Scripture to use. There is more knowledge to accompany The Holy Bible. Translations were difficult. We do not talk or read in the manner of The Holy Bible. We have lost concepts in the manner of speaking and writing with our technology. We don't write much anymore. With television, we do not have the experience to relate to and have lost the ability to *form concepts with our own brain*. The Savior has provided other works translated in our day. Those scriptures are The Book of Mormon, The Doctrine and Covenants, and The Pearl of Great Price.

The Savior would tell us not to worry about our dignity or what others are thinking about us now. This is not important now. Grace and dignity will come after individuals cross their Red Sea. It is a trial of faith. The Savior would remind us that we have had to have faith in doctors, lawyers, real estate agents, car salesmen, insurances, unions, stocks, landlords, banks, government officials, utility companies, various industries, and recreational industries. It is time to have faith in the Savior and compare the results.

If animals can acknowledge the master of their lives, humans can, too. We can have faith in our Savior who died so that we might change the things that need changing in our lives. Others will get the same experience when they cross their Red Sea. They will understand then.

Seventh, become familiar with a term called sin. Sin is one of those words we like to avoid, especially when we know we could have done better. Sin is not a four-lettered word. It is a three-lettered word that is overcome with three principles or three bonds to free us.

Christ, the Savior of the World and the Great Physician, died to pay the price so that these bonds are negotiable and priceless for everyone forever. In other words, someone's blood stands behind these bonds, not gold or silver.

The first bond our Savior provided for us in times of trial is *repentance*. Let me define repentance for you. What is the first thing you do if your child comes to you with a wound? Do you bandage it? Do you ignore the wound or cover it, leaving in dirt and debris? Do you cover it with a type of dressing that incubates bacteria in wounds? Of course, the answer is "No" to all of these questions. We clean the wound with clean water, apply some balm, and the wound is bandaged. When the wound is healed, we remove the bandage. This is repentance.

For complete cleansing, some will need to visit with their minister or religious leader, their parents, and spouses. However, repentance will not be complete unless it is done with someone who has the authority to forgive, such as a bishop in The Church of Jesus Christ. We are not going to be better by someone who only has the authority to tell us to forgive, forget, and not feel bad that we are hurting. We need all of the keys or answers to problems in our families.

The second bond is forgiveness for yourself. Many are dealing with severe depression. They have wayward children and wayward spouses in various states of predicaments. They have wayward behavior within themselves. Naturally, mothers blame themselves. They wished they could do more for their children and feel guilty when they cannot.

The third bond is gratitude. Be grateful for what you have. Each individual has problems. Others may feel that you have an attention deficit disorder as well as an addiction. Many people do not have what you have. You have worked hard to have what you have. Be grateful there is a way provided for you to enlarge your borders and feel good about yourself.

Learn how to deal with sin, especially your own sins. We cannot live a mortal life without a liver, kidneys, and intestines. Repentance will be the way that we will eliminate waste from our spirits when we are separated from our bodies at our deaths. Those wasteful things in our spirits do not have to accumulate within us to bear, weigh us down, and make us sick. We do not have to live with regret all of our lives.

Eighth, make righteous judgements. The Savior taught us how to judge.[168] With the same verse, He warned of judging others excessively, harshly, and casting others out. He warned of not taking the time to judge what impact various things, our behavior, and even people would have in our lives.[169] An alcoholic who has killed someone in a drunken driving accident judged not. He went his own way. He did not weigh what impact that first drink would have not only on his life, but on the life of everyone with whom he comes in contact forever. There will many victims of his careless and absent judgement. Naturally, this drunken driver is now going to be judged. He is going to be judged in a manner that he judged. Sadly, for many victims there will be a lack of judging until several offenses have been committed against many victims.

Individuals are overtaken by sins, faults, judgements, and the lack of judgement. Learn the difference by using the SOAP Method. S represents subjective, or what the person complains about. O represents objective, or the things we see or cannot change. A represents analysis, and P represents your plan. More information about judging situations instead of people can be found in the scriptures. Do not make final judgements by the movies you view. There is repentance.

A word of caution. Many times we are being treated how we judged and treated others. We want to blame others, or we feel someone has reported on us. The Holy Ghost has

---

[168]Matthew 7:1-2, The Holy Bible, p. 1197.

[169]Mormon 8:19, The Book of Mormon, p. 482.

147

withdrawn from us. He would be speaking against the Lord's Anointed and God's Anointed by going against the natural order of things. Ministering angels leave for the same reasons the Holy Ghost leaves. It is not attention deficit disorder or attention deficit disorder with hyperactivity. Ministering angels are allowed to judge situations, too.

Ninth, name your price of yourself and the worth of your talents. The Savior has declared His price for us. It is time for you to declare the value of your talents, not just your career, friendships, wants, needs, and desires. Remember. These talents belong to the Savior. What is the talent of the Savior worth? What are your convictions worth? What is the going price for a family?

Make a list of what you would like to see, do, learn about, experience, or change with your talents and with the Savior in your lifetime. Constantly update your list. Some things are only worth doing one time or reading about one time. Now, you are ready to bloom where you are planted. However, it is through righteous judgements that we learn to control our body and our spirits. The body and spirit must work in concert with each other.

Tenth, be aware that others will be uncomfortable with positive changes in you. For every positive change in your life, there will be an equal, opposite or negative change in others. It's a law of chemistry that carries into personal lives, too. This can cause the fear of man and many hurt and guilty feelings. This tells you that you are on the right course.

It is a law of nature that others want to make sure you are committed to this new way of life. They also feel guilty about the things they have not changed in their life. They do not feel so guilty if others are doing the same things with and for them. Misery really does love company, and they won't let their company leave either. Individuals may have to go on alone for awhile. However, this time you will not be alone. The Savior and Holy Ghost and some new friends will be there with you and will he helping and tutoring you along the way.

Stay on course, and in the future you will be able to help your family and friends help themselves. They need to see that you are committed and that change works. You may be their only source of help in the future. It will be a great blessing to be able to help others and know that you can be a source of pleasure not pain once again.

Eleventh, ask for a blessing. This blessing comes from two elders or two high priests of The Church of Jesus Christ of Latter-day Saints. Individuals do not have to be a member of The Church of Jesus Christ of Latter-day Saints for this blessing. All that is required is your faith.[170]

Twelfth, a Lamb has been prepared for you, just as was prepared for Isaac, son of Abraham. Many parents and children, spouses, and friends are feeling like Isaac did when his hands were tied. The Lord provided Himself a lamb for Abraham so he did not have to sacrifice, his son, Isaac. Abraham was able to untie his son's hands. The lamb was sacrificed in place of Isaac.[171] Parents do not have to sacrifice themselves or their son or daughter either. The Lamb has taught us how to untie our own hands and the hands of our children with prayer.

Many diseases are caused by wayward behavior. Here are a few examples. Alcoholism leads to cirrhosis of the liver and affects every organ of the body. Smoking leads to emphysema

---

[170]Matthew 17:20-21, The Holy Bible, p. 1217.

[171]Genesis 22:1-13, The Holy Bible, p. 31.

and various cancers. Drug addiction has painful ups and downs as the patient has access to his or her drug of choice. The method of choice leads to hepatitis and AIDS. Adultery leads to syphilis, gonorrhea, herpes, hepatitis, and AIDS. Excessive worry over loved ones with these behaviors leads to ulcers, heart attacks, strokes, fibromyalgia, cancer, diabetes, and arthritis.

These conditions and behaviors make one feel like an Isaac with his or her hands tied for forever and no way of getting loose. These things result in helplessness, anger, depression and thoughts of suicide for the victim and the victimizer.[172] If you feel like Isaac felt, this is not attention deficit disorder or attention deficit disorder with hyperactivity. You are without hope.

To all of you Isaacs out there. A Lamb was prepared for you, too. If everyone can get pass the word sin, the word repent, and the "Thou shalt not's," there are many messages of comfort and love provided for the many Isaac's of this world. My favorite is:

7 Have ye any that are sick among you? Bring them hither. Have ye any that are lame, or blind, or halt, or maimed, or leprous, or that are withered, or that are deaf, or that are afflicted in any manner? Bring them hither and I will heal them, for I have compassion upon you; my bowels are filled with mercy.

3 Nephi 17:7, The Book of Mormon

Lastly, many addicts get in trouble with the law and are assigned to weekly classes. They are taught in these classes the many defense mechanisms that we use to justify partaking of illegal drugs and alcohol and endangering others and ourselves.

These defense mechanisms are not the weaknesses that will make you stronger. These defense mechanisms are your spirit crying. This is how you learn how to discern your own cries for help and can recognize cries for help in others. If we do not help ourselves or ignore our cries for help, we usually get bolder (aggressive). Bolder does not mean stronger. We are actually becoming weaker, or we would not have to be so bold. There is no way to become assertive (positive) with defense mechanisms.

I learned the same information in a college communication class. My instructor had us write out conversations with people and identify the principle that each participant was using with each statement. It was a difficult class because we could not identify the principles of communication. Experience has taught me that defense mechanisms are the principles of communication. The defense mechanisms which we use to cover our anxiety, shame, and guilt, and lack of self-confidence with others are the principles of communication in our lives. With defense mechanisms, we cannot guarantee that the correct message was sent or received.

Our weakness for mercy, love, faith, forgiveness, justice, endurance, etc. are our weak areas that will become strong. We will become humble and have some of the graces that the Savior learned. We do not have to endure with addictions and alcoholism.

Write out some conversations with your children. Discuss the principle behind your communications. It took me years to figure out that my college instructors were trying to teach me the gift of tongues. It is a gift to be able to communicate with others. Do you want to

---

[172]Mormon 2:14, The Book of Mormon, p. 471.

communicate that you are sad and hurting all the time? One look, and people know if you are happy, sad, or mad. My instructor as yours, were trying to teach me how to communicate what I wanted to communicate. More importantly, she taught me how to discern that my message sent was or was not received. She taught me to communicate peace to my patients.

There are other ways to relax your mind and body without breaking the law of our land. Learn them. This information may save your life, your family's lives, and the lives of others. Go to your classes and participate with an open mind. There are many more defense mechanisms now. However, there is another world out there for you. You do not need them.

Stop here. Do you have any parents or children in your family who are lame, blind, crippled, leprous, withered, deaf, spiritually as well as physically? Are these handicaps a result of physical disabilities, faults, and/or sins? Are you aware that you can train your brain and slow those racing thoughts down with journals? As you learn to write, your brain follows the pattern and speed of your writing. Eventually, your speech will follow the pace of your writing.

How does each member of your family or step family magnify their distress? How does each member of your family magnify their calling as a parent, step parent, son, daughter, step son, step daughter, sister, brother, step sister, step brother, grandparent and step grandparent? Learn the difference between magnifying distress and magnifying your calling.

How does each member of your step family take peace and order from the home? Is their behavior a result of an addiction? Learn the difference between addictions caused by problems and addictions requiring energy boosters. Addicted family members usually have both types of addictions–psychological and physical dependence. Mother and father, will your child have to resort to an addictive energy booster to keep up the pace you have set between sports, vacations, and homework? Is this why your child blames you for his addiction? Is this why there are so many teenagers using drugs? Children get tired.

Parent	*Teenager*	*Communication Principle*
Son, we want you to come in earlier. You are waking us up, and Dad has to work.	*This is my day off. I want to spend it with my friends. I am almost twenty,*	*Puberty and menopause do not mix.* *Apathy to others' needs*
We are older parents, and we need our sleep to function well the next day.	*Function well! You should take a look at yourself.*	*By projection, he has switched the conversation to my behavior. It is now my fault, not his.*
We are concerned that you might get hurt or into trouble after midnight.	*I am just with my friends. I will stay over night with them.*	*Fixation–same response, different day*
Your friends' parents have to work, too. It will be disturbing to them, too.	*Their parents' do not care if we stay up late.*	*Fantasy; Aggressive.*

Chapter Twenty-Two

Your Cold, Failing Heart

When we examine the last layer of attention deficit disorders, we discover many of the difficulties with attention deficit disorders are caused by a form of cardiomyopathy. I call this condition spiritual cardiomyopathy. Spiritual cardiomyopathy comes from a cold, failing heart which is enlarged with pride, power, and passion. Our hearts fail over all the commotions of the Earth that never cease to plague us. (Doctrine and Covenants 45:26)

Cardiomyopathy. Cardiomyopathy in your heart in your physical body is known as an enlarged heart. Enlarged hearts gradually become paper-thin. In some types of cardiomyopathy, the walls of the chambers are stiffer than normal. Though the heart is enlarged, the heart cannot pump sufficient blood to circulate to all of the various organ systems in the body. One chamber tries to do the work of all four chambers. The heart cannot receive blood since it is pumping out poorly. The blood receives less oxygen as fluid accumulates in the lungs. The heart beat becomes irregular. Other organs try to perform tasks the heart is unable to do to preserve a heart beat and blood flow to the organs. Blood pressure is elevated and then becomes low with the many medications required to ease the work of the heart and help the heart beat stronger. Other body organs become engorged, overworked, and under-oxygenated. These organs cannot perform their tasks.

Enlarged hearts lead to congestive heart failure. The digestive and vascular systems become engorged with fluid which the kidneys cannot eliminate. Often, you can see the level of congestion in distended neck veins and edema in the feet and ankles. The heart enlarges to compensate for the excess fluid in the heart. High blood pressure, coronary heart disease, previous heart attacks, valve damage, drugs and chemicals, alcoholism, viral or bacterial infections, and excessive stress are some of the causes of enlarged hearts.

Patients with failing hearts cannot perform simple tasks. They experience shortness of breath with the slightest of exertion and are cold all of the time. Their thinking is affected by lack of oxygen and fear. They do not have energy to organize and carry out a plan of action.

Spiritual Cardiomyopathy. Spiritual cardiomyopathy is strikingly similar to cardiomyopathy. Our spiritual hearts do not pump properly. The pump of a spiritual heart is a broken or tamed heart and a contrite spirit. Our spiritual systems cannot drain properly through repentance. Excess guilt, shame, and sorrow accumulate. Many fears accompany these emotions. As our hearts become hardened, the systems that stimulate the spiritual heart beat are interrupted or become non-existent. Hearts become engorged with ambition, rage, pride, lies, and weapons of rebellion which affect how well the entire physical body and spiritual mind work together. Our many spiritual systems do not receive adequate nourishment. There is no room to breath and no spiritual nourishment to grow. The normal pathways which affects how well we perform our tasks are not developed. We become depressed and angry and try other things to compensate for the way we perform daily tasks and control our fears.

151

Treatment of Spiritual Cardiomyopathy. Individuals with spiritual cardiomyopathy often turn down the simple things which alleviate or prevent spiritual cardiomyopathy. They have the right to refuse treatment and find alternative methods. They demand mercy for themselves and justice for others. These individuals want others to do their tasks for them and have learned to stall until they do. If others do not do their tasks, they must pay and pay dearly. Individuals with spiritual cardiomyopathy will forgive if it is profitable for them to forgive, but they will never forget. They do not need to drain their soul. Others do. They certainly do not need to be under the care of the Great Physician. He is too expensive and His ideas too strange.

Learning by Trial and Error. As a result, individuals with cardiomyopathy must learn by trial and error. They want others to learn by trial and error, too. Everyone usually learns by some trial and error. After a lot of embarrassment, inconvenience, and debt, we usually do not want to make the same mistakes twice.

However, adults and children with an attention deficit disorder are not learning by trial and error. Why? Their parents and step parents may be trying to learn solely by trial and error. Parents and step parents may minimize their mistakes and the mistakes of their children too much. If adults cannot keep up the pace that the false doctrines of the world has set for us, children and step children are not going to be able to keep up the pace of a pile of mistakes either. Learning by experience in a variety of things is often just learning by trial and error.

I suspect the following verse explains why we and our children are not learning from our mistakes. Denial or minimizing our mistakes does not make our mistakes go away.

> *But behold, there are many that harden their hearts against the Holy Spirit,*
> *that it hath no place in them; wherefore, they cast many things away which*
> *are written and esteem them as things of naught.*

2 Nephi 33:2, The Book of Mormon

In other words, paying attention, interrupting others, falling behind in work, poor performances, following through, not waiting their turn, listening, being unorganized, being a self-starter, etc. is not important. If there are no standards in your home, then these things are not errors. What your children want to do or focus on is important–movies and video games.

Many people feel that grace is going to save them in spite of what they do to others and themselves. This is not working. There is only grace for some–and a very few at that. Grace has not saved us from adults with an attention deficit disorder who are charging outrageous prices for food, gas, utilities, shelter, and medical care. We are forced to live in others' sins, or God's children commit sins to make a living for themselves.

Grace is not working for parents and our children. Learning by trial and error is not working. Living without standards is not working. So where does a parent and step parent start in helping your child overcome his or her behavior? We begin with the parents and step parents of the world. They arouse their faculties by experimenting on the Savior's words which are standards that are fair. These standards do not change. (Alma 32:27, The Book of Mormon)

The teachers of our children's heart are parents, not idols. In His Plan of Salvation for us, the Lord determined who the teachers of the hearts of His children would be. His children would be raised and taught in families by parents. Step parents would join this family–just like His own father, Joseph of Bethlehem. Honoring our parents is included in the Ten Commandments. This keeps us and our parents and step parents from becoming neither root nor branch. How severely we dishonor our parents and step parents determines how much we become neither root nor branch. We become depressed.

Parents and step parents are the teachers because they have been given the responsibility to develop their children's hearts–not just physically, but emotionally, intellectually, financially, morally, spiritually, socially, and by service, persistence, work, and sacrifice. Like the Savior, parents know more about their children's hearts. Parents spend the most time with their children. They know the efforts that children and step children can make. Parents and step parents are to teach their children how to survive in the temporal and spiritual world that exists around them because parents and step parents extend mercy to their children. No one else does. Many of our children's idols have cold hearts and will teach your child how to have a cold heart.

There is a gentleness and a meekness that comes when a child allows parents and step parents to impart of their wisdom to them, and the child builds on this wisdom. This will increase gradually. There is a gentleness and peace that comes to a child when a child no longer views his parents and step parents as stupid, ugly, clumsy barriers to their happiness. There is a gentleness and meekness that comes to parents and step parents when they are able to teach their children. Parents and step parents cannot make up for the missed years of this kind of a parental education in themselves or their children and step children. This education is priceless. It is an education that will rise with us when we discard those mortal degrees for an eternal degree.

When a child is not willing to be taught by his parents, he or she takes agency from parents. The battles between parent and child take agency from the entire family, your community, and our nation. This determines the choices which parents and step parents can make for their children and step children and the kinds of choices our community and national leaders make for their citizens. The battles between parent and child take agency from our Heavenly Father. He is forced to withdraw blessings that He has accumulated for us.

Prepare for the time when your child or step child wants to be taught by his parents or step parents. This time will come. It may be in a brief visit, a few questions, or on the other side of the veil. Learn the things that parents should teach children which have substance. Teaching them about sports and camping will not help children when they are suffering from depression, suicidal thoughts, drug addiction, a death, or a divorce in the family, or they cannot play sports due to disease and disability.

Provide a Spiritual Education. If you do not want your child to have a cold heart, teach your children of the Lord. Many parents and step parents started this when the child was young. Don't stop just because your child is now learning a temporal education. There is a Savior. We have been forced to give up the Ten Commandments and prayer by individuals who could not reconcile with the Savior. So what is next? Do we have to give up the Lord's Prayer and His great Intercessory Prayer for us?

Many children complain that parents and step parent did not give them any self-esteem. Your child's self-esteem will come from his spiritual education. Adults and children have to make an effort with their spiritual education if they want self-esteem. This spiritual education will save parents and step parents much frustration when children are blaming you for not giving them self-esteem. If parents and step parents did not provide a spiritual education, parents and step parents did not provide their children enough self-esteem. (See page 182.)

Peace comes to our children when they are taught of the Lord. Peace comes to us as children learn about the Lord precept by precept, line upon line. Again, to obtain peace, children must make some effort. We all reap what we sow. Children will, too, especially if they are over the age of eight years of age.

> *And all thy children shall be taught of the LORD; and great shall be the*
> *peace of thy children.*
> *Isaiah 54:13, <u>The Holy Bible</u>*

Return to Church. If you want a college education, you go to college. If you want eternal truths taught to your children and step children, you will have to take your children and step children to church. Parents and step parents pay tithes and offering to be enrolled in their church. This is an implied contract. If families do these truths, there are blessings for them. Find a church that uses all the eternal truths instead of one that omits truths so they can accommodate rich paying patrons. We would not pay to go to a college who did this.

Repeat the principles and blessing you learn at church to your family on a day sat aside for you to be together. The Church of Jesus Christ calls this day Family Home Evening. Share your knowledge and experiences. Eternal truths cannot be learned by a moment of silence in the wilderness. Wilderness training will not help your child when his or her spouse is ill or their spouse or child has passed away.

John, the Revelator, told us: "And ye shall know the truth, and the truth shall make you free. (John 8:32) John the Revelator saw the world from the beginning to the end. He saw how sin is cumbersome and restricting. He saw how sin limits our growth and potential and how sin constricts and hardens our hearts. John the Revelator saw that the Savior and His teachings free us spiritually from the bondage of sin. We would do well to follow his teachings.

Teach the Children. The Savior has asked us to be pure in heart instead of stubborn of heart and cold-hearted. Thus, there must be a way to eliminate the stubbornness, (unyielding behavior), our hardheartedness, (lacking compassion), and our foolishness, (lacking good sense), in our spiritual hearts and the spiritual hearts of our children and step children. The removal of these yokes come from our spiritual education. We experiment on His words and plant spiritual seeds. These spiritual seeds swell, sprout, and begin to grow. This is how we know the seed is good. (Alma 32:33, <u>The Book</u> of <u>Mormon</u>) Which seeds will eliminate stubbornness, hardheartedness, and foolishness? What would be the label on this seed packet? I suspect this seed packet will be labeled "The Weightier Matters of the Law." With this seed packet, we will never be starved spiritually.

Teach the Weightier Matters of the Law. The weightier matters of the law teach judgement, mercy, and faith. (Matthew 23:23) Adults and children with attention deficit disorders lack judgement, mercy, and faith. With the weightier matters of the law, we learn how to apply our temporal and spiritual education to our life's experiences. We learn when justice and mercy are needed. We learn to speak peacefully and use the principles of mathematics and science to everyone's benefit. We learn good common sense.

Weightier matters of the law, your foundation, teach the first principles of the gospel. The first principles will be the building blocks for all the good in your children's life. Your child will learn faith when his prayers are answered. We will not repent if we do not know how to pray. Repentance is our spiritual drainage system. If we will not repent, we cannot drain the soul. Your child and you must carry around unnecessary layers of stress and attention deficit disorders that have accumulated over the years. Your child and you can learn to love God with all his heart and love his neighbor as his self with the weightier matters of the law and learn how to make judgements at the same time.

The following scriptures provide a list of some of the weightier matters of the law. These weightier matters will give our spiritual hearts a good work-out. There is a Comforter who sets our pace while gaining these kinds of expertise.

And their children shall be baptized for the remission of their sins when eight years old, and receive the laying on of the hands.
And they shall also teach their children to pray, and to walk uprightly before the Lord.
And the inhabitants of Zion shall also observe the Sabbath day to keep it holy.
And the inhabitants of Zion also shall remember their labors, inasmuch as they are appointed to labor, in all faithfulness; for the idler shall be had in remembrance before the Lord.
Now, I, the Lord, am not well pleased with the inhabitants of Zion, for there are idlers among them; and their children are also growing up in wickedness; they also seek not earnestly the riches of eternity, but their eyes are full off greediness.

Doctrine and Covenants 68:27 - 31

And by them their children were taught to read and write, having a language which was pure and undefiled.
Moses 6:6, The Pearl of Great Price

And they were preachers of righteousness, and spake and prophesied, and called upon all men, everywhere, to repent; and faith was taught unto the children of men.

Moses 6:23, The Pearl of Great Price

Provide a Temporal Education. Children and step children need to learn how to get along in this world. They need to be taught traffic safety, food safety, stranger safety, how to cook, sew, plant, and harvest a crop as well as reading, writing, mathematics, language skills, and history. Children need to learn how to keep working when they are sad as well as when they are happy. They need to learn a trade to support them and their future family.

School changes our children. I suspect that what is changing our children's hearts is the things that we are teaching our children–either as a parent, step parent, in the schools, or as a nation. Since schools are receiving state and federal money, schools now have to accommodate every philosophy known to man because all children and their parents have their rights. As a result, our children our tossed to and fro between many false doctrines. With so many ideas and causes floating around the schools, children have no real main idea to focus on. As a result, there is a lack of enthusiasm for learning by both teacher and child. Even the adults do not focus on education. They focus on philosophies and sports. Sports receives more money than homework and teachers. Teachers try to obtain the attention of children with sports stars.

The atmosphere is intense at school. Swearing and bulling by children are prevalent in schools. Instead of being united as a school, there is much positioning for power and popularity. It amazes me how much security we have to have in schools to keep children from harming other children in school. The children and we parents and step parents put up with this. Parents and step parents receive the blame for the lack of progress in children and step children. Parents and step parents pay heavily for this lack of progress in our property taxes.

No one learns when they are being insulted or constantly tempted. No one learns when there are no standards. The best rocket scientist would not learn basic arithmetic if he was fearful all day of being beat up at school and at home afterward, and there were no standards to learn. Of course, if students do not want other students to learn because they want customers in their drug business, this works wonders. Many parents do not like to face it, but they have children selling drugs in school to make money, and they make lots of money. The children may even be working in their family drug business just like other family businesses. Children feel they do not need to go to the trouble of an education. They only need customers. Their customers have to feel terrible about themselves in order to keep buying drugs.

To compensate for this lack of peace in our schools, parents and step parents have to provide a peaceful environment in their homes. More and more parents are home schooling their children. If you do not home school, I suggest you buy the books that home schools use.

Since schools will not let books come home, and you cannot depend on children to bring homework home, I recommend purchasing a GED book for yourselves and your children. In order to teach children, adults need to learn the basics of education themselves. A General Education Diploma book explains things better. It is a great book to send off to college with your college student. If you have a child with an attention deficit disorder, he may quit school and have to take the GED test for a diploma. Keep in mind. If you get 100 percent on this test, this is only an eighth grade education. If you keep a GED book in your home, parents have the material that can be copied for repetitive use. Adults can review the material before they take those employment tests for job advancement. I got my book at a library sale for 25 cents.

Your child's intellectual development is dependent on the basics of an elementary education. Your child's identity and personality are dependent on both a temporal education and a spiritual education. A child receives an F if he only does fifty-percent of the work. A temporal education without a spiritual education is fifty percent of the work.

Parents and step parents are working. They will contract out some of the things that develop their children's physical bodies, personalities, and identities. Coaches and schools are an example. Parents have paid money to enroll their child on a team or in a school. Many parents are willing to support the team and coach. They are not willing to support the teacher in the same manner. When joining a team or a school, there is an implied contract that the parent and child will do certain things that the coach or teacher asks. If the parent only follows through with the coach and not the teacher, this tells the child that school is not important.

Repetition. Teaching children how to acquire a broken or tamed heart and contrite spirit with a spiritual and temporal education will require a lot of repetition. There is no ten-second rule in learning concepts that will be with us for eternity. Our efforts, our identity, and our dignity will be determined by what concepts we were willing to learn and experience in this life.

Much of your child's inattentive, impulsive behavior is a result of the kinds of choices your child repeatedly makes for himself. The kinds of choices that parents repeatedly make for their children may increase their child's attention deficit disorders. Your children will make their choices from the things that are repeated over and over at home and at school. Unfortunately, hostility and recess are the things that are repeated over and over at school by peers and at home by family members. Life was not meant to remain at the kindergarten level. If you recall your kindergarten days, children had frequent recesses and play time because five year old and six year old children have short attention spans. They became frustrated easily, too.

We have been given agency, the freedom to choose for ourselves what concepts we will learn. This freedom was given to us to choose good over evil. This is how we sprout, bloom, produce, harvest, and preserve our fruits. Agency was not given to us to choose between evil, more evil, and most evil. This is how our fruit falls prematurely to the ground by the winds of the world and in our homes. There is no opposition for learning to take place. Your child needs to see that families function better with repeated love instead of repeated hostility in their homes. Repeated recesses will not make up for repeated hostility in your homes.

To prevent a cold, failing heart, our children must turn their hearts to their fathers. Fathers must turn their hearts to their children.[173] Parents and step parents may provide the best spiritual and temporal education for their children and step children. Hearts still must be turned to children and to fathers. This begins with our biological fathers, includes our ancestors back to the time of Adam, and includes our Heavenly Father and Jesus Christ.

Turning the hearts to fathers and to children is not limited to genealogy. There are many aspects to this responsibility. In our day and age, we call turning the hearts of fathers to children and children to fathers bonding. Elijah the prophet may oversee this work in the kingdom. We are responsible to develop the binding love between fathers and children. Turning our hearts to family develops feelings of softness and mercy between parent and child. Bonding occurs with acts of sacrifice, mercy, and love. Many siblings, divorced parents, and grandparents will not allow this bonding and feelings of mercy to happen. Punishing fathers and their spouses and taking the possessions of their fathers has turned their heads and their personalities. We are affecting many generations and many nationalities of mankind if we do not develop forgiveness and mercy for the many children of our Heavenly Father. We are affecting families and step families adversely if we do not allow children and step children to develop mercy and forgiveness for their fathers. Our salvation is affected for we are forgiven as we forgive.

One of the signs this softness is developing between parent and child is the assignment and performance of household chores. Parents and step parents are going to assign chores. They expect chores to be done. If the child refuses to obey, parents doubt their children's affection for them. Parents and step parents doubt many other things about their children, especially their ability to stay on task. Parents become angry and assign more burdensome

---

[173]Malachi 4:5-6, The Holy Bible, p. 1184; Doctrine and Covenants 2:1-3, p. 5.

chores. Even the Savior said: "If ye love me, keep my commandments." (John 14:15) He added: "If you keep not my commandments, the love of the Father shall not continue with you, therefore you shall walk in darkness." (Doctrine and Covenants 95:12)

Household chores are an issue in households. Children and even adults do not like to do them. Children will check to see if chores are assigned fairly. They will become stubborn and hard-hearted if one sibling is shown favoritism, especially by a step parent. It does not take rocket science understanding to know that if parents are working several jobs, household chores and yard work still need to be done by someone. Children usually think that if you are working three or more jobs, parents can pay well for the chores. Be fair with your child or step child. Do not give them assignments that an adult would be overwhelmed to fulfill. A yard full of weeds is not going to be pulled in one hour or one evening. It will take many individuals many days working at this job. Break the yard down into sections. Assign sections. Have a contest with a reward. My husband made yard work more pleasant by cooking a meat dish and a cobbler nearby in Dutch ovens. I could help out because I did not have dinner to prepare and dishes facing me. Out of respect to my step son and grandsons, I did not expect them to do things in the yard that my husband had difficulty doing.

When I was trying to do homework with my children I should have used the same method as my husband. I should have baked bread or a cake or something while we were trying to learn. The smell of bread or cookies or a cake baking often keeps children home. By small things, great things come to pass. (Alma 37:6, The Book of Mormon) Box mixes are not as nutritious nor do they taste the same.

If you decide to ground your child because he has not done his chores, you are grounded. If your child loses a privilege because he did not do his chores, it does not help to entertain him in other ways. Your child does not have to learn follow through if you are rewarding him for not doing chores and homework. Have him do these things instead of the fun thing he planned. Some things even chores and homework has to wait.

When adults are sick, children should be taught where they can take over. They can take over cooking simple meals for the family, doing dishes, tending younger children, and housework. Children have to be taught how to do these things if you want them to give you a hand without being commanded. When you are sick is not the most opportune time to be trying to teach children how to do household chores. When children begin to do household chores, cook simple meals, and do yard work for parents and step parents to assist their parents and step parents, they are beginning to turn their hearts to their fathers and mothers. When parents and step parents realize that children need care and order in their home and conscientiously try to provide this, they are turning their hearts to their children.

Remember. Without this concern between parent and child, the Lord will smite the Earth with a curse. The Savior would not curse the earth because someone did not look up birth and death dates for their family and do their temple work. There are too many who are related and who are willing to do this work. They, of course, will receive the blessings of staying with this task, especially if they have performed this work in the correct manner.

I suspect, the Savior would curse the earth if children take free agency from their parents and step parents and their children and step children. He would curse the Earth if parents gave up their agency to take accountability from children. He would curse the earth if parents and children were not willing to forgive each other when either or both had repented. The Savior would curse the earth if parent and child had no mercy for each other. He died for everyone to develop personal agency, not just their children's agency. The Savior atoned for our mistakes so everyone would have mercy while they were fine tuning their agency as an adult.

To help children avoid developing a cold heart, teach your children the proper ways to make and keep promises. In Doctrine and Covenants 2:2, we learn that some how Elijah the prophet shall plant in the hearts of the children the promises they made to the fathers. From this, we learn that children and step children have made promises to their fathers. Elijah is the planter of these promises. We are the gardeners or the keepers of the promises made to our fathers. The many promises made to our fathers and our children will return to our memories.

We do not know how well we knew our fathers before us. Most of us know our Earthly fathers and grandfathers. We have promised things to our Earthly Fathers. Our Heavenly Father and Jesus Christ know us well enough to know our hearts so we must have known them, too. We knew them all well enough to make promises to them.

If Elijah is assigned to this work, it must be important. There also must be a way to teach children how to keep promises instead of teaching children how to escape the promises made to parents and step parents.

The Lord teaches through covenants. Covenants are promises. Covenants and promises are similar. Covenants are more solemn and formal than a promise. There are Earthly promises, known as contracts. Fulfillment of contracts is a fulfillment of an obligation. Both are legal binding arrangements between parties.

Children and step children under the age of eighteen cannot make binding contracts. This is to protect the buyer and the seller, especially the parent and child. Children can be taken advantage with inferior merchandise. There are children who have no intention of keeping the contracts they make.

Covenants are also known as commandments. I find it interesting that spiritually, a child is accountable to God at the age of eight. With his parent's permission, a child can make a covenant with Heavenly Father to take upon himself or herself the name of Jesus Christ and keep commandments. The child can be baptized. Why the difference? In Earthly contracts, there is no mercy if the child falls behind. In a Heavenly contract, there is mercy and forgiveness of the debt by repentance. If the child makes a mistake, he does not have to live with guilt and shame all his life. Most debts are forgiven if the child is taught and uses the proper steps of repentance.

I also find it interesting that both our Heavenly Father and the Savior subdue their fruits through covenants, a formal agreement with God to do or not do something. For example, the Savior was baptized before He began his ministry. Our Heavenly Father has a lot of children to bless. We may not be A students, but we continue to bloom with every covenant and promise we keep with our Heavenly Father. There must be more to this than just one covenant of baptism. I suspect parents and step parents subdue their children by teaching them the proper way to make and keep promises, covenants, and temporal contracts.

From my experience in making and keeping covenants with our Heavenly Father, I have noticed there are steps in keeping promises: spiritually able to make promise, promise made, principle behind the promise, feelings of obligation to keep promise, blessings for keeping

159

promises, wisdom learned, and stature gained. I may not understand the promise I made or the principle behind the promise, but I get a definite feeling of obligation. This is why we were given a conscience. The understanding comes when I receive the blessings and wisdom for keeping a covenant. The blessings of stature I can feel. This stature neither moth nor rust can corrupt. Thieves cannot break through and steal this stature from me. I do not have to be fidgety, inattentive, and impulsive all day or month long because I was distraught over making and not keeping particular covenants. I do not have to worry what people were thinking of me.

If your child is a poor keeper of promises, parents and step parents, children and step children may be eliminating the steps in the covenant-keeping and promise-making process. To fresh your memory, those steps are: mentally able to make promise, promise made, principle behind the promise, feelings of obligation to keep promise, blessings for keeping promises, wisdom learned, and stature gained. When your child makes a promise to you, make sure he understand the principle behind the promise. Do not give him the blessings or rewards for keeping promises when he does not keep promises. Notice how long your child acts guilty and what measures he uses to avoid keeping his promises. Notice the distractions that he uses. In the future, gather those distractions up. (Game systems, cell phones, IPODs, MP3 Players) Children know how to stall well. Children like to push your buttons. They get out of keeping promises by being forced to spend time in time-out. Try time-out after the promise is kept.

Children must know they are accountable at age eight. Give them things to do at their level which children can make and keep promises. Gradually increase the level of difficulty and time required to increase their attention span. Teach your children the difference between logical and illogical promises. Children make promises without thinking. Their promises were what father and mother and peers wanted to hear. Their false promises got children out of trouble or shortened a lecture. The promises of children sound good until they see the amount of work and time involved. Have compassion so your child will make other promises to you.

Children will copy parents in how they fulfill Earthly contracts and covenants. Be wise. Do not make illogical promises that parents cannot keep. Don't whine while you keep your promises. Give your child a chance to tell you what he can perform logically in the amount of time you give him.

Your child may have said he was sorry many times before for broken promises. However, he is not refraining from breaking promises. The steps of repentance are not complete. I suspect other acts of repentance are not complete. Former sins are returned. (Doctrine and Covenants 82:7) This is why your child is so fidgety, impulsive, inattentive, and aggressive, etc. He or she is bearing the burden of many acts of misbehavior. Parents just do not know all of them, but we can see them in their countenance and behavior.

Evaluate the Traditions of Your Fathers. The traditions of our fathers affect many things in our lives such as the food we eat and drink, how we spend our time, our talents, which church we belong to, the location where we live, the kind of schooling we receive, our hobbies, and our occupations. Usually, we relieve stressful situations like our fathers did. I suspect that the kinds of sins we have are a result of the traditions of our fathers. We copy what we see. We are told that the iniquity of the fathers will be upon the children unto the third and fourth generation of them that hate me. (Exodus 20:5) Your fathers had agency, a period of time to develop their identities, and a time to discard their sins in this life. You do, too. You are accountable for the development of your agency, not the development of the agency of your fathers. There will be conflict when children want to bloom differently than their Earthly father.

Many of the incorrect traditions of our fathers are centered around holidays. Holidays in the past were created to remember family, deceased family members, and the Savior. In this day, holidays have been created for us to have time to travel. These are retailer holidays supposedly to help our economy. After all the preparations and anticipation, we are too tired to think of anyone. Meanwhile, you and your budget are paralyzed by an incorrect tradition of your father and your favorite retailer. We are teaching our children to be idle and then we complain when they are idle.

When I was young, one two-week vacation in the year was the norm. We looked forward to this all year long. In this day and age, people like to travel. Many vacations are planned throughout the year. Everyone says it's a tradition to do this with family and friends every holiday. It takes weeks of planning, preparing, and paying for these frequent trips. It is a lot of work for the mothers of the world. Fathers work hard for the money often in the heat or the cold of the day. Mother has to worry how to provide the money for this trip out of her budget. Frequent trips affect the energy level of parent and child at the very minimum of a week before the trip and a week after the trip.

When I tried to do the things my father was doing, I noticed it was hard to get my grand children back on track even though we had a great time together. Their excitement before the trip affected their attention span. The large amount of fatty food and carbonated drinks did not help either. They were too tired to work on homework. I was too tired to help them after the trip. We missed important things on Sunday, too. I could not ground my grandchildren because they knew we were going on another trip soon. Children do not have to keep their grades up all year long. They do not have to be courteous and productive. Whether the child keeps his promises to his parents or not does not matter. The family is still going on another trip next week or next month with parents and step parents.

We decided to eliminate some family traditions that were really "retailer traditions." I evaluated other family traditions. We took our children and grandchildren to church. We had more energy, and we were not so broke. We taught our children the ways to achieve peace and financial stability in their lives with the light and truths of the gospel of Jesus Christ. You will have to evaluate your family traditions, too, to increase your own potential and the potential of your children. Children may not accept these truths, but parents have taught peaceful methods to their children. This is a stress reducer. Parents will be tried and tested in these truths along with children. Don't quit. You find things within yourself that you are not aware that you have when you overcome these tests.

Families are not meant to be "jet set families." The great work that we have to do with families will be in our own homes. This work is not family recess. This work is educating our families so they can educate their families. Individuals have developed many ideas to lure people away from their homes into excessive travel. There are many who feel that if you can afford to travel, you can afford to pay the many expenses of travel. Thus, travel is expensive. Hotel rooms are taxed. Gas and food prices are outrageous. Alcohol and drugs and other unsavory things are available as services to the traveler. You may not participate, but your children see these things.

161

There is a rule of thumb for the traditions of our fathers. Correct traditions do not take agency, the way of achieving things, from parent and child, step parent and step child. There is room for both to grow. Our fathers' traditions should not cause our fruits to fall prematurely to the ground. The traditions of our fathers should not pull up the seeds that parents have planted in their children.

> *And that wicked one cometh and taketh away light and truth, through disobedience,*
> *from the children of men, and because of the tradition of their fathers.*
> *But I have commanded you to bring up your children in light and truth.*

<u>Doctrine and Covenants</u> 93:39 - 40

Heart Trouble in God's Children. Patients and parents of patients hate to hear that anything is wrong with their heart or the heart of their child. They feel helpless. Heart trouble is expensive to fix and to maintain. Heart patients want to know what caused their heart trouble. Was it something they were born with or something they did? They want to know "why me?"

The Lord hates heart trouble in His children, especially spiritual heart trouble. The Lord states there are seven things which He hates. I suspect he hates these things because these things develop a cold, failing heart and attention deficit disorders in His children. These things certainly do not develop a broken heart and contrite spirit. His children will not turn their hearts to their fathers. One of their fathers died for them. An Earthly mother nearly died for them. These are the things which many children and adults do, resulting in spiritual cardiomyopathy.

> *¶ These six things doth the LORD hate: yea, seven are an abomination unto him:*
> *A proud look, a lying tongue, and hands that shed innocent blood,*
> *An heart that deviseth wicked imaginations, feet that be swift in running to mischief,*
> *A false witness that speaketh lies, and he that soweth discord among brethren.*

Proverbs 6:16 - 19, <u>The Holy Bible</u>

Parents and step parents hate these things, too. Just do not hate your child or step child. This will consume you. This is not the type of consumer that you want to be. I know that parents and step parents do many things for their children. Their children still develop cold, failing hearts instead of a broken heart and a contrite spirit. They develop many secret combinations to carry out their behaviors. It feels like your many sacrifices are wasted.

The behaviors described in the verses in Proverbs 6:16-19 cause much contention in your home. Your child's deceptions wear on the emotions of parents and step parents. Order in the home cannot be achieved. Parents and step parents particularly want to know how not to be victimized by their children's and step children's cold, failing heart. Parents and step parents also want to know how to change their child's or step child's heart.

First, do not treat distractions with more distractions. Excessive recreation and sports will not help your child turn from this behavior. Excessive recreation and sports becomes just another way to control parents and step parents. More than likely, your child has to keep misbehaving to keep the excessive sports and recreation coming. Parents and step parents cannot use recreation as a reward for good behavior. Your child knows there are always other vacations or outings. Children do their destructive behaviors when you are having fun together.

Second, parents and step parents, notice what false doctrines of the world that your child is falling for. Notice how your child or step child absorbs the false doctrines of the world. Your children have difficulty accepting and performing the true doctrines that parents and step parents try to teach their children. They easily absorb the false doctrines. I suspect your child has too much exposure to the false doctrines of the world and too less exposure to truth. Your child learns what he is exposed to. Expose more truths of this world than false doctrines. These truths come from the Savior and prophets. Parents must be able to detect false doctrines.

Third, learn how to compel your children. Compel means to cause a person to act or move in spite of resistance. This does not have to be done in a very aggressive manner. (negative) Parents and step parents can do this in an assertive manner. (positive) This is not a new concept. In our day, we call this type of learning–child psychology.

The Savior was teaching us child psychology when He told us "to resist not evil." The more you resist your child's evil behavior, the more they will cling to their evil ways. Parents feel they must punish harshly to get children to refrain from their evil behavior. If we do not resist evil, parents and step parents will not discipline their children in an eye for an eye, and a tooth for a tooth manner. Eye for an eye methods increase hostility instead of relieve hostility.

The Savior added that whosoever smites (hits or cause suffering) on the right cheek, turn to him the other cheek. (Matthew 5:38 - 39) It is illegal for children to beat parents and step parents and for parents and step parents to beat children on their face. The parent will be taking the sins of their children upon their heads if they become abusive to a distracted, impulsive child. So what was the Savior trying to teach us about that elusive, other cheek? Was He telling us to ignore evil? Ignoring evil is not the same as not resisting evil. Ignoring evil is denial.

We are thinking cheeks of the face. I suspect that the Savior was telling us not to be impudent, arrogant, and argumentative with our children. Cheeky behavior is just that. Children do not like to be compelled. They do not like to do things when you want them done. If you argue with them, they become argumentative and impudent with you. Nothing is solved. The other cheek is a broken heart and a contrite spirit. The Holy Ghost can give us soft answers to the behavior problems in our family and comfort us at the same time.

Lead your children to their chores this way. I learned not to argue with my patients and children. This method even works on spouses. Doctors ordered me to do treatments which the patient did not want to do. I knew they did not feel good so I gave my patients a choice. For example, the doctor ordered a heart patient or a patient with crutches to walk so many steps the first day they were able to ambulate. I gave them a choice by giving them the amount of steps the doctor wanted them to walk and then a higher number. I was surprised all my patients did the higher number. When I used this method on my children and step children, this worked until they discovered that they did not get out of chores. My patients and spouse were not in a power struggle with me. My children and step children were. Use this method as long as you can. It decreases contention in your home and yourselves.

Children may be seeking the attention of father or testing the limits of their fathers with misbehavior. It is okay to say "no" to your children and step children and set limits. Otherwise, children will set limits on their fathers and mothers. It is okay to designate consequences when your limits are tested or broken. Just do not discipline with an eye for an eye method. We set our limits by turning to the other cheek and by saying yes or no softly, using silence–the look, or using soft answers such as please, may I, thank you. We do not feel guilty over these limits.

Parents and step parents cannot compel children and step children to be humble. Some religions define humble or humility as being teachable. Being teachable is a choice that a child must make for himself. There are blessings that are connected to the character of being humble and teachable. These blessings must be greater than the blessings of a distracted life or what parents can provide for children. To be teachable, your child must turn his heart to his fathers.

> *Yea, he that truly humbleth himself, and repenteth of his sins, and endureth*
> *to the end, the same shall be blessed—yea, much more blessed than they who*
> *are compelled to be humble because of their exceeding poverty.*
> *Therefore, blessed are they who humble themselves without being compelled*
> *to be humble; or rather, in other words, blessed is he that believeth in the word*
> *of God, and is baptized without stubbornness of heart, yea, without being brought*
> *to know the word, or even compelled to know, before they will believe.*
> *Alma 32:15 - 16, The Book of Mormon*

> *For behold, it is not meet that I should command in all things; for he that is*
> *compelled in all things, the same is a slothful and not a wise servant; wherefore he*
> *receiveth no reward.*
> *Verily I say, men should be anxiously engaged in a good cause, and do many things of*
> *their own free will, and bring to pass much righteousness;*
> *For the power is in them, wherein they are agents unto themselves. And inasmuch as*
> *men do good they shall in nowise lose their reward.*
> *But he that doeth not anything until he is commanded, and receiveth a commandment*
> *with doubtful heart, and keepeth it with slothfulness, the same is damned.*
> *Who am I that made man, saith the Lord, that will hold him guiltless that obeys not my*
> *commandments?*
> *Who am I, saith the Lord, that have promised and have not fulfilled?*
> *I command and men obey not; I revoke and they receive not the blessing.*
> *Then they say in their hearts: This is not the work of the Lord, for his promises are not*
> *fulfilled. But wo unto such, for their reward lurketh beneath, and not from above.*

> *Doctrine and Covenants 58:25 - 33*

Parents and step parents often feel compelled or controlled by the behavior and lack of action in their children and step children. When your children and step children compel you to go a mile in their footsteps, do as the Savior taught everyone on the Sermon on the Mount. Go with them twain. Do not participate in their behavior. Keep a watchful eye. Pray for help in that second mile. Often, children do not want that close parental introspection and supervision in the second mile that prayer gives us.

Parents and step parents become lonely without companionship. So do children and step children. Children will befriend anyone just to have a friend. Make time for your children and step children in the first mile. This is a planned time that can be a time of fun. Make time when you are just together without any demands on money and chores, etc. Talk with your children and step children. Hopefully, your child can tell you about his burdens that he is carrying. We are to help our children bear their burdens, not just needy neighbors. Children who do not stay on task are expert manipulators. They will compel parents to help them.

And whosoever shall compel thee to go a mile, go with him twain.
Matthew 5:41, The Holy Bible

Enduring to the End. In His first instructions to His Apostles, the Savior told His Apostles to endure to the end, and they would be saved.[174] These instructions were for His disciples, too. We are all His disciples in some degree.

Doing What You Have to Do. Enduring to the end is more than doing what you have to do. If you have a child with a disease of the heart, parents have to learn how to multitask in order to care for their child, his wounds, yourselves, your spouse, other children, work, and do household chores. Parents and step parents have to learn how to go the extra miles with many members of their families. Parents have to learn how to extend their borders or extend themselves with every member of the family, not just the sick child. If you have a child or children with spiritual cardiomyopathy, parents and step parents need to control their emotions and extend themselves in healthy ways to preserve what health parents have.

Children with spiritual cardiomyopathy can consume the whole family. The Savior is aware of our difficulties with our children. He knows their hearts. The Savior knows that parents and step parents must endure to the end when they are distraught, tired, sick, pregnant, and broke. Parents and step parents cannot just exist and pray for the day their child moves out. A child with an attention deficit disorder has no where to go. If you do not learn how to endure to the end, parents and step parents will become fatigued mentally and physically. There are more things than just diet and exercise that will increase your energy physically and mentally when dealing with distracted, impatient, impulsive children.

Enduring to the end involves commitment. Many parents and step parents are paralyzed by their fears for their child with attention deficit disorders. Most parents and step parents feel that it is their duty to care for spouse and children. This is not commitment. Commitment requires a course of action to follow while caring for your children. Commitment is not a course of inaction.

A course of action helps you perform your duties. It gives you something to work toward. There are civil laws that parents, step parents, and spouses are expected to follow. The best course of action to follow is The Plan of Salvation. This gives parents and step parents a path to follow and a path to direct our children to. The Savior called His path, the narrow path. He told us that broad paths would lead to destruction. (Matthew 7:13-14) Children and adults with attention deficit disorders have trouble focusing in too liberal or broad paths.

---

[174]Matthew 10:22, The Holy Bible, p. 1203.

We learn best when we go from small to large gradually, not large to small. Broad paths also take too much agency from parents and step parents. Without a course of action, children with attention deficit disorders become the leaders of the family and do not stay on task.

Parenthood and step parenthood will test how committed you are to the Savior's Plan of Salvation. However, parenthood and step parenthood gives the repetition and opposition from which we learn. This repetition and opposition will explain the Plan of Salvation to you in terms you can understand. You can see why our Heavenly Father and Jesus Christ developed this plan once you try to follow the plan. Performance or experience is the best teacher.

Understand our Mission with our families. We cannot understand our mission with our children until we understand the Savior's mission to us. There was a war in heaven in our pre-existence. Our Heavenly Father lost one-third of His children before they were ever born. Heavenly Father understands your pain of losing children. Heavenly Father created a Plan of Salvation for those who would be born on Earth. Jesus Christ, His Son, offered himself as a Sacrifice for all who would come to Earth. All would be saved to immortality. Not all will receive Eternal Life in the Celestial Kingdom because of various efforts in keeping God's commandments, His Plan of Salvation. Our mission is to direct our children to the Celestial Kingdom with the Plan of Salvation created by Jesus Christ. Children who are extremely talented in this world must develop the talents of the Celestial Kingdom. (1 Corinthians Chapter 13) Parts of Earthly talents are not going to save us or help us endure to the end.

God, the Father, and His Son, Jesus Christ, realized when the Savior came to Earth that many families would not follow the Plan of Salvation while on Earth. Family members would isolate, intimidate, manipulate, and stonewall any family members who wanted to keep any part of the Plan of Salvation. Children would oppose parents or step parents when parents and step parents taught their children about a Messiah and about the weightier matters of the law. There would be families and individuals deteriorate in pursing their own ways and agency. We have forgotten that the Messiah, the Savior, saves us from our sins, not in our sins. The Savior died to save parents and step parents from their sins and mistakes, too. If the Savior refuses or cannot save us in our sins, parents and step parents will not be able to save their children and step children in their sins either. Parents have to find the way that will save their children from their sins. Their children will have to make an effort. Parents and step parents role is to love, nourish, and provide shelter as children learn the Plan of Salvation.

The Savior knew peace would be taken from our homes by children and step children who oppose the Plan of Salvation. The agency of children would conflict with the agency of parents and step parents and cause both many heartaches. The Savior told us:

Think not that I am come to send peace on earth: I came not to send peace,
but a sword.
For I am come to set a man at variance against his father, and the daughter
against her mother, and the daughter in law against her mother in law.
And a man's foes shall be they of his own household.

Matthew 10:34 - 36, The Holy Bible

In other words, in spite of all their hard work and sacrifices, parents and step parents will not completely achieve peace in their homes. Children will not walk a mile with parents and step parents. Many disagreements in your home will occur when parents and step parents try to teach the Lord's Plan of Salvation to their children. Children feel that the Lord's Plan of Salvation takes too many rights and their agency from them. The disagreements come from changing the Lord's Plan of Salvation to our ideas of salvation. Avoiding the Plan of Salvation does not bring peace to your home and child either. Avoiding the Plan of Salvation consumes that self-esteem, dignity, and identity that you want to develop in your self and your children.

Control the two-edged sword that comes from your mouth. John the Revelator saw in his vision in Revelation one liken unto the Son of Man, another name for the Savior. Out of His mouth went a two-edged sword. (Revelation 1:16) We have a two-edged sword coming from our mouth, too–the tongue. Unfortunately, we have not developed the skills which will help us control this two-edged sword in our mouths: say nothing, yes or no answers, and soft answers.

There is too much screaming in our homes. The screaming occurs over little things. Children and step children cannot build confidence while parents and step parents are screaming every day all day long. Backseat driving in cars does not work. Backseat driving in our homes does not work either.

There is too much belittling of spouses in front of children and step children. Children begin to feel that the spouse of their parent has no worth. It does not matter that this is their natural father or mother. They are not going to be obedient to them. You are not obedient.

Our children are viewing this screaming and belittling as acceptable behavior. They do it with their friends and teachers. Our children scream at and belittle their spouse and children. Remember. With repetition, your child learns. If your child hears repeated screaming, swearing, and belittling, that will be what he learns instead of listening to you. Create an atmosphere where your child wants to learn with you over and over. If you have a tendency to speak loud, test your hearing. Act, not react.

The Savior, in His mortal ministry, went to great lengths to teach us how to live peacefully. He taught us parables. When Peter cut off the ear of the servant of the high priest, the Savior restored the servant's ear. The Savior told the Apostles gathered in the garden around Him that those who take up the sword shall perish by the sword. (Matthew 26:52) The Savior rode into Jerusalem on a colt of a donkey signifying He came in peace. (John 12: 15) Don't cut off your child's spiritual ears with screaming, swearing, and belittling.

The Apostle Paul told us the word of God was quick and powerful and sharper than any two-edged sword. I suspect this sword from the Son of Man's mouth is the word of God. In latter-day scripture, we are told to reprove with sharpness, when inspired by the Holy Ghost; and then show afterwards an increase of love to those we have reproved, lest they view us as an enemy. (Doctrine and Covenants 121:43) In other words, one edge of our two-edged sword is to reprove and the other edge is to show forth love and speak peace to our loved ones. This how we turn the other cheek. (Matthew 5:39)

Penitence or Repentance. If you do not control the two-edged sword that comes from your mouth, your conscience will be pricked and will cause a feeling for the need for repentance. Parents and step parents have asked me and probably many counselors how much penitence do they have to do for their mistakes with their children and step children. The answer is simple.

None. Parents and step parents are confusing penitence with repentance. These terms are similar, but they are very different.

Penitence use to mean that one feels sorry for his mistakes. They do not stop the mistake, they just feel sorry. In this day and age, penitence has come to mean blaming others, especially parents and step parents, for children's and step children's sins. Children and step children expect parents to make an offering to children and step children for parents' and step parents' mistakes. Children keep sinning, and parents keep offering.

Children and step children with attention deficit disorders are expert manipulators. They may not be working at age level, but they know how to take advantage and exaggerate parents,' step parents,' and siblings' feelings about their personal mistakes. Children and step children know how to make parents and step parents feel guilty. When feeling guilty, parents and step parents do many things for children and step children–things they would not normally do.

Children are recognizing that parents and step parents are always doing wrong. Children and step children do not recognize and admit that they have done wrong. This is projection. Through penitence, children and step children skillfully punish parents and step parents for children's and step children's behavior. Children and step children now have parents and step parents trying to repent for their children's and step children's behavior in a myriad of ways. Parents may do a lot of things to try to obtain forgiveness from their children. The children never forgive. Parental burdens are not lifted. They are increased. This is not repentance. This is penitence. Repentance eases burdens and guilt. Penitence increases burdens and guilt. If you obey the law of the land, then God and the Savior will be the judge on how much repentance you need–not children and step children. Remember. We are remorseful over our own sins, not remorseful for the sins of others. One cannot refrain from doing another's behavior!

Go back and review the chapter on repentance. There are five steps of repentance, not numberless steps of penitence. All you have to do is recognize your mistakes, be truly sorry for your mistake, ask forgiveness, make restitution if possible, and refrain from doing what you think you might have done to hurt your children. Ask only once for forgiveness of children and step children. We have agency to repent and forgive. Forcing others to repent is penitence. There are many children and step children who live in penitentiaries because they would not repent and refrain, forgive, listen to their parents and step parents, or they forced others to penitence.

The Miracle of a Garden. Christ performed many miracles in His ministry. Yet, His miracles were not a sign for the Israelites. The Herodians, Sadducees, Pharisees, and Scribes could not or would not believe their own eyes anyway. They wanted another sign and another sign and another sign, etc. The Savior did His Mighty Miracle for us in The Garden of Gethsemane. Most everyone wants to partake of the blessings of this miracle in The Garden of Gethsemane, but they do not want to till, plant, weed, water, harvest, and preserve the benefits and blessings of this Mighty Miracle.

Many parents and step parents do mighty miracles for their children and step children in a garden, too. I call it the Miracle of a Garden. After working hard for their family or step family, many parents and step parents plant a garden of peas, corn, beans, beets, radishes, onions, spinach, squash, cucumbers, tomatoes, a zucchini, and some fruit trees. Quickly, they discover that all want to partake. No one wants to help till, plant, water, weed, harvest, preserve, and cook–just like in the Story of the little Red Hen and her bread.

Many step fathers and step mothers pray over and persist with their gardens. The Lord blesses their efforts. The family has no idea where their food is coming from. They assumed mother or step mother was charging their food on a credit card, or their mother and step mother was holding out money again. The children would not partake of the fruits and vegetables which was provided for them by the Lord and the hard work of parents and step parents. Children and step children stonewalled parents and step parents efforts. They may not realize it. They were also stonewalling, and trying to manipulate, intimidate, and isolate the prayers to and the blessings from our Father in Heaven.

Through gardens, I have learned to appreciate what the Creator of this World has done for us and how difficult it is to subdue a small piece of land. Remember. The Lord has already subdued the Earth for us to use. We have to live with and subdue its fruits. Hopefully, our behavior and habits will not cause an absence of fruits.

Experience the miracles of a family garden as well as the Miracle in the Garden of Gethsemane. Both have much to teach you, your children, and step children. Both Miracles in the Garden will benefit your health and family budget, too. With good seed and effort, you sow and reap a good crop. Experience the miracle of home-baked bread with your garden. With a garden, food storage and the Word of Wisdom are easier to keep. With gardens, we always have something to share. You cannot share a petunia or a geranium. Do not kill the pollinators of your garden with pesticide spray. Soapy water will usually help and is cheaper. It is that way spiritually, too. We need our natural pollinators in our gardens for a spiritual harvest. They are called parents and step parents.

Food Pyramids. Current food pyramid charts recommend five fruits and five vegetables a day for an individual. I do not believe this is accurate. In a family of seven, a mother would have to buy and prepare seventy servings of fruits and vegetables a day, four hundred and ninety servings per week. This is not logical or affordable with current minimum wages, high food prices, high gas prices, high home heating fuel, high water prices, and ridiculous real estate prices. We are even forced to replace appliances that we do not need. We cannot buy this many fruits and vegetables for our family, the things that will give them energy and that has substance, with society leaning strongly in these ways. We can serve moderate servings. Moderate servings are not excessive or small, but sensible. This depends on your activity level.

It would be interesting if fruits and vegetables have a natural anti-depressant in them as well as the energy we need. Energy-enhancers with no substances are not working. The B vitamins have to have food present to start and complete the energy cycle of breaking down glucose in food, storing glucose as glycogen, and retrieving glycogen when energy is needed.

With the high prices of gas, food, utilities, etc., the best alternative is gardens. Prophets in The Church of Jesus Christ have asked members to plant gardens. Notice. They did not say a patch. A tomato patch, one zucchini plant, and a few strawberries are not going to provide the nutrients and energy which a family needs in the winter and all year long. A patch will not help you endure the times when you are out of work or when you want to save some money for something important. Gardens are how we replenish the earth in times of pollution.

Learn how to deal with depression. If you do not do so, you will become neither root nor branch with your children and step children. In other words, both parent and child become like a piece of driftwood. Children will control you. Often, we become depressed because things are never done or the same. We have an eternity where things will not remain the same or things will never be done. We must learn how to control depression. I have written another book on understanding and relieving our depressions titled, <u>Neither Root Nor Branch</u>.[175] This book is about to be released, too. It will be our disaster manual for depression. There are many things in the scriptures that help us ease and drain those depressions. The weightier matters of the law will help you endure to the end even in times of sadness and will help you stay on task. The weightier matters of the law will increase your initiative and decrease your depressions.

"An ounce of prevention is worth a pound of cure." This is why the Savior taught us how to pray. What would the Savior's ounce of prevention be? I suspect it would this scripture.

> 9 After this manner therefore pray ye: Our Father which art in heaven,
> Hallowed be thy name.
> 10 Thy kingdom come. Thy will be done in earth, as it is in heaven.
> 11 Give us this day our daily bread.
> 12 And forgive us our debts, as we forgive our debtors.
> 13 And lead us not into temptation, but deliver us from evil: For thine
> is the kingdom, and the power, and the glory, for ever. Amen.

Matthew 6:9 - 13, <u>The Holy Bible</u>

Prayer is our "ounce of prevention" for attention deficit disorder and attention deficit disorder with hyperactivity. Prayer eases burdens. The Savior and the Holy Ghost can warn us about paths we do not want to be compelled down before we arrive at the path. Perhaps, this is why the Savior told us to pray and not to faint.[176] This is where we begin teaching and preparing our children and ourselves for their greatest responsibility on this earth—the work in their homes. Prayer helps us endure to the end especially when children refuse to turn their hearts to family. However, we have to ask for these answers to prayer.

Whatever is sealed on Earth is sealed in Heaven. Why will turning the hearts of the children to the fathers and the fathers to children help us with attention deficit disorders? Why is keeping promises and enduring to the end with our fathers and our children so important? I suspect that turning our hearts to our fathers and to our children is more than a prevention of the Earth being smitten with a curse. The Savior told us whatsoever we bind on earth shall be bound in heaven. Whatever we loose on Earth will be loosed in Heaven. (Matthew 16:19)

The process of binding and loosing requites the keys of the kingdom. Keys are the method of achieving this blessing. This process of binding begins with family relationships. However, this process includes our knowledge and behavior. Our intelligence and our sins rise with us. (<u>Doctrine and Covenants</u> 130:18; <u>Doctrine and Covenants</u> 132:44) Somehow our intelligence and our sins are bound to us. Your level of education will rise with you when you die—not passing fancies, sports, coaches, movie stars, and your idols.

---

[175]Grange, Mary Jane, <u>Neither Root Nor Branch</u>, Trafford Publishing, 2010.

[176]Luke 18:1, <u>The Holy Bible</u>, p. 1309; 2 Nephi 32:9, <u>The Book of Mormon</u>, pp. 115-116.

Education and behavior are a matter of your efforts. However, family relationships are sealed in one of the temples of The Church of Jesus Christ in a very sacred ceremony. You can perform this work for yourself or as a proxy for your deceased family members. I am aware of the conflicts this causes in nonmembers of The Church of Jesus Christ. There are conflicts about this work in members of The Church of Jesus Christ, too. Dysfunctional families and divorces occur in members as well as nonmembers of The Church of Jesus Christ.

In a bitter divorce, children do not want to be sealed for an eternity to a father or a mother who has caused much pain in the family with wayward behavior. Spouses do not want to be sealed to wayward spouses. Personal attacks may have occurred on parents, children, and spouses. Wayward spouses and wayward children are not worthy to be sealed to spouses or parents. Wayward spouses and wayward children have to refrain from wayward behavior. Otherwise, sin binds to their life, and they live for an eternity in their sins.

Divorced spouses like to agitate ex spouses and grandparents by telling you that your children or grandchildren will not be sealed to their mother or father and grandparents. Mothers are not going to be separated from children. Fathers may. This is frightening and confusing to parents and children. There are rules that are followed when there are multiple spouses. The truth of the matter is that we do not know how these sealings will be bound in heaven. Who someone lives with for an eternity will be their choice. We only know that we did the sealing of parent and child or spouses in an orderly, sacred way so all of Heavenly Father's children could return to Him and use their agency according to what they learned on Earth.

We will not have the Adversary following us around in Heaven. We are going to feel a lot different about God, family, ourselves, and religion when we die. There are going to be surprises. The biggest surprise is that the pattern that was established in the pre-existence still continues: faith, repentance, baptism, and the Gift of the Holy Ghost, effort, education, temple marriage, and family relationships.

Family members have trouble letting other family members repent. The steps of repentance only work for controlling individuals, not in other family members. Besides, the traditions of their fathers or even the lack of traditions are going to save their family. Offended family members feel they get to decide when family members can repent and progress. This is not true. These controlling individuals have decided when their own repentance is accepted.

It takes a lot of effort and time to seal family members to correct family members. Members of The Church of Jesus Christ try diligently in not putting any marriage asunder. When someone performs this ordinance in one of the temples of The Church of Jesus Christ, they are not making a choice on which church your family member is a part of. This decision is made in chapels when someone who is alive decides they want to be baptized.

Families are sealing families. This sealing in the temple has open the way for deceased family members to break the many yokes they were burdened with on Earth. They do not have to live forever in their sins. They can complete the steps of repentance. This may be the first time the deceased family member settled down long enough to evaluate their behavior to repent. If you refuse, you are stopping their progression.

Many deceased family members are allowed to be ministering angels to their families and countrymen who are suffering on Earth. They cannot do this until they are baptized and sealed to their family on Earth with the proper authority. Even the Savior was baptized on Earth with the proper authority before He made his Supreme Sacrifice for us. Your family member must be baptized by one having authority and have the Gift of the Holy Ghost bestowed on them to minister to others. Deceased family members are entitled to the Great Comforter, too. Otherwise, they must wait till the millennium to be comforted. This is a long wait.

Everyone hates to be ready to go somewhere and has to wait. Do not force your family to live in their sins without the Great Comforter. This sealing will save them from their sins. There are many countries who are at war and who are suffering. They have countrymen who have passed on and who can speak peace to them. They may know how to solve the problems in their countries. This is a great resource that we have not tapped into.

Who suffers from spiritual cardiomyopathy in your family? Is this the root of their attention deficit disorders? Who feels they have the right to develop or control your children's and step children's hearts?

Are you compelling your children more than you are teaching your children? Are members of your family resisting each other for no good reason? Do your children and step children refuse to walk a mile and that second mile with parents and step parents?

When you make a mistake with your children, are you repenting or doing penitence to regain your child's approval? Does the two-edged sword in your mouth control you and the way your family and neighborhood view you or do you control your tongue? Can you give soft answers instead of screaming and belittling and swearing?

Does each member of your family have enough spiritual nutrition within your hearts and minds to last till your deaths, through the Second Coming of Christ, and for eternity? Do you or your child have enough spiritual food stores to last even twenty-four hours or for your comforting angels to speak peace to you in sad moments? Are you trying to sustain yourselves with just a patch of spiritual food? Are you giving yourself chemical autism to achieve some energy in your trials?

To what and who have you turned your heart? Is your heart turned to your children, parents, and your spouse, or have you turned your heart to coaches, friends, idols, sports, recreation, movie stars, and addictions? Do you have the same kind of mercy for your parents and step parents as you do your coaches, friends, favorite movie stars, and idols? Is the things that you have turned your heart to controlling you and taking away your agency?

Evaluate the traditions of your fathers. Will their traditions support you in this day and age and in the eternities or do you need more knowledge? Do their traditions take agency from you as you mature?

Do you allow your family members and step family members to have peace in their lives? Are you or any family members privileged to have the Gift of the Holy Ghost? Do you allow your family to develop their agency with the Gift of the Holy Ghost and to be comforted by the Holy Ghost? Are you willing to grow and mature by keeping promises made to parents and step parents, the Savior, and God? Are you willing to help the Lord till His kingdom?

To what are you sealed on Earth? Are children sealed to their fathers? Are fathers turned to their children? Are you sealed to the things which should be loosed on Earth such as those seven sins the Lord hates? Have you loosed the things which you should be turned to and sealed to on Earth such as fathers and children, level of education, and the Great Comforter, the Holy Ghost? Are you sealed to the Lord's Plan of Salvation?

Epilogue

At the close of each shift, every nurse gives a report about her patients to the oncoming shift. Naturally, the oncoming nurses are told the room number, name of the patient, and his or her diagnosis. The diploma nurses who trained me always taught our group of student nurses to remember that it was Mrs. Smith who had gall bladder surgery in room 6W14, bed 2, not a gall bladder in 6W14, bed two. Student nurses were to give report in this manner. We started with Mrs. Smith's vital signs. We acknowledged any wounds, drainage tubes, and any significant problems or stumbling blocks in her recovery.

The oncoming nurses wanted to know if Mrs. Smith was receiving intravenous fluids. They wanted to know how much fluid remained in Mrs. Smith's IV bottle. Would that amount be sufficient for the nurses to get out of report, get organized, and check on her?

The night nurses always wanted to know if her side rails were up! Nurses do not like to have patients fall out of bed on their shift. There is a lot of paper work, and they have some explaining to do, especially to the patient's attending physician and family. No one seems to understand that the night nurse is not cloned nor does the night nurse have eyes in the back of her head. The night nurses will be in other parts of the ward all through the night.

Patients have given nurses some very interesting stories on why they do not need to have both of their side rails up. Their stories can compete with the stories that the nurse tries to give the patient when she wants to get them out of bed eight hours after surgery. The nurse tells them with a straight face that getting up will be good for them, even though she knows it will hurt. Nurses who have had surgery knows it feels like everything inside them is falling out on the floor.

Though the head nurse is not happy about it, nurses usually compromise with one side rail being up during the night. The patient has to be oriented to person, place, time, and situation. In other words, they have to know who they are and what is going on to have this privilege. Invariably, someone will fall out of bed with one side rail down and one side rail up.

After my surgery, it was my turn to have both side rails up. My nurse did not listen to my excuses any more than I listened to my patients' excuses. However, I discovered that I could scoot and turn easier by holding onto both side rails. It was a little difficult getting back into bed. The nurse was there to help, and she put the side rail up or down for me when needed.

Likewise, there are ministering angels receiving reports on those whom they will be in charge. They want to know if our side rails are up and if we have enough spiritual nourishment on board to speak peace to us. Hopefully, we are oriented to person, place, and time in a spiritual sense. We also need physical nourishment that has substance.

Spiritually, we have been asked to hold to the rod at all times, not just at night. If we hold to the rod, the Lord has said that He will be our rearward and our forward.[177] We will still have problems to solve. He will go before us, behind us, and in the middle of us as we solve those problems. He will point out the hazards and their solutions as well as the blessings. Holding to

---

[177]Isaiah 58:8, The Holy Bible, p. 931.

the rod is another term for holding to the scriptures. The scriptures will be our comfort.[178] The scriptures will also teach us many things. The scriptures are our standards.

Why must we hold to the rod while we learn how to glean our fields? We are not completely oriented to person, place, time, and situation spiritually. We do not want to glean the wrong field or be chased from the right fields. If we are easily distracted, there will be ones who will dig bottomless pits for us in our experiences, especially if we are heading for the right fields of life. Bottomless pits are excellent methods to hedge our way in families and step families.

Your Final Report. Your time of duty with children and step children will end. After the close of your time of duty with your children and step children, parents and step parents will give a report to the Savior and our Heavenly Father on what they tried to accomplish with their families. I suspect the Savior will want to know about the vital signs in parent and child, step parent and step child, especially their faith, their spiritual blood pressure. We will acknowledge any wounds and significant problems or stumbling blocks in the earthly sojourn of ourselves and our children. Were these wounds self-inflicted or were they caused by the actions of parents, children, or by others in which they came in contact? What kinds of nourishment did everyone receive on Earth? Was this amount sufficient for parents, step parents, children and step children to get organized, prepare needful things, make good use of time, and raise their families? What kind of fields did everyone glean? Did everyone try to glean these fields with a cold, failing heart or with a broken heart and contrite spirit? Did parents and step parents teach God's children about the rules for self care, His commandments? How did parent and child, step parent and step child respond to the Lord's Health Care Plan for us, the Plan of Salvation?

At this time, parents and step parents, children and step children may discover their children are not sealed to them. This is the effects of a sinful life on earth. Families may not have had the opportunities or the understanding to be sealed. Parents and step parents will discover to what and to whom they and their children are sealed to. Families will also discover that parts or whole families must wait till the last resurrection. This will be a sad experience for parent and child. They will need the Great Comforter as they begin their repentance process.

There were so many issues facing us on Earth. It will be difficult to know where to start. To restore accountability for our agency, I suspect the Lord will ask: How far did we stray from the Plan of Salvation which includes all of His children? What replaced the Plan of Salvation for us? Did we endure to the end? In this final report, we will find out what truly is normal for a child of God.

If you recall, normal is inconsistent in attention deficit disorders. Parents and step parents become irritated trying to achieve normal in a distracted child. Their teenagers need more babysitting and more repetition than they did as a young child.

Parents and step parents watch their children develop. Most parents compare their child with other children and with the expected patterns of development. They breath a sigh of relief when their children seems to be following normal patterns of development. As their child received more freedom and school work became harder, there were less and less patterns of normal development. Their child could pay attention and perform while working in a one-on-one relationship with parents and teachers. They cannot stay with their tasks when unsupervised. In

---

[178]Psalm 23:4, The Holy Bible, p. 727.

addition, their child has lost skills he had already learned. Why? Learning to control structure is different than learning to control function. Learning how to control function of various things is harder. Learning how to be entertained is not hard.

Reflexive Behavior. Children learn quickly when doing something they enjoy. Children can sit and play difficult electronic games or watch TV for hours on end. Afterwards, they can recite the script and sing the songs word for word. They cannot do this with homework. So what changed? Why could our children not keep up in homework and in behavior with other children in their age group? Why could they not apply the same skills they were using in front of the arcade games, movies, and sports to homework and parents and family? Perhaps, our children were using the same skills they developed in front of the arcade games, movies, and sports games. Children developed a short range of reflexive behavior to solve a variety of trials. Reflexive behavior does not develop intra personal aspects and interpersonal relationships. Reflexive behavior is meant to be quick. It occurs without thinking and planning to protect us from danger, not to make choices.

So what changed in the behavior of our children? Perhaps, when we were comparing ourselves and our children to our peers, we were not comparing ourselves and our children to what is normal. We were comparing our children to what is accepted behavior in their day and age. Accepted behavior has no limits today–just like in Medieval times or the old West. We do not know the hearts of our children's peers and idols anymore than we do the hearts of our peers and idols. Perhaps, this is one of the reasons for this earthly existence–to discover and receive a testimony (a confirmation) of what really is "normal" for a child of God.

Now, let's return to the story of Joseph and his "coat of many colors." This time it is the remnants of Joseph's brothers who are in the various pits of the world. Joseph's descendants, which include us, seem to travel from one pit to another all the time. We have a "coat of many colors" to assist us in staying away from these pits. This "coat of many colors" has blessings that help us deal with the virtual realities and falsehoods that we are exposed to daily by many media and by our peers. Scriptures teach us how to handle mocking when we try to avoid these pits. We have prayer and fasting which teaches us how to avoid these pits. There is a Comforter provided for us while in these pits. (John 14:16: John 14:26)

Our "coat of many colors" will assist us in caring for Joseph's descendants in the manner that Joseph of Egypt cared for his family. I am sure Joseph would like all of his descendants cared for regardless of ability, nationality, color, or creed. Our "coat of many colors" will then become a coat of many nationalities and many generations, "a coat of many colors." Your "coat of many colors" was given to you to help you endure to the end of your lifetime. Your "coat of many colors" will assist you in all of your trials.

Many prophets, even the latter-day prophets, have done works for or with the descendants of Manasseh. Their works are similar to the works for the descendants of Ephraim. This is another aspect of turning our hearts to the fathers and to the children. Joseph was blessed through his seed or generations of two children and many great-great grandchildren. When everyone is reunited, Joseph is not going to reunite with just one son and his descendants. He will reunite with both of his sons, Manasseh and Ephraim, and their descendants. Manasseh and the other tribes of Jacob, father of Joseph of Egypt, have not been forgotten. The tribe of Ephraim has descendants of Manasseh and other tribes by marriage, birth, or civil adoption.

The tribes of Manasseh and Ephraim are so similar. One would think they are related. Manasseh and Ephraim are both affected by jealousy. This jealousy takes them off task quickly. Both tribes care more about their land than they do their people. Both Manasseh and Ephraim do not want to give up the ways of their fathers because they want to be free to smoke pot or do whatever comes to mind to relieve their stress. They have not relieved their stress. They have created and added to their stress layer upon layer–especially to parents, mothers, and spouses.

In both tribes, their homes have become emasculated. Women run the homes or the tribes. The Indians in North America are not allowed to have male chiefs. They might rise up against the Whites again. To make up for this control, the tribes of Manasseh were given fishing rights which the tribe of Ephraim cannot have. The tribe of Ephraim would just rather fish.

Individuals in both tribes have friends who have problems with alcohol, drugs, and immorality. If individuals of both tribes return to the same friends, they pick up the same habits again. Both like to vex each other and have for centuries for the same ideas. Are we truly vexing each other because of jealousy, or are we walking a mile in each other's shoes?

The descendants of Manasseh and Ephraim may vex each other. They may create more laws for one which does not apply to the other. However, both tribes are going to bow before Joseph, our great-great grandfather of many generations ago. Joseph told us so in one of his dreams in Genesis.

The sun, moon, and stars will bow to Joseph.[179] I suspect that this dream has not been fulfilled yet. Joseph's fruitful bows in the Celestial Kingdom (Sun) and the Terrestrial Kingdom (Moon), plus the unfruitful ones of the Telestial Kingdom (Stars) will bow before their great-great grandfather of many generations ago, Joseph of Egypt. I have wondered if this will be the time when the generations from Father Adam to our Grandfather Joseph will then bow before the Savior. They will return the authority of the Earth back to Jesus Christ and Heavenly Father.

Even the Kings of the Earth will return their authority of their country to their previous rulers who will eventually return the authority of the earth to Father Adam. He will return this authority to the Savior, the King of Kings. It is no wonder that the Kings of the Earth are fought in every peaceful move they make. After so many problems in their countries, the various kings and queens and presidents of the Earth probably will be more than willing to give the authority and control back to Father Adam and the Savior.

However, this time, there will not be a war in Heaven. It will not be a matter of pride and who has the best weapons of rebellion. This gathering will be a matter of honor, love, respect, and obedience. However it happens. It is going to be a very moving moment for us to see and participate in. It is not going to be an experience where we will be giving up our land. It will be an experience where we find out what land we acquire next. As expected, we will prefer the view from the Celestial Kingdom with all of our family united. We want to enjoy this moment without regret and retaliation. A lot of work and effort got the inhabitants of Earth to this point.

Until that time happens, the stone that was cut out of the mountains without hands will keep rolling forth.[180] Truth is marching on as well as time. There are many children with

---

[179]Genesis 37:9, The Holy Bible, p. 57.

[180]Daniel 2:34-35, The Holy Bible, p. 1103.

176

attention deficit disorders who will need to listen to their parents and must learn to be obedient. They should bow to their mother and father for their struggles with them while they were distracted and impulsive because they would not listen to or obey their parents and step parents or any authority figure.

There are many fields which are white and ready to harvest in us! We have to learn how to control their various structures and control their various functions to have a harvest. There are other worlds in which to sing–right here. We do not have to die to have this experience or to be comforted. We do not have to rely on reflexive behavior to protect us. We do not have to have a separate circulation from families and step families for satisfaction. All have been given a "coat of many colors" to help in their personal harvest and the harvest of others. *If we cannot harvest and preserve what is in ourselves, we cannot help others with their harvest!* People with attention deficit disorders and even retarded children are included in this harvest.

Everyone's "coat of many colors" is different, but follows a pattern. In a family, there are several "coats of many colors." Families are hectic. Parents and step parents try to provide just one style of "coat of many colors" to save time and money. However, each child has a different personality and potential. One child's "coat of many colors" does not work in a household with a full quiver. Parents and step parents feel like they lose their "coat of many colors" while trying to provide for the many different "coats of many colors" in their home. The pattern of the Savior's "coat of many colors," the gospel of Jesus Christ, allows for many different "coats of many colors" while following one pattern. Notice, the Savior does not have one color to His "coat of many colors."

Journal. If you have a child who is having difficulty learning in school and is falling behind in school, don't panic and pigeonhole yourself and your child. Analyze the situation. Keep your own records about your children. Although a teacher keeps daily records, it may take months for the teacher to notify you that your child is behind. It is very hard to catch up and try to do the daily tasks at the same time, especially if the child has an attention deficit disorder.

Keep in mind. If your child will not do the work, even though he has the capacity to do the work, your child will still fall behind. He will be labeled with an attention deficit disorder. This tag will follow him along with guilt and shame and anger all his life. If your child can learn the difficult, fun things of life, but refuses to learn the basics of education, be suspicious. There are many things that can side-track a child at school. In our day, gangs, drugs, alcohol, and sexual promiscuity are prevalent in our schools. This affects your child's performance and ability to focus. Some parents have moved away from the city or school to control this behavior. Some have home-schooled their children to keep them from the problems at school.

Gird up. I suspect that our level of retention is determined by how we have girded ourselves. Gird is an old word meaning to encircle and prepare one's self. We live in an age of advanced preparation. There is schooling and seminars for every disaster that might occur in our lives such as: earthquakes, tornadoes, death, disease, divorce, and loss of wages.

It is a painful experience for parents and step parents when they discover they have children who prefer a stubborn, hard heart instead of a broken heart and contrite spirit. Parents may have a hard, stubborn heart. You and your child prefer to gird up or prepare and protect yourselves with lies, smoking, truancy, theft, drugs, alcohol, fornication, adultery, pornography, homosexuality, and contention. Everyone's ability to concentrate and perform tasks decreases with these things. Parents and step parents know there is no strength that comes from these things. These things consume physical health and potential instead of encircle and protect.

Our physical bodies are encircled with skin, clothing, and shoes to protect us. I suspect that we gird our minds with reverence. Reverence is more than just being quiet. Reverence is what we are devoted to and who we adore. Reverence is respect, sometimes a solemn respect. We turn to whatever or whomever we revere. Our personalities and our identities are determined by whom we adore and to what cause we are devoted. What we have reverence for affects how well we perform our tasks. I suspect this is why the Savior commanded us to have no other idols before the Savior. He did not want rough ways, passing fancies, or cravings to gird us up.

Mankind has looked for or developed many treasures in the world. The Savior said:

For where your treasure is, there will your heart be also.
The light of the body is the eye: if therefore thine eye be
single, thy whole body shall be full of light.
But if thine eye be evil, thy whole body shall be full of darkness.
If therefore the light that is in thee be darkness, how great is that darkness!

Matthew 6:21 - 23, The Holy Bible

In other words, what and who you treasure or see as having great value will determine where your heart is. The amount of light of the body is in the eye. The eye of the body is single or focuses to a distinct part. The eye of a part is the most intensely, active central part. Focus means to direct to a common center as well as devote oneself to a task. If the eye of your heart focuses on evil or calls good evil and evil good, you and your personality will be full of darkness. It will be hard to stay on task. If the eye of your heart is full of good works, your personality and life with be full of light. It will be easier for you to stay on task. You have been given agency to choose how much light and darkness you want in your life. You do not have to call dark things light to avoid conflict within yourselves and others.

Questions were asked at the end of each chapter to help you become aware of how you and children are accumulating the layers of attention deficit disorders. These questions were to help you focus or direct you to the eye of your heart. They were not meant for you to beat upon yourself. Once these layers are identified, determine where you and your child perform and need to change. The Gift of the Holy Ghost helps you change the eye of your heart. Parents can identify gaps in themselves and their children can tell what they have done for their children and step children in their final report.

Our Heavenly Father provided ways to make the rough spots smooth in this life. The Adversary deepens our rough spots. God blesses those who turn their hearts to their children and to their fathers. He will bless you as you smooth out the rough spots in your life. We do not have to be lame ducks in our thoughts and actions in our maturing process. There is a standard that we can follow which will help us concentrate, retain, and stay on task. Be willing to go beyond the lame duck stage. Your treasure is not a cigarette, an alcoholic beverage, jewels, money, an expensive car, or a big house. Your treasures are you, your children, and extended family. Christ is the pattern for the development of our treasures.   *Mary Jane Grange, R.N.*

Attention Deficit Disorder Checklist

LISTENING:

☹ Your child is daydreaming a lot.
- ☹ Bored
- ☹ Hungry
- ☹ Tired
- ☹ Sick
- ☹ Worried
- ☺ Initiative
- ☹ Sugar, caffeine, carbonation in system
- ☹ Drugs and/or alcohol in system

☹ Child does not pay attention to what is going on.
☹ He missed details of instructions.
☹ He cannot follow instructions.
☹ Child cannot start or complete tasks with or without instructions.
☹ He cannot remember simple things.
☹ Tasks performed by guess work.
☹ Poor performance brings criticism and anger.
☹ Child has trouble starting tasks or completing tasks that require planning or long term effort.
☹ Child receives no attention, appreciation, or praise for a job well done.
☹ Child is not prepared now. He will not be prepared for harder tasks in his future.
☹ Your child refuses to do tasks.
☹ Your child is lonely.
☹ Your child is starved for attention and affection.
☹
☹

IMPULSIVE

☹ Angry.
☹ Defensive.
☹ Jealous
☹ Won't talk
☹ Mood doesn't fit the occasion
☹ Verbally impulsive with adults and peers
☹ Attack physically and/or verbally
☹ Consequences do not change behavior
☹ Fidgety
☹ Distant
☹ Do anything for acceptance
☹ Lying
☹ Manipulative

☹ Territorial
☹ Road rage
☹ Likes to agitate or tease
☹ Sugar, caffeine, carbonation present
☹ Low blood sugar
☹ Extremely self-conscious
☹ Drugs and/or alcohol is in system.

☞

HIS NEEDS ARE MORE IMPORTANT THAN OTHERS.

☹ He feels no one meets his or her needs.
☹ Rules do not apply to him.
☹ He is unable to wait his turn.
☹ He misplaces things frequently.
☹ "I forgot" is his excuse.
☹ How are his needs being met?
☹ Is anyone playing "The Hitler Game" with parents or themselves?
☹ Is anyone playing "The Nothing will ever happen to me game?"

CHILD CANNOT ORGANIZE, PLAN, AND MANAGE IMPORTANT AREAS OF HIS OR HER LIFE.

☹ He is too young for this to apply.
☹ Lack of organization affects relationships with others.
☹ Behavior affects running a home.
☹ He or she has trouble keeping track of finances.
☹ Others take advantage because this person can be stirred up easily with anger.
☹ Others will not trust these individuals with anything important.
☹ How much homework are you doing for your child?
☹
☹

YOUR CHILD BECOMES RESTRICTED IN SOME WAY.

☺ He has to work one-on-one with some one to help him make up his work.
☺ This child has great ability and potential.
☺ He is able to pay attention while working one-on-one with someone.
☺ He has "steel trap" memories for complex issues.
☺ He cannot focus on things that have no interest.
☺ He can focus intensely on subjects that interest them.
☺
☺

HE DOES NOT HAVE THESE PROBLEMS ALL OF THE TIME.

☹ He goes back to the same behavior when not one-to-one.
☹ His learning becomes inconsistent.
☹ He seems like an absent-minded professor.
☹ He has poor handwriting.
☹   ☞

PHYSICAL CAUSES

☹ Eyes
☹ Hearing
☹ Diet
    ☺ Do you eat together as a family?
    ☹ How much sugar or foods with no substance does your child consume?
☹ Television time
☺☹ Game time
☹ Do you spend time together without being forced into a one-to one situations?
☹ Emotional distress
    ☹ Stress at home:
        ☹ Illness present in home or child.
        ☹ Both parents are working two and three jobs.
        ☹ Mother is working.
        ☹ Contention present in home.
        ☹ Parents are divorced.
    ☹ Trouble at school:
        ☹ Teachers
        ☹ Friends
        ☹ Have friends
    ☹ Weapons of rebellion:
        ☹
        ☹
        ☹
        ☹
        ☹

☺ *Family time*:	☺ *Education time*:
☺ Monday	☺ Monday
☺ Tuesday	☺ Tuesday
☺ Wednesday	☺ Wednesday
☺ Thursday	☺ Thursday
☺ Friday	☺ Friday
☺ Saturday	☺ Saturday
☺ Sunday	☺ Sunday

Language skills:	*Your child's five senses:*
☺ Hearing or speaking problems	☺ Seeing
☺ Can express words, ideas, groups of ideas	☺ Hearing
☺ Can or will read, write, and study	☺ Touch
☺ Can communicate without offense or defense	☺ Taste
☺ Can communicate peace and love	☺ Smell ☞

Your Child's Spiritual Education–His Coat of Many Colors

☺ Church most Sundays   ☺ Develop eye of your heart

☹ No church attendance   ☹ Develop eye of the storm

☺ Knows Jesus is the Christ, the Messiah, who atoned for our mistakes.

☺ Knows how to manage in the Kingdom of our Heavenly Father

    ☺ Love the Lord with all their heart   ☺ Love thy neighbor as thy self.

    ☺ Keep Sabbath Day Holy.   ☺ Tithing and fast offerings

☺ Teach reverence for God, Christ, family, and self

☺ Teach to pray   ☺ Family prays together.   ☺ Individual Prayers a.m. and p.m.

☺ Teach and keep the Ten Commandments–law given to Moses.

☺ Taught about the weightier matters of the law–law given by Jesus Christ:

    ☺ Faith in Jesus Christ: ☺ Repentance ☺ Baptism–the gate to Christ's Kingdom

    ☺ Gift of the Holy Ghost–Great Comforter in His Kingdom   ☺ Teach charity with charity

☺ Repeat teachings in home during the week.   ☺ Teach comforting music

☺ Develop agency in children and ourselves   ☺ Teach to not call: ☺ Evil good & good evil

    ☺ Sweet bitter & bitter sweet, ☺ Dark light & light dark

☺ Teach the saving ordinances in Christ's Kingdom: ☺ Blessing of infants

    ☺ Baptism at age eight or more ☺ Sacrament ☺ Patriarchal Blessing ☺ Temple marriage

    ☺ Baptism for deceased family members ☺ Anointing of sick by elders

    ☺ Dedication of grave ☺ Priesthood Functions

☺ Follow Savior–Child cannot follow Christ if child does not know what Christ teaches.

☺ Follow prophets–Child cannot follow prophets if child does not know what prophets teach.

☺ Believe in word of God.   ☺ Read scriptures with them.

☺ Teach to turn to the father with peaceful methods.   ☺ Acts of service to family and others

    ☺☹ Household chores   ☺ Keeping promises to parents and children   ☺ Genealogy

☺ Teach children about making and keeping covenants and promises to God and parents.

☺ Keep Word of Wisdom   ☺ Healthy food–meat sparingly, lots of fruits and vegetables

    ☺ Be sober.   ☺ No alcohol ☺ No caffeine ☺ Less sugar in food ☺ Abstain from drugs

☺ Teach how to distinguish sound doctrine versus false doctrine. Child and parent must know

    sound doctrine.   ☺ Teach how to not resist evil.   ☺ Teach how to overcome opposition.

☺ Be temperate and patient.   ☺ Avoid pride.   ☺ Control tongue   ☺ Control Emotions

    ☺ No lies ☺ Stay away from false accusations   ☺ No swearing ☺ how to handle mocking

☺ Be Charitable.   ☺ Concern for all ☺ Mercy ☺ Forgiving ☺ Humanitarian projects

☺ Be chaste–no fornication or adultery in home.

☺ Be keepers of a home.   ☺ Cooking ☺ Cleaning ☺ Gardens ☺ Budgeting ☺ Yard work

    ☺ Sewing ☺ Pick up after self ☺ Fair delegation ☺ Whistle while you work

☺ Walk uprightly ☺ Obey the law of the land ☺ Keep commandments of God ☺ Schooling

☺ Not to be idle ☺ Don't run faster than can walk ☺ Be anxiously engaged in a good cause.

☺ Teach how to walk the first and second mile with parents and step parents

☺ Teach how to turn to the other cheek. ☺ Broken heart and contrite spirit.

☺ Spiritual education controls temporal education not vice versa.

☺ These things and many more from spiritual education help with attention deficit disorders.

And if men come unto me I will show unto them their weakness. I give unto men weakness that they may be humble; and my grace is sufficient for all men that humble themselves before me; for if they humble themselves before me, and have faith in me, then will I make weak things become strong unto them.

Behold, I will show unto the Gentiles their weakness, and I will show unto them that faith, hope and charity bringeth unto me—the fountain of all righteousness.

Ether 12: 27 - 28,
<u>The Book of Mormon</u>

INDEX

G

Gifts of the Spirit, continued
    greatest gift, 61
    interpret tongues, 64 - 65
    knowledge, 63
    little children, 60
    ministrations, 62 - 63
    obtain, 65
    prophecy, 64
    self-esteem, 59 - 60, 61, 67
    speaking in tongues, 64 - 65
    Word of Wisdom, 63
Gird up, 177 - 178
Gossip, 36, 40-44, 47, 73-76, 85, 88, 128
Grange, Mary Jane, 97, 129, 170

H

Handwriting, poor, 17, 135-136
Heavenly Father, 10, 16, 34, 41, 53, 54, 56,
    58, 60, 61, 64, 66-68, 74, 80, 82, 87-
    88, 91-92, 110, 111, 114, 115, 117,
    126, 128, 130, 137, 153 157, 159,
    166, 171, 174, 176, 178, 182
Holy Ghost, 39, 63-66, 69, 72, 79, 84, 92,
    114, 115, 137, 138, 140, 147-148,
    163, 167, 170, -172, 178, 182
Holy Ghost, learning, 139 - 138
Homosexuality, 47, 53, 57, 95, 115, 118,
    119, 120, 102-123, 177
Husband, does not cleave, 128
Husbands, need slack, 129
Heimlich Maneuver in Isaiah, 144 - 145

I

In Flanders Field, 81 - 82
Initiative, 11, 43, 158
Instructions, following, 77 - 82
    angry, 77 - 78
    cramming, 78
    feel cannot learn, 77

I

Instructions, following,
    feel no need, 78
    intimated by over-achievers, 77
    lame instructions, 79 - 80
    no instructions given, 79
    parents not available for children, 78
    prophets, 80
    self-confidence, none, 77
    two masters, 79
Interpretation of tongues, 63, 64-65, 67,
    106, 116, 138-139, 140, 149-150, 156
Isaac, 12, 15, 16, 34, 80, 121, 132, 148, 149
Isaiah, 10, 16, 48, 49, 51, 69, 108, 144-145

J

Jesus, anointed one, 10, 41-44, 68, 123, 176
Jesus, Atonement, 11, 67, 107, 111, 126, 146
    182
Jesus Christ, head of His church, 16, 75,
    166
Jesus, Giver of Spiritual Gifts, 60-65, 67
Jesus, promises to, 159
Jesus, teachings, 93-95, 114-115, 134, 145,
    161, 177
Jesus, tested, 34
Jesus, turn to, 157
Jacob, 12-14, 15, 111, 112, 134
Jacob, blessing of Joseph's children, 14-15
Jacob's ladder, 16
John, The Revelator, 80, 107-108, 154, 167
Joseph of Egypt, 12-16, 80, 111, 152
    dream, 13 - 14, 155
    father of Manasseh and Ephraim, 12,
        14, 104, 175
    our great-great-grandfather, 9, 12,
        14, 175 - 176
Joshua, 15
Journal, 177
Judgements, 12, 75, 79, 86, 106, 108, 147

Author

Mary Jane Grange

Mary Jane Grange was born in Sheridan, Wyoming in 1946. She graduated from the University of Wyoming in 1970 with a Bachelor of Science Degree in Nursing. She has worked in doctors offices and several hospitals in Wyoming and Utah. She worked ten years at LDS Hospital in Salt Lake City, Utah, in obstetrics, neuro-intensive care, and the PRN Pool. She is a member of The Church of Jesus Christ of Latter-day Saints and worked in several organizations as a teacher and as an officer. She has been a cub and boy scout first-aid merit badge counselor, Sunday School teacher, building scheduler, emergency preparedness consultant, and Relief Society teacher in the wards she has resided.

She is married to Joseph E. Grange. She has one daughter, eight step children, and many grandchildren and step grandchildren from which she has learned several Ph.D. degrees from the University of Step Parenting (Hard Knocks). She has learned several degrees from the University of Attention Deficit Disorders (Harder Knocks) with many individuals. This book on attention deficit disorders is Mary Jane's second book. She is now working on her fifth book.

Other Books by Mary Jane Grange

The Medicine Wheel for Step Parents
A Disaster Manual When Someone
Has More Rights Than Step Parents

Neither Root Nor Branch
The Disaster Manual for Depression

The Nurse and the Prophet

Grandma's School